TYPE TALK

TYPE TALK

THE 16 PERSONALITY TYPES THAT DETERMINE HOW WE LIVE, LOVE, AND WORK

Otto Kroeger and Janet M. Thuesen

A Tilden Press Book

Delta

A Delta Book
Published by
Dell Publishing
a division of
Bantam Doubleday Dell Publishing Group, Inc.
666 Fifth Avenue
New York, New York 10103

The trademark Delta® is registered in the U.S. Patent and Trademark Office.
ISBN: 0-385-29828-5
Reprinted by arrangement with Delacorte Press

Printed in the United States of America
Published Simultaneously in Canada

October 1989
10 9 8 7 6 5
BG

*For our children—Amy, Jill, Kären,
Scott, Stephen, and Susan—a constant
reminder of the power
and beauty of differences*

Contents

How types play the dating game
Do opposites attract?
What's a "small" wedding?
Gift giving
Fair fighting
Love, sex, and type

"Would you please look with your eyes instead of your mouth?"

How Introverts and Extraverts invade space
Sensing-iNtuitive communication problems
Thinking and Feeling role models
Judgers shape kids up; Perceivers lack guidance
Some case histories

"Have a cookie. You'll feel better."

Type, teaching, and learning
Who does well on tests?
Career choices of the sixteen types
How types behave at parties
Money management: Who saves, who spends?
Weight: Who gains, who loses?
Humor: How types tell jokes
Sexual antics
Sports: winners and losers
Religion: the true believers
Politics: Who make the best leaders?

"How could we lose when we were so sincere?"

Acknowledgments

This is a book about people and life, and the list of people to thank could conceivably include the thousands of people with whom we've interacted over the years. However, many people contributed particularly generously to this effort, and they deserve recognition and thanks.

First and foremost, two Introverted women, Katharine Briggs and Isabel Briggs Myers, formulated the background for this book. It was their intent to take the obvious, make it understandable, put it in a measurable psychological instrument, and use it to help people understand their differences and deal with them in a constructive manner.

Mary H. McCaulley, president of the Center for the Application of Psychological Type, and certainly among the most knowledgeable people in the world on the subject of type, has been a fount of intellectual inspiration and always helpful when specific details were needed.

Katharine D. Myers and Peter Briggs Myers have each been a constant source of information, support, encouragement, and interest each step of the way. As stewards of the Myers-Briggs Type Indicator, they are constantly bombarded with others' pet thoughts, new ideas, improvements, and schemes. That goes with the turf. Despite such pressures, we felt, are grateful for, their genuine support.

Susan Scanlon gave us license to use freely from her fine publication, *The Type Reporter,* the results of which appear among the boxes throughout this book. Her generosity has been a valuable contribution. Similarly, Consulting Psychologists

Press, and its president, Loren Letendre, have been extremely helpful.

The actual book would not have happened without the efforts of Joel Makower, an unending resource, who was able to take our disparate thoughts and ideas and craft them into the very readable prose that follows—at times cajoling, sometimes directing and confronting, but always with a concern for excellence. We consider him singularly to be the most significant reason why this book came into being. We must also acknowledge a debt to Kari Fischer, who introduced Joel to us.

The enthusiasm of Susan Moldow at Dell has kept us on course and provided us with considerable encouragement about Typewatching's practical applications. As one who knew virtually nothing of Typewatching prior to meeting us, she has become a deft and skilled Typewatcher. Editor Beth Rashbaum provided valuable fine-tuning to the early drafts. Literary agent Raphael Sagalyn played a key role in bringing this book to the marketplace.

David Keirsey deserves a special thank-you. He is always open and eager to discuss the concepts of Typewatching. Willing to engage and glad to influence, he has been most supportive. Thanks also to two other colleagues: Alan Brownsword, who was responsible for introducing the two of us and who encouraged us to move beyond our initial skepticism of typology; and Charles Seashore, a personal friend and mentor, for his insights and encouragement.

Several people have read and commented on our manuscript, providing constructive feedback, including Marie Rasmussen, R. W. Higgins, and Mary Sklar. We especially want to thank Marilynn and Jim Johnson and Terry Newell, whose efforts went well beyond the call of duty.

Many of our clients have provided examples, support, and encouragement: the Air Force Air War College, U.S. Army War College, Arthur Young International, AT&T, Bell Communications Research Inc., C&P Telephone, Citicorp, Exxon, Ford Motor Company, Harley-Davidson, IBM, Internal Revenue Service, Marine Midland Bank, Marine Corps Command and Staff College, National Defense University Armed Forces Staff College, Naval Education and Training Center, NTL Institute, Sovran Bank, Student Loan Marketing Association, U.S. Army Intern Training Center, U.S. Department of Education, and the University of Richmond, among many others.

Our office staff—Susan L. Mendelson, Jill Marie Esbeck, Pat Hutson, and Fern Quinn—have been most helpful and patient throughout this project. Without the backbone of their support, we would have been unable to free ourselves from the demands of our business to attend to this book. Our blended family, as always, have been supportive—and have provided a wealth of the day-to-day illustrations of Typewatching in family life that appear in these chapters.

There are many others: Aïda Bound, Eleanor Corlett, Jack Diehl, Michael Esnard, Patrick Falvey, Sandra Falvey, Gloria Fauth, Janet Gates, Louise Gates, William Jeffries, Donald M. and Shirley G. Kroeger, James A. and Carm Kroeger, Robert C. and Shirley G. Kroeger, Al and Jean Ledebuhr, Dan and Elizabeth Ann Mannen, Tom and Karen Overocker, Chum Robert, Edith W. Seashore, Richard Sklar, Major General Perry Smith (Ret.), Alice M. Thuesen, Richard and Marie Thuesen, Mark Williams. Each plays a special role in our lives, and they have provided, among their many differences, vast resources for this book.

Finally, we owe a sincere debt of gratitude to the thousands of participants in our Typewatching seminars for their generous sharing—of themselves and their ideas. They will find themselves on every page of this book in the form of quotes, anecdotes, and applications.

—O.K. and J.M.T.
Falls Church, Virginia

Foreword

by Dr. Charles Seashore

Know Thyself. What Will the Neighbors Think?

These are but two of the items on my parents' agenda during my early childhood. Little did I appreciate all that was involved in pursuing these two matters to the end of the line—or, should I say, to the bottom of a bottomless pit. Indeed, despite all the theories, books, films, and discussions I have had on these subjects, I still lack satisfactory answers as to the ultimate responses to these issues. You probably have your own list of admonitions, euphemisms, wise sayings, or free-floating bits of advice that haunt you from your past.

Still, I am intrigued with ideas and concepts that help me find a new angle on who I am and what others think of me. These days, there are compelling reasons to do so.

Diversity is upon us. Whatever the merits of living in a relatively homogeneous world of people somewhat like us, we find ourselves continually challenged, confronted, even assaulted with others' differences—differences in perspectives, styles, beliefs, and feelings, to name just a few of the categories. It is clear that our individual pursuits will bear fruit only to the degree to which we can not only understand these differences, but actually value and capitalize on them. At work, at home, and in our communities, our satisfactions are increasingly tied to our skills in building relationships with a wide variety of people, not just those who share our own particular perspective.

That is why the Myers-Briggs Type Indicator has been a welcome relief in the psychological-testing world—relief from the barrage of instruments built on assessments of weaknesses, "good" and "bad" characteristics, or evidence of pathology.

The explosion of interest and use of the MBTI by the general public can be accounted for in large part by its descriptive and neutral characterization of the ways we perceive and relate to our world. It allows us to look at our uniqueness as our strength, our styles as useful, and our perceptions as assets. All told, that can be a strong foundation on which to pursue our goals and desires. And the benefits extend beyond ourselves: accepting the contributions of those who are fundamentally different from us can begin only when we start from the premise that there is no one "best" style.

Otto Kroeger and Janet Thuesen have been among the principal explorers and adaptors of the Myers-Briggs research instrument for use in the practical settings of everyday life. The framework of their book—Typewatching—is one that will appeal to the entire spectrum of psychological types and temperaments.

This is a book about interdependence and how to join with others in mutually enhancing ways. We all require others to reach beyond the simple and the obvious. A profound appreciation of the whole orchestra can lead to a richness in playing our own part. The challenge for most of our loftier ambitions is to work through our differences—not avoiding, denying, or overriding those whose perspectives are different from our own.

The surprise, as you will see, is that so much complexity and diversity can be captured through Typewatching using only four dimensions of human behavior. Of course, even the sixteen personality types and the four temperaments explored in these pages will never capture all the nuances of our individual uniqueness. But what is amazing is just how much ground can be covered.

Typewatching has proven to be an enormously productive way of looking at ourselves in a wide variety of settings, from time management to weight management. It is a tool that can be used across a wide span of age groups to help us reach challenging and commonly valued objectives. The combinations of eight letters help us to move easily from alphabet soup to a direct, plain-folks understanding of behavior. Typewatching is a skill for expanding ourselves and contributing to others.

In the pages that follow, Otto and Janet help us tolerate our foibles and frustrations with examples from our shared day-to-day activities. Laughing at ourselves and others is a delightful bonus of their illustrations of our jousting with the inevitable dilemmas of our existence. As one reads, it soon becomes clear that impossible conflicts, unreconcilable differences, and personality conflicts are amenable to new types of solutions when seen through the lens of Typewatching. Our hopeless dilemmas are turned to the light in such a way that vivid colors soon replace dull and draining grays. The differences that block us can be translated into differences that empower us.

Psychological tests and theories are controversial, to be sure, and the Myers-Briggs is no exception. For those of us who have used this instrument, however, it is reassuring that informed and articulate skeptics often find a new edge or perspective on familiar or old puzzles and problems. Categorizing people may well be inevitable. But how we choose to categorize, for what purposes, and how we change and modify those perceptions over time is what this book is all about.

For those with profound doubts about any such scheme, this book may still challenge you to be clearer about how you conceive of and relate to our intricate world. At the very least, it may help you to answer those two questions: What do you know about yourself? And why in the world do the neighbors think what they think?

Dr. Charles Seashore, ENTP, a Washington, D.C., psychologist, is on the faculty of several prestigious institutions, including the Fielding Institute in Santa Barbara, California, The American University in Washington, D.C., Johns Hopkins University in Baltimore, and the NTL Institute in Arlington, Va.

1

Name-calling

"There are three fingers pointing back at you."

This is a book about name-calling. In one way or another we do it all the time. You know the lines: "He's such a *space cadet.*" Hey, *smarty pants,* what's the answer?" "She's such a *brain!*" "My boss is so *uptight.*" "She's such a *big mouth.*" "He's a real *mover and shaker!*" That's just for starters.

The point is, it's almost second nature for us to pigeonhole and catalog people around us, though not always accurately or positively. But name-calling isn't necessarily bad. Without labels and pigeonholes, a lot less communication would likely take place. Name-calling creates communication shortcuts that often facilitate our dealings with one another at work and at home, with friends, relatives, and veritable strangers. If someone tells you about a friend who is a "bundle of energy" or who is "happy-go-lucky," you know pretty much what that means. Unfortunately, such labels can also lead to negative stereotypes and misunderstandings, sometimes hindering communications and creating self-fulfilling prophesies.

Why do we name-call? It starts when we become aware that someone displays a distinctive, identifying characteristic, whether it's something we like or dislike. Name-calling is a method of cataloging people—much as we catalog animals, buildings, and types of art—a handy device to help us remember those identifying characteristics and store that information for future reference. You know that co-worker who likes things explained thoroughly and in detail before she can try something new? You've likely dubbed her a "slow learner" and made a mental note to take five minutes to explain to her something *you* could grasp in three. That friend who insists on reading every sign out loud during a car trip is the "chatterbox." You learn to think twice before asking him to take a lazy Sunday drive to the mountains. And then there's the "administrator," the friend who can walk into a room and organize something— the furniture, a business, an event—in a matter of minutes. That's someone you like to have around when chaos abounds, but not necessarily when you want to have a lazy day.

Convenient and natural as this business of name-calling is, we tend to have mixed feelings about it, especially when it is done in the name of science. When a psychologist or other behavioral scientist creates a personality "coding" scheme—even one based on sound research and psychological theory—many of us become resistant and negative to the idea of typing while continuing our own personal classifying and name-calling. The response itself often involves name-calling: "Those *shrinks*—what do they know with their *touchy-feely stuff*?" In one sentence, someone resistant to being categorized unfairly categorizes an entire profession and belittles the good work many in that profession do.

The Scientific Approach

Typewatching is a constructive response to the inevitability of name-calling. It is based on the notion that as long as we're going to do it, we might as well do it as skillfully, objectively, and constructively as possible. That's what *Type Talk* is all about.

Type Talk is about Typewatching, an organized, scientifically validated approach to name-calling that has been used for more than forty years by individuals, families, corporations, and governments who want to communicate better. Typewatching is easy to learn and natural to use. With even moderate practice, it can help teachers teach and students learn, workers work and bosses boss. It can help lovers love, parents parent, and everyone to accept themselves and others more easily. Best of all, Typewatching can be fun.

One curiosity about name-calling is that it often says as much about the *caller* as the *callee*. It's like that old adage: When you point a finger at someone there are three fingers pointing back at you. Try it. And so it is with name-calling. Often, when you put another person in a box or use a label, especially a negative one, it reflects as much on you as on the one you're describing. Typewatching, then, is also about self-awareness.

Who We Are

The ideas in *Type Talk* stem from the work of a small cast of characters—more about them in a moment—but they also come from a cumulative total of fifteen years of personal and professional Typewatching on the part of your authors—not to mention many more years of people-watching. Otto came into Typewatching by a rather circuitous path. He was a clergyman in the late 1950s and a psychologist and behavioral scientist in the 1960s. The 1970s were spent as a consultant in "organizational development," a discipline that assesses the impact of human behavior on productivity in the workplace, during which time he was introduced to the psychological instruments on which Typewatching is based. In the late seventies, as an organizational development consultant, he helped to establish the Center for the Application of Psychological Type (CAPT), which is now the largest research center on Typewatching in the world. In 1978, he focused his business entirely on Typewatching.

Janet, too, has a varied background, which includes teaching —everything from preschool to elementary school to high school, and everyone from emotionally disturbed adolescents to chemically dependent inner-city women. In the late 1970s, she received a degree in counseling and organizational development, which she then put to use while working at the White House as assistant director of organizational development—the first time "OD" was formally used at that level of government. She spent a year at the Department of Education before becoming associated with Otto in 1981.

That association became more complete in 1985 when we were married. Together, through our seminars, lectures, and individual counseling, the two of us have introduced more than ten thousand people to Typewatching, from Pentagon generals to parents and their teenage children. We apply Typewatching to everything, including friends, associates, children, pets, and the plans for our own wedding.

One of the great advantages of Typewatching, as we've learned over the years, is that it is a judgment-free psychological system, a way of explaining "normal" rather than abnormal psychology. There are no good or bad "types" in Typewatching, there are only differences. Typewatching celebrates those differences, using them creatively and constructively rather than to create strife. Typewatching removes negative attitudes, highlights obvious differences, and fosters inter- and intrapersonal growth. It enables us to view objectively actions that we might otherwise take personally. With Typewatching, the tendency for a friend to be frequently late, for example, might be viewed as a typological characteristic rather than a personal affront or a character defect. Typewatching elevates name-calling from a negative, "put-down" tactic that mainly produces distance and distrust between people to a positive, healthy exercise with the potential for producing, not just harmony, but synergy at home as well as in the workplace.

A Brief History

Typewatching's roots date back more than sixty years, when the Swiss-born psychiatrist C. G. Jung suggested that human behavior was not random but was in fact predictable and, therefore, classifiable. At the start, Jung was out of step with many of his colleagues because he suggested that the categories he proposed, for which he coined some new words, were not based on psychological sicknesses, abnormalities, or disproportionate drives. Instead, Jung said, differences in behavior, which seem so obvious to the eye, are a result of *preferences* related to the basic functions our personalities perform throughout life. These preferences emerge early in life, forming the foundation of our personalities. Subsequent issues of life are translated through each of our basic personality preferences. Such preferences, said Jung, become the core of our attractions to and repulsions from people, tasks, and events all life long. (Jung's 1923 work *Psychological Types* brilliantly outlines his classifications. However, unless you are either a very serious student of psychological typology or a masochist, the book is not likely to appeal to the lay reader.)

Fortunately for Jung's work, two women, neither of whom were psychologists, became very interested in classifying people's observable behavior. One of them, Katharine Briggs, independently of Jung had begun as early as the turn of the century to classify the people around her based on their differences in living styles. Simply put, she came to the conclusion that different people approach life differently. When Jung's works appeared in English in 1923, Briggs set aside her own work and became an exhaustive student of Jung's. With her exceptionally gifted daughter, Isabel Briggs Myers, she spent the 1930s observing and developing better ways to measure these differences. Spurred by the onslaught of World War II and the observation that many people in the war effort were working in tasks unsuited to their abilities, the two women set out to design a psychological instrument that would explain, in scientifically rigorous and reliable terms, differences according to Jung's Theory of Personality Preferences. And so was born the Myers-Briggs Type Indicator (MBTI). The idea behind the MBTI was that it could be used to establish individual preferences and then to promote a more constructive use of the differences between people. Jung's theory has become increasingly popular in the 1980s, due largely to the landmark accomplishments of this mother-daughter team.

More about the origins of MBTI in Appendix One. For now, it is important only that you understand that much of your attraction toward specific people in your life is the result of your personality preferences. In this book we will attempt to identify and understand these preferences, then to show how such an understanding can make your life easier, happier, and more productive. After you are able to identify your preferences (and those of your friends, colleagues, and family), we will show you how to fit Typewatching into your work, home, school, play, or wherever.

Same or Opposite?

Do you prefer people who are the same as you, or people who are different? If you're like most people, you are initially attracted to people who are different but over time you find that those differences don't wear well. In fact, at work, or with mates or children, after the initial attraction has subsided, you may even demand that these differences be eliminated: "Shape up or ship out." Or, if you are not in a position to make such demands, you may simply become alienated.

It is interesting that we think we prefer differences, yet in reality few of us make much allowance for them. Though we may say "different strokes for different folks," we are nonetheless resistant to those who buck conformity to "do their own thing." In a family, company, or other organization, such non-conformity may be viewed as disloyal at best, dangerous or destructive at worst. But with Typewatching you will gain enough insight to understand the attractiveness of some of those differences and will develop the patience to allow them to exist for the benefit of those whose lives you touch—as well as your own.

It all starts with greater self-awareness. By understanding what the Jung and Myers-Briggs classifications mean, you can then begin to identify your personal preferences and how you are similar to and different from those closest to you. You can identify where those similarities and differences make for harmony and where they cause discord.

With that in mind let's take a look at how your preferences are formed and what they mean for your life. Such self-insight is the key to Typewatching.

The Birth of a Type

As we said, according to Jungian theory you are born with a predisposition for certain personality preferences. In Typewatching, there are four pairs of preference alternatives. You are either

Extraverted	or	Introverted
Sensing	or	iNtuitive
Thinking	or	Feeling
Judging	or	Perceiving

These leanings, say Jung, reflect both genetic predispositions and whatever else is part of your earliest moments. As life develops, your environment greatly influences the direction your preferences will take.

Take, for example, the preference for Extraversion,* which we'll examine in depth in Chapter Three. If you are predisposed to a preference for Extraversion, you will, barring an environment that is utterly hostile to Extraverted behavior, become an Extravert, but you still must translate that preference within the context of your particular situation in life. Birth order, the behavior of other family members, and other environmental factors are all part of the life forces affecting that context. For example, if you are an Extravert in a family of Introverts, you may be different from how you would be if you grew up in a family of other Extraverts—where "survival of the loudest" was the rule. You'd be an Extravert in either case, but a different one.

As you grow and develop, your Extraversion also develops and matures. Over the years it takes on many different forms;

---

* While the preferred dictionary spelling of this word is "extroversion," Jung preferred "*extra*version," which is the way it is spelled throughout his writings —and throughout Typewatching literature, including this book.

you may appear to be quite different from decade to decade. Though your preference will continue to be for Extraversion, its strength or quality may give it a very different "flavor" at different stages of life.

Remember that we're talking about *preferences.* By way of analogy, think of left- versus right-handedness. If you are right-handed, it doesn't mean you never use your left hand. It simply means you *prefer* the right. And you may prefer it strongly, in which case you make relatively little use of your left hand, or you may prefer it barely if at all, in which case you border on being ambidextrous. The same is true for the preferences involved with Typewatching. You may prefer one characteristic a great deal, and another only slightly. As we further examine the Typewatching preferences, as we describe the two sides of each pair, you may find that you identify with both. Within each pair, however, there is one that you prefer—that you rely upon and to which you more naturally gravitate.

The Foundations of Our Lives

According to Typewatching theory, each of us develops a preference early in life and sticks with it. And the more we practice those preferences—intentionally or unintentionally—the more we rely on them with confidence and strength. That doesn't mean we're incapable of using our nonpreferences from time to time. In fact, the more we mature, the more our nonpreferences add richness and dimension to our lives. However, they never take the place of our original preferences. So, Extraverts never become Introverts, and vice versa. (Back to the left-hand, right-hand analogy. Right-handers do not become left-handers, and vice versa. The longer they live, the more they learn to use effectively their nonpreferred hand. But no matter how long a right-hander lives, he or she will never become a left-hander.)

Perhaps another way to view this is to liken an individual's type development to a house. Your type is like the foundation of a house: it doesn't really experience many radical changes through life. The rest of the house, and especially that part readily seen by others, can be likened to your behavior, the outward appearance of your type. Over time, the house experiences many changes—an added room, a coat of paint, landscaping, interior renovations, and all the rest. The house, after twenty years of living, is changed significantly from what it was when it was built—but the foundation is still intact. So, too, with our personalities and behavior. Over the years, we experience many changes and may appear to be considerably different to a friend we haven't seen in years. But like the house's foundation, our personalities remain pretty much intact and the changes are, for the most part, merely behavioral.

This is not to rule out real change, growth, and development, or to imply that we are all hopelessly rigid. But it does mean that change comes slowly to our more basic selves and that to affect change and growth in the malleable parts of our lives is a full-time job, day in, day out. Just to manage yourself and your own growth constitutes a busy day—never mind trying to "psych out" the rest of the world. Hence, it is our intention in this book to direct your energy primarily toward yourself—where Type-watching skills can best be used to maximize every waking hour.

2

What's Your Type?

"Is it three fifty-two, or a little before four?"

You needn't take the Myers-Briggs Type Indicator and know your "official" type to be a Typewatcher or derive benefit from applying Typewatching's insights to your life. The Indicator is a finely tuned psychological instrument, which only trained, qualified individuals are allowed to purchase and administer. Anyway, many people don't like to take formal psychological tests, although they may still have natural skills and instincts that make them good Typewatchers. The material in this chapter will give you a good working framework that will enable you to obtain an informal determination of your own and other people's preferences.

If, however, you want a more in-depth reading and are interested in taking the Myers-Briggs Type Indicator, write us (Otto Kroeger Associates, 3605-C Chain Bridge Road, Fairfax, VA 22030) and include a stamped, self-addressed legal-size envelope. We'll provide you with information about MBTI resources in your area.

As this book unfolds, you will gradually develop an increasing understanding of your own preferences, as well as those of others. But to start out we're going to give you some shortcuts to help you translate your everyday behavior into Typewatching terms. By counting how many of the statements in each section you agree with, you will see your own preferences beginning to emerge.

As you read the statements below, you'll find that you agree with some strongly, some a little, and some not at all. You'll also find that you may agree strongly with some of the statements attributed to, say, Extraverts, as well as some of those attributed to Introverts; the same will probably be true for each of the other three pairs of preferences. This is quite natural. Remember, what we're dealing with are *preferences.* Each of us has some Extraversion and some Introversion (as well as some of each of the other six characteristics). What Typewatching is all about is determining which alternatives you *prefer* to use.

As we stated earlier we'll be looking at four pairs of preference alternatives, the meaning of which we'll explain more thoroughly in Chapter Three.

- Extraversion vs. Introversion
- Sensing vs. iNtuition
- Thinking vs. Feeling
- Judging vs. Perceiving

First, we'll deal with the way people prefer to interact with the world and the way they prefer to receive stimulation and energy: as Extraverts (E) or as Introverts (I).

If you are an Extravert (E), you probably:

- tend to talk first, think later, and don't know what you'll say until you hear yourself say it; it's not uncommon for you to berate yourself with something like "Will I *ever* learn to keep my mouth shut?"
- know a lot of people, and count many of them among your "close friends"; you like to include as many people as possible in your activities.
- don't mind reading or having a conversation while the TV or radio is on in the background; in fact, you may well be oblivious to this "distraction."
- are approachable and easily engaged by friends and strangers alike, though perhaps somewhat dominating in a conversation.
- find telephone calls to be welcome interruptions; you don't hesitate to pick up the phone whenever you have something to tell someone.
- like going to parties and prefer to talk with many people

instead of just a few; your conversations aren't necessarily limited to those you already know, and you aren't beyond revealing relatively personal things to veritable strangers.

■ prefer generating ideas with a group than by yourself; you become drained if you spend too much time in reflective thinking without being able to bounce your thoughts off others.

■ find listening more difficult than talking; you don't like to give up the limelight and often get bored when you can't participate actively in a conversation.

■ "look" with your mouth instead of your eyes—"I lost my glasses. Has anyone seen my glasses? Who knows where my glasses are?"—and when you lose your train of thought, verbally "find" your way back—"Now, what was I saying? I think it had something to do with last night's dinner. Oh, yes, it was about what Harriet said."

■ need affirmation from friends and associates about who you are, what you do, how you look, and just about everything else; you may think you're doing a good job, but until you hear someone tell you, you don't truly believe it.

If you are an Introvert (I), you probably:

■ rehearse things before saying them and prefer that others would do the same; you often respond with "I'll have to think about that" or "Let me tell you later."

■ enjoy the peace and quiet of having time to yourself; you find your private time too easily invaded and tend to adapt by developing a high power of concentration that can shut out TV, noisy kids, or nearby conversations.

■ are perceived as "a great listener" but feel that others take advantage of you.

■ have been called "shy" from time to time; whether or not you agree, you may come across to others as somewhat reserved and reflective.

■ like to share special occasions with just one other person or perhaps a few close friends.

■ wish that you could get your ideas out more forcefully; you resent those who blurt out things you were just about to say.

■ like stating your thoughts or feelings without interruption;

you allow others to do the same in the hope that they will reciprocate when it comes time for you to speak.

▪ need to "recharge" alone after you've spent time socializing with a group; the more intense the encounter, the greater the chance you'll feel drained afterward.

▪ were told by your parents to "go outside and play with your friends" when you were a child; your parents probably worried about you because you liked to be by yourself.

▪ believe that "talk is cheap"; you get suspicious if people are too complimentary, or irritated if they say something that's already been said by someone else. The phrase "reinventing the wheel" may occur to you as you hear others chattering away.

Again, keep in mind that these are preferences. It is likely that you've agreed with some statements under each preference. That's to be expected. Remember, also, that everything is relative. Some people may agree with *every* Extraverted statement and *none* of the Introverted ones. They are probably strong Extraverts. Others may agree with half the Extraverted statements and half the Introverted ones; their preference for one over the other is not as clear, although they probably do have a preference, if only a very slight one. There's nothing at all wrong with having a very strong or a very weak preference, or entertaining strong but conflicting preferences. In fact, that's perfectly natural.

We can't emphasize enough that there are no right or wrong choices. The beauty of Typewatching, as we've already said, is that there are no good or bad types; there are only differences.

Now we'll take a look at the two ways people prefer to gather data: as Sensors (S) or as iNtuitives (N).

If you are a Sensor (S), you probably:

▪ prefer specific answers to specific questions; when you ask someone the time, you prefer "three fifty-two" and get irritated if the answer is "a little before four" or "almost time to go."

▪ like to concentrate on what you're doing at the moment and generally don't wonder about what's next; moreover, you would rather *do* something than *think* about it.

▪ find most satisfying those jobs that yield some tangible result;

as much as you may hate doing housekeeping, you would rather clean your office than think about where your career is headed.
- believe that "if it ain't broke, don't fix it"; you don't understand why some people have to try to improve *everything*.
- would rather work with facts and figures than ideas and theories; you like to hear things sequentially instead of randomly.
- think that *fantasy* is a dirty word; you wonder about people who seem to spend too much time indulging their imagination.
- read magazines from front to back; you don't understand why some people prefer to dive into them anywhere they please.
- get frustrated when people don't give you clear instructions, or when someone says "Here's the overall plan—we'll take care of the details later"; or worse, when you've heard clear instructions and others treat them as vague guidelines.
- are very literal in your use of words; you also take things literally and often find yourself asking, and being asked, "Are you serious or is that a joke?"
- find it easier to see the individual trees than the forest; at work, you are happy to focus in on your own job, and aren't as concerned about how it fits into the larger scheme of things.
- subscribe to the notion that "seeing is believing"; if someone tells you "the train is here," you know it really isn't "here" until you can get on board.

If you are an iNtuitive (N), you probably:

- tend to think about several things at once; you are often accused by friends and colleagues of being absentminded.
- find the future and its possibilities more intriguing than frightening; you are usually more excited about where you're going than where you are.
- believe that "boring details" is a redundancy.
- believe that time is relative; no matter what the hour, you aren't late unless the meeting/meal/party has started without you.
- like figuring out how things work just for the sheer pleasure of doing so.
- are prone to puns and word games (you may even do these things standing up).
- find yourself seeking the connections and interrelatedness

behind most things rather than accepting them at face value;
you're always asking "What does that *mean?*"

▪ tend to give general answers to most questions; you don't
understand why so many people can't follow your directions,
and you get irritated when people push you for specifics.

▪ would rather fantasize about spending your next paycheck
than sit and balance your checkbook.

Again, you probably see yourself as having some of both preferences. Everyone has some Sensing characteristics and some
iNtuitive ones. Besides, it is quite natural for the same person to
perceive things differently at different times. Every April 15,
for example, even the most iNtuitive individual must deal with
the objective, hard facts and figures of taxes.

As you read these statements and try to identify your preferences, you'll probably find some preferences emerging more
clearly than others. This, too, is natural. You might, for example,
be a very clear Extravert, a slight iNtuitive, a moderate
Thinker, and a very clear Judger. In such a case, you'd identify
with a lot of the Extravert and Judger statements, and fewer of
the other two.

Next, we'll look at how people prefer to make decisions: as
Thinkers (T) or as Feelers (F).

If you are a Thinker (T), you probably:

▪ are able to stay cool, calm, and objective in situations when
everyone else is upset.

▪ would rather settle a dispute based on what is fair and truthful
rather than what will make people happy.

▪ enjoy proving a point for the sake of clarity; it's not beyond
you to argue both sides in a discussion simply to expand your
intellectional horizons.

▪ are more firm-minded than gentle-hearted; if you disagree
with people, you would rather tell them than say nothing and
let them think they're right.

▪ pride yourself on your objectivity despite the fact that some
people accuse you of being cold and uncaring (you know this
couldn't be farther from the truth).

▪ don't mind making difficult decisions and can't understand why so many people get upset about things that aren't relevant to the issue at hand.

■ think it's more important to be right than liked; you don't believe it is necessary to like people in order to be able to work with them and do a good job.

■ are impressed with and lend more credence to things that are logical and scientific; until you receive more information to justify Typewatching's benefits, you are skeptical about what it can do.

■ remember numbers and figures more readily than faces and names.

If you are a Feeler (F), you probably:

■ consider a "good decision" one that takes others' feelings into account.

■ feel that "love" cannot be defined; you take great offense at those who try to do so.

■ will overextend yourself meeting other people's needs; you'll do almost anything to accommodate others, even at the expense of your own comfort.

■ put yourself in other people's moccasins; you are likely to be the one in a meeting who asks, "How will this affect the people involved?"

■ enjoy providing needed services to people although you find that some people take advantage of you.

■ find yourself wondering, "Doesn't anyone care about what *I* want?" although you may have difficulty actually saying this to anyone.

■ won't hesitate to take back something you've said that you perceive has offended someone; as a result, you're accused of being wishy-washy.

■ prefer harmony over clarity; you are embarrassed by conflict in groups or family gatherings and will either try to avoid it ("Let's change the subject") or smother it with love ("Let's kiss and make up").

■ are often accused of taking things too personally.

Interestingly enough, Thinking and Feeling are the only two preferences that have gender-related issues. About two-thirds of all males are Thinkers and about the same proportion of females are Feelers. Again, this is neither good nor bad, right nor wrong. And not conforming to your sex's preference is also neither good nor bad (though it may be inconvenient at times). We'll get into this much more in subsequent chapters.

Type Resisters

Some people, for a variety of reasons, are very resistant to the idea of Typewatching—and to psychology in general.
- **Introverts,** in their need for privacy, are often reluctant to reveal themselves. They may object to Typewatching, even if they believe in its virtues, simply out of fear of being "exposed." As a result, they may become closet Typewatchers—doing it, but not sharing it.
- **Sensors,** in their quest for immediacy, can resist Typewatching because it is theoretical and abstract. Without being able to see its positive and immediate applicability, they will quickly become bored with it.
- **Thinkers,** in particular, are leery of the "soft" science of psychology. Unless you can objectively prove Typewatching's validity and reliability, it may be brushed aside as being too "touchy-feely."
- **Feelers,** on the other hand, can be initially resistant because "It puts people in boxes and takes away their individuality." In general, Feelers prefer not to engage in activities that have any chance of hurting others' feelings.
- **Perceivers,** who prefer to find alternatives to everything, may be resistant if they find sixteen different personality types to be too limiting. They may ask, "Why only sixteen types?"

As you continue reading through these statements, you should consider checking your self-perceptions against a mate's or colleague's perception of you. Sometimes others see us in ways we can't see ourselves.

Now on to the last set of preferences, which pertain to how people prefer to orient their lives—as structured and organized

Judgers (J) or as spontaneous and adaptive Perceivers (P). Among other things, this preference determines what you most naturally share when you first open your mouth.

If you are a Judger (J), you probably:

- are always waiting for others, who never seem to be on time.
- have a place for everything, and aren't satisfied until everything is in its place.
- "know" that if everyone would simply do what they're supposed to do (and when they're supposed to do it), the world be a better place.
- wake up in the morning and know fairly well what your day is going to be like; you have a schedule and follow it and can become unraveled if things don't go as planned.
- don't like surprises, and make this well known to everyone.
- keep lists and use them; if you do something that's not on your list, you may even add it to the list just so you can cross it off.
- thrive on order; you have a special system for keeping things in the refrigerator and dish drainer, hangers in your closets, and pictures on your walls.
- are accused of being angry when you're not; you're only stating your opinion.
- like to work things through to completion and get them out of the way, even if you know you're going to have to do it over again later to get it right.

If you are a Perceiver (P), you probably:

- are easily distracted; you can get 'lost' between the front door and the car.
- love to explore the unknown, even if it's something as simple as a new route home from work.
- don't plan a task but wait and see what it demands; people accuse you of being disorganized, although you know better.
- have to depend on last-minute spurts of energy to meet deadlines; you usually make the deadline, although you may drive everyone else crazy in the process.
- don't believe that "neatness counts," even though you would prefer to have things in order; what's important is creativity, spontaneity, and responsiveness.

▪ turn most work into play; if it can't be made into fun, it probably isn't worth doing.

▪ change the subject often in conversations; the new topic can be anything that enters your mind or walks into the room.

▪ don't like to be pinned down about most things; you'd rather keep your options open.

▪ tend to usually make things less than definite from time to time, but not always—it all depends.

Did you agree with more of the Extraverted statements than the Introverted ones? If so, enter "E" on the first line below; if you agree with more Introverted statements, enter "I." Then do the same with each of the other three pairs of preferences.

E or I   S or N   T or F   J or P

_____   _____   _____   _____

These letters shouldn't be carved in stone—or even written in ink. You may want to verify your results by turning to Chapter Ten and reading your four-letter profile. As you read through the rest of the book and hone your Typewatching skills, you may find yourself erasing one or more of these letters, because you'll be increasing your knowledge of how each of the eight preferences come into play in a variety of life's situations, as well as gaining a fuller understanding of your own preferences—and how to use them constructively through Typewatching.

3

Celebrating Differences: The Eight Preferences

**"I know the answer.
Let me start talking until it becomes clear."**

You now have some idea of the four basic preferences. But what do they mean? Before we describe them, it is important to understand that while some preferences are very clear and obvious and easily codified, others are far more difficult to discern. In the following pages, we will help you to apply Typewatching to yourself first. In the process you will not only learn many new things about yourself (and some new ways to describe things you already know), but you will also develop Typewatching skills that can be applied to others. As with most other skills—from speed-reading to speaking French—practice makes perfect.

With that thought in mind, let's do a more in-depth exploration of the basic principles behind Typewatching.

In Jungian theory, the basic functions involve *gathering information* about one's world and *making decisions* based on it. We'll call the first the "information-gathering function" and the second the "decision-making function."* Although Jung said that these were functions of the personality, we suggest that they are in some ways part of the very processes of life. The animal world "gathers information" and then "makes a decision": it hears a sound or smells a scent (information), and it climbs a tree, purrs, growls, or runs away (decision). It then gets

---

* Jung hypothesized these theories in his landmark work, *Psychological Types* (Harcourt Brace), which first appeared in English in 1923.

more information, makes another decision, and the process continues. Even the plant world behaves in this manner. It gathers "information" (water, nutrients, sunlight, wind) and based on an evaluation of the information offers some kind of a response (it grows, bends, or withers). We realize the analogy has limits for the lower forms of life, but the point is that the life process involves these two functions: gathering information and making some decision about it.

The Information-Gathering Function: Sensors vs. iNtuitives

Let's focus in on the information-gathering function, the never-ending process of taking in information about the world around us. (Although this is the second of the four Typewatching letters, we will begin with this preference, because nothing else takes place without our first gathering some information. For example, when the alarm clock rings in the morning, that is only "information." Whether you greet the new day with joy or terror is a "decision"—another matter altogether.)

According to the Typewatching paradigm, there are two different ways that we can conduct this process:

Sensors (S)	vs.	iNtuitives (N)
Sequential		Random
Present		Future
Realistic		Conceptual
Perspiration		Inspiration
Actual		Theoretical
Down-to-earth		Head-in-clouds
Fact		Fantasy
Practicality		Ingenuity
Specific		General

■ As you perceive, observe, or collect data about your world, do you prefer to be quite *literal* about it all? Do you prefer to be *practical* and *realistic* and enjoy the *tactile* side of life? Are you more interested in the *experience*, in the *hands-on, tangible, here-and-now* parts of a situation? If so, your information-gathering preference is toward *Sensing*, designated with the letter *S*. You are a Sensor if you like things presented to you in an *exact* and *sequential* manner and if you have come to rely primarily on your five *senses* as a means of gathering information—you are certain about only those things you can taste, touch, see, hear, and smell. Sensors prefer to focus on the *facts* and *details* of something and have less need to interpret what they mean. About 70 percent of the U.S. population prefers to gather information about the world this way.*

■ Instead of preferring the above ways of gathering information, it is possible you would rather be *figurative* about it all. As you gather information from your five senses, do you immediately translate it through your intuition, looking for *possibilities, meanings,* and the *relationships* between and among various things? Do you prefer to look at the *grand scheme*, the *holistic* aspect of things, and try to put things into some *theoretical framework?* Are words like *approximate* ("close enough for government work") and *random* to your liking? If so, then you have come to rely on your intuition as a means of information gathering. About 30 percent of the U.S. population prefers to gather information that way. They are iNtuitives, designated with the letter *N*. (We do this because the letter *I*, as you'll see in a moment, is used to describe another.)

S-N Interactions

The difference between Ss and Ns is very crucial because the way we gather information is the starting point for most human

---

* Population projections are just that—projections based on samples. Unfortunately, those samples are often skewed. A group of high school or college students, for example, will not score the same as the overall population. In the MBTI samples, as with most psychological tests, there is insufficient representation of minorities and certain other population segments. Still, a variety of researchers in the field of type—including Isabel Briggs Myers, David Keirsey, the Center for the Application of Psychological Type, and ourselves—have all arrived at similar figures. The population figures we are using here and elsewhere, unless stated otherwise, are reasonable estimates based on the entire body of research and observation. For further reading on this subject, consult the *Journal of Psychological Type* (1985), Volume 9.

interactions. Consider the following common S-N conversation, based on a relatively simple request:

Sensor: "What time is it?"
iNtuitive: "It's late!"
Sensor (somewhat surprised): "What time is it?"
iNtuitive (insistent): "It's time to go!"
Sensor (getting impatient): "Hey, read my lips! I asked, 'What *time* is it?'"
iNtuitive (equally impatient): "It's past three."
Sensor (exasperated): "Close, but no cigar! I shouldn't have to ask a simple question four times to get a close answer."
iNtuitive (perturbed, because he believes he answered correctly the first time): "You shouldn't be so picky."

And so it goes with a typical S-N communication problem. Remember: Sensors are literal; they ask a specific question, for which they want a specific answer. The iNtuitive, in contrast, may find a hundred ways to provide an answer—none of which may be the one the Sensor was looking for.

For iNtuitives, everything is relational: it must have meaning. If an iNtuitive isn't looking for something in particular, he or she may walk right by it, never recognizing its existence. Sensors find that very difficult to comprehend. For them, something is real, it exists, it is there—how can you not see it?

One night we visited some friends—a Sensing wife and an iNtuitive husband. Because there was a large group of people, the wife had rearranged the living room to accommodate everyone. Her husband, walking through the room, tripped and fell over the newly moved coffee table. The wife laughed. "How could you be so stupid?" The husband swore he didn't see it. "But it's there," she insisted. "How could you miss it?"

But as an iNtuitive, there was no real "need" for him to see that the table had been moved. Had he needed to pick up a magazine, for example, or put down a glass, he would probably have spotted the change. But because it wasn't needed, the coffee table, for him, failed to exist.

Here's another S-N dilemma, this one from the Book of Exodus. Imagine Moses' plight when he sent twelve spies to check out the Holy Land. It's clear from their responses that ten members of the group were Sensors, two were iNtuitives. The Sensors, according to the biblical account, reported with precise detail about the size of the people, their numbers, what they did, and where they spent their time, as well as an assortment of other facts. The iNtuitives, on the other hand, looking at the same scene reported that it "was a land flowing with milk and honey." That certainly must have been laughable to the Sensors, who couldn't even perceive that the land was flowing with *water*.

The S-N dilemma can be laughable indeed, and has been the basis for some of our great comedic acts: Gracie Allen, playing to George Burns; Jean Stapleton as Edith Bunker; or Suzanne Somers as Chrissy in *Three's Company*. All have been known to get a laugh or two simply by giving literal answers to questions, thereby distorting their meaning. (Question: "Can you reach the salt?" Answer: "Yes." Or, Question: "What was the book about?" Answer: "About three hundred pages.")

Of course, iNtuitives can be funny too. They are the absent-minded professors and "space cadets" of the world, the ones prone to "lose" glasses sitting on top of their heads or try to get in the wrong car in a parking lot. Their tendency not to focus on specific details can make them great sources of humor—especially for Sensors.

In real life, the S-N dilemma often isn't funny. So many of our communication difficulties begin with S-N misperceptions: one person sees a forest, the other sees trees. The refreshing part of Typewatching is that it offers a nonjudgmental way of coping with this age-old interpersonal difficulty.

The Sensing-iNtuitive difference plays a major role in the way we learn throughout our lives, particularly in school. Sensors prefer to learn through facts, which they prefer to be given sequentially ("Today we will discuss the three events that led to World War I. The first is . . .") In contrast, iNtuitives gather things in a more random fashion, making "leaps" along the way. ("Let's examine Germany's political system at the turn of the century and how it might have instigated the first world war.") The differences exist long past school, continuing throughout life.

The Decision-making Function: Thinkers vs. Feelers

Now let's look at the decision-making function, the process of making decisions about the information we've gathered. Unlike the information-gathering function, which is open-ended and nondirected (because it is the process of taking in information before doing anything with it), the decision-making function seeks closure and is very focused. Its purpose is to make judgments and decisions. When you bite into a steak, for example, you may *see* that it is big, tender, and juicy; your *decision* is that the steak is exactly how you wanted it, and that it is good.

As with our information gathering so, too, our way of decision making can be separated into two different camps:

Thinkers (T)	vs.	Feelers (F)
Objective		Subjective
Firm-minded		Fair-hearted
Laws		Circumstances
Firmness		Persuasion
Just		Humane
Clarity		Harmony
Critique		Appreciate
Policy		Social values
Detached		Involved

▪ You may be among those who, in the decision-making process, prefer to be very *logical, detached, analytical,* and driven by *objective* values as you come to conclusions. As a group, such individuals tend not to get *personally involved* in a decision and would prefer that the *consequences of the action* be the driving factor wherever possible. This group strives for *justice* and *clarity;* they are also often called *firm-minded.* In Typewatching terms, these individuals have a preference for Thinking decisions, designated with the letter *T.*

■ For others, the decision-making process is driven by an *interpersonal involvement* that comes from *subjective* values. Words like *harmony, mercy,* and *tenderhearted* come to mind with this group. The *impact of the decision on people* is extremely important to this group's final action. These people have a tendency to *identify with* and *assume others' emotional pain.* In Typewatching terms, such individuals prefer to make Feeling decisions, designated by the letter *F.*

Understanding this preference may have profound effects on how you function within your family, workplace, or classroom in any given situation. Unfortunately, Jung used terminology— Thinking and Feeling—that in our society denote intellect and emotion. As a result there often are misunderstandings about the meanings of these preferences. It is important to remember that Thinking types do not have a corner on the intellectual market and Feeling types don't necessarily wear their hearts on their sleeves. Let us make it perfectly clear: Thinkers feel and Feelers think. What we're talking about is the process one *prefers* in making a decision. At their worst, Thinking types *think* that Feeling types are fuzzy-headed and Feeling types *feel* that Thinkers have ice for blood. At their best, the Thinking decision maker brings objectivity to any given decision-making situation and the Feeling decision maker brings an awareness of how that decision will be received by those whom it affects. Too frequently, in the more intimate issues of life, Ts and Fs pass like ships in the night, often with negative feelings, resulting in unresolved issues and much interpersonal dissatisfaction for both.

How Thinkers and Feelers Make Decisions

Let's look at both T and F parents as they try to make a decision regarding a teenager and the family car. The car was promised earlier in the week to the teenage daughter for traveling to a Friday night party, but, alas, an unexpected snowstorm has begun and road conditions leave a lot to be desired. New "data" are on the scene and the decision must be reevaluated. Examine the thought processes of both the T and F parents—and note that it's possible for Ts and Fs to arrive at the same conclusion via their different paths, or for people who employ similar modes of decision making to come to opposite conclusions. It's the *route* to the decision, not the decision itself, that characterizes them. We've italicized the key words in each rumination that typify Thinkers and Feelers:

Arguments for Her Getting the Car:

Thinker: "We can each *learn a lesson* from this. Parenting involves *learning how to take risks* and growing up requires *learning how to take responsibility.* Parenting involves training yourself to let go and this will be good practice for *letting go* when she is no longer under this roof. According to my *calculations,* the risks here are *outweighed* by the benefits of the *learning experience.*"

Feeler: "How would I *feel* if the car was indiscriminately snatched out from under me without any regard for *my personal feelings*? She will *feel embarrassed* if she has to call her friends and ask for a ride when she was going to be one of the drivers. *If I were she* I would be *crushed* and understandably so. There is no way I could be so *insensitive.*"

Arguments Against Her Getting the Car:

Thinker: "Parenting is a *tough role* and *difficult decisions* must be made. They are *not always decisions liked by everyone* and sometimes they lead to temporary unhappiness. However, *I am not called upon as a parent to be liked* or to make others happy. As a parent I must make *responsible decisions* that reflect a *competent role model* and that are *in the best interest* of everyone."

Feeler: "*I remember when I was a teenager,* one of the ways my parents told me they *loved* me was to *not always give* me what I wanted. Even though I felt *crushed and wounded* at the time, when I got over it I really felt as though *they cared about me* enough to look out for my best interests. *The only loving thing to do* is to not let her use the car."

Individual Thinkers or Feelers can be very decisive or very indecisive. The issue here is the process, and in this example note the Thinker is objective and removed while the Feeler is totally involved. Both care, both think, and both feel, but the routes by which each arrives at the final conclusion are so very different. More often than not, one doesn't understand the other and both can fall into the common trap of name-calling or other interpersonal put-downs.

As we said earlier of the four Typewatching delineators, the decision-making function is the only one that conforms to a gender bias: roughly two-thirds of all American males prefer Thinking decisions and the same percentage of American females prefer Feeling decisions. Over the short term, men and women may be charmed by this difference between them: opposites usually do attract—for a while. Over the long haul, this factor becomes a major source of interpersonal problems. Further, when a female who prefers to make Thinking decisions behaves in ways for which similar behavior in a male would be lauded, she is called a variety of bad names, as is a male who prefers Feeling decisions. "Real men," as conventional wisdom has it, don't show feelings. Real women, it would follow, can't make the "tough" decisions, those that require that personal feelings be put aside. Both statements, of course, are simply untrue.

This Thinking-Feeling male-female dilemma haunts the workplace. The Thinking woman swims upstream against a rather swift negative current in most aspects of her life, especially in the workplace. If she is objective and decisive, she is viewed as "hard" and "unfeminine" and may be subject to a variety of even harsher names. The Feeling male is similarly presented with some special problems at work; he may be called a wimp simply for his caring nature. As is frequently the case, however, being male does have its advantages: While he still must swim upstream, the current against which the Feeling male must swim is not as swift as that opposing the Thinking female.

We believe the T-F function to be the one most closely related to how intimacy is defined: an F wants to *experience* intimacy, a T wants to *understand* it. Given the gender difference on this function, it is easy to see how this sets many couples up for some serious relationship struggles. (See Chapter Seven for more on this subject.)

The Source of Energy: Extraverts vs. Introverts

So far, we've described preferences involved with information gathering and decision making. Another important issue is the source of one's energy, which will determine how and where one performs those two functions. Once again, there are two basic preferences:

Extraverts (E)	vs.	Introverts (I)
Sociability		Territoriality
Interaction		Concentration
External		Internal
Breadth		Depth
Extensive		Intensive
Multiple relationships		Limited relationships
Energy expenditure		Energy conservation
External events		Internal reactions
Gregarious		Reflective
Speak, then think		Think, then speak

▪ As you observe and make decisions about your world, do you *verbalize* much of what you are observing and deciding—that is, do you prefer to perform these functions in the *outer* world of other people? Do you tend to open mouth and then engage brain? Are you energized by *people* and *action*? Do you become drained if you spend too much time by yourself? Would you rather *talk* than listen? Do you tend to leave meetings or parties saying, "Will I ever learn to keep my mouth shut"? If so, you are probably an Extravert, designated by the letter *E*. You are an

Extravert if words like *lively* or *popular* are more to your liking than *calm* and *private*.

▪ Or would you rather keep your observations and decisions *inside*? Are you energized by *thoughts* and *ideas* but drained by intense discussions? Would you rather *listen* than talk? Do you often leave a meeting thinking, "Why didn't I say . . ."? If so, you likely have a preference for Introversion, designated by the letter *I*. You are an Introvert if you find it necessary to "recharge"—to be alone with yourself and your thoughts—after spending a few hours with one or several people.

Of all the Typewatching letters, according to Jung, the division between Extraverts and Introverts is the most important distinction between people, because it describes the source, direction, and focus for one's energy. A lack of understanding between these two types can lead to some serious interpersonal difficulties.

The Extravert, as we said, is energized by the outer world and, as a result, all those activities that Extraverts find exhilarating, uplifting, and exciting drain the Introvert. And the reverse is equally true: the reflection, introspection, and solitude that produce energy, focus, and attention for the Introvert are a drain on the energy of an Extravert. So, at home, school, or work, the degree to which one is allowed to resort to the preferred source of one's energy has a fundamental effect on the quality of one's day and one's life. And it is very, very important that Is and Es come to understand how their opposites work.

How Es and Is Cope

In American society, Introverts are outnumbered about three to one. As a result, they must develop extra coping skills early in life because there will be an inordinate amount of pressure on them to "shape up," to act like the rest of the world. The Introvert is pressured daily, almost from the moment of awakening, to respond and conform to the outer world.

Classroom teachers unwittingly pressure Introverted students by announcing that "One-third of your grade will be based on classroom participation." Prior to such a statement, both Extraverts and Introverts are on a level playing field. But the moment that new realization hits, the Extraverts have an advantage. When the teacher poses a question to the class, the Introvert responds by thinking, "I know the answer. I just need to get it in focus." The Extravert, meanwhile, says, "I know the answer. Let me start talking until it becomes clear," and then raises a hand—or, better yet, blurts something out, perhaps: "Well, let me see. I think that the answer to your question is . . ." And *plop,* the answer becomes clear, just in the nick of time. A second Extravert inevitably repeats the answer in his own words—and there's nothing more repugnant to a true Introvert than to say a third time something that's already been said correctly once or twice; Introverts are not ones to waste words. (Extraverts, on the other hand, have advanced degrees in redundancy.) So, who do you think gets the better grade for "classroom participation"?

It's important to understand that neither approach to answering a question is better than the other. Both are quite natural. The problem begins when we make judgments about these differing preferences by passing out grades, promotions, or other rewards.

Extraverts can be a problem even to other Extraverts. For example, those who lose something—be it the car keys or their train of thought—want to "talk their way back" until they find it. ("Now, what was I saying? Let's see, I was talking about *Knots Landing* because last week's show reminded me of my husband's secretary's daughter and the French guy she's going out with, which I got to when I was telling you about—oh, yes, I was trying to find that soufflé recipe I tried the other night.") In doing so, the Extravert not only invades everybody else's space but often fills the air with seemingly empty words. It's at this point that the Introvert, with some sense of righteousness, jumps in with something like "Look with your eyes instead of your mouth," or some such statement. Ultimately, such comments become subtle (or not so subtle) messages that there are preferred, socially approved ways to behave—even when looking for lost possessions.

Extraverts can be particularly difficult for Introverts to put up with. Consider what happens when an Introvert needs time alone. Typically, Extraverts not only invade that time, they may actually try to take it away. It's not uncommon, for example, for an Extraverted parent to force an Introverted child out to play with others ("What are you *doing* up there alone in your room?") or for an Extraverted boss to force Introverted employees to engage in group discussion or some other Extraverted activity. In management circles, we see such things as Introverts working in "bullpens" divided only by short partitions, no floor-to-ceiling walls. Ironically, such environments, designed to facilitate worker productivity, facilitate mostly headaches for the Introverts, who need space to themselves to reflect on things and sift through information. Such "alone time" is essential to Introverts for making good, clear decisions. They don't want someone else's phone calls to be an invasion of their space.

Not that Introverts do all the suffering. The opposite problem occurs when an Extraverted manager who had made it to the top is rewarded with a private office and a door that closes—shutting him or her off from all the other workers who have provided the inspiration and energy for the rise *to* the top! This is the manager who establishes an "open-door policy," who makes employees feel guilty for not "stopping in," and engages in "management by walking around"; often, he or she may be found running down the hall glad-handing whoever is within arm's length, finding out "what's going on," often minding everyone's business but you-know-who's.

What's important to remember is that both kinds of behavior are perfectly normal, depending on who's doing the behaving. It is from their respective behaviors that Introverts and Extraverts draw their energies and strength. And for anyone of either type to operate for too long a period outside their preferred attitude, regardless of how successful one becomes at it, is ultimately bad news.

There are more Introvert-Extravert problems than you can imagine. Extraverts, for example, typically need a great many more overt "strokes" than Introverts. Introverts, in contrast, tend to be suspicious of those same overt "strokes." True, both need affirmation, but too much affirmation makes the Introvert wonder why so much is needed, while to the Extravert "too much affirmation" is a contradiction in terms. As a result, Extraverted managers (or parents) tend to overpraise employees (or children); the other Extravert recipients of the praise love it, but the Introverts begin to wonder if such praise isn't superficial, unnecessary, or maybe even phony. This, in turn, can make praisers feel uneasy and wonder "whether it's worth it" to proffer such praise—though their natural tendency would be to pile it on. Conversely, Introverted managers (parents) often refrain from stroking, even when they know that their employees (children) would like it, because they feel like phonies doing it. This, in turn, makes the Extravert feel rejected or, at best, unappreciated. Both are being true to their respective types while sending the wrong signals to each other.

Extraverts can be amazing beasts indeed. A true-blue Extravert can walk into the room, present a situation, ask for an opinion, arrive at his own conclusion, thank anyone who happens to be in the room, and walk out, while never interrupting his own thought process. Introverts are not only amazed (and sometimes amused) by such behavior, they often wonder whether the Extravert ever really wanted an answer in the first place. An Introvert reverses the process—he works inwardly, explores a number of possible scenarios, reaches some kind of conclusion about them, and never says a word to anyone. Moreover, if confronted, he may even *swear*—in all good faith—he told the Extravert what he decided. The Introvert does this because, having rehearsed the issues so thoroughly inside his head, including imagining what the other person might have said in return, it seems clear to him that he has communicated his thoughts—without his actually ever having spoken a word on the subject. Needless to say, arguments result from such communication gaps. The sad part is that in both situations— the Extravert letting it all out and the Introvert keeping it all in —each party could likely have benefited from the other's perspective, if only they had been able to communicate.

It's very important to keep in mind that in most real-life situations, we are not dealing with extremes. That is, Extraverts need to introvert and Introverts need to extravert. And we all do both. As we've stated repeatedly, Typewatching deals with *preferences*.

Life-style Orientation: Judgers vs. Perceivers

So we've now examined the information-gathering function, in which you are either a Sensor or an iNtuitive, and the decision-making function, in which you are either a Thinker or a Feeler. We've looked at how and where you prefer to perform these functions—in the outer world, as an Extravert, or in the inner world, as an Introvert. That covers three of the four letters that make up a Typewatching "type." Finally comes the area we believe to be the most significant source of interpersonal tension. It deals with which function—information gathering or decision making—you most naturally use as you relate to the outer world, verbally and behaviorally.

Once again, there are two preferences:

Judgers (J) vs.	Perceivers (P)
Resolved	Pending
Decided	Wait and see
Fixed	Flexible
Control	Adapt
Closure	Openness
Planned	Open-ended
Structure	Flow
Definite	Tentative
Scheduled	Spontaneous
Deadline	What deadline?

■ If the environment you have created around you is *structured, scheduled, ordered, planned,* and *controlled,* and if you are *decisive, deliberate,* and able to make *decisions* with a minimum of stress, chances are you prefer to use the decision-making function as you relate to life; you are a Judger, designated by the letter *J.* Judgers *plan their work* and *work their plan.* Even playtime is organized. For Js there's usually a "right way" and a "wrong way" to do anything.

MOPPING UP

*J: "Every morning, I usually have my day planned.
When someone comes to me and asks me to do something I
didn't plan, I feel like they've just tracked mud all over my
clean floor."*

▪ If, however, you have created an environment that allows you
to be *flexible, spontaneous, adaptive,* and *responsive* to a variety
of situations, if making and sticking to decisions causes anxiety,
if other people often have trouble understanding where you
stand on a particular issue, you are more likely to use the information-gathering function as you relate to life. That makes you
a Perceiver, designated by the letter *P.* Perceivers prefer to
take a *wait-and-see* attitude on most things—what work needs
to be done, how to solve a particular problem, what to do today.

Put another way, Perceivers have a tendency to perceive—to
keep collecting new information—rather than to draw conclusions (judgments) on any subject. Judgers, in contrast, have a
tendency to judge—to make decisions—rather than to respond
to new information, even (or perhaps especially) if that information might change their decision. At their respective extremes,
Perceivers are virtually incapable of making decisions while
Judgers find it almost impossible to change theirs. Such extremes, however, are not the rule.

DON'T FOLLOW ME, I'M LOST

*We've found that the creativity of an iNtuitive-Perceiver is
constrained by maps. They're not above driving off wrong
exits, taking unintentional side trips, and exploring un-
charted routes. They often come out okay, but it can be
nerve-racking to another type. To an NP, getting there is
half the fun.*

The Most Difficult Preference to Hide

Why, as we stated earlier, is the J-P preference the source of the greatest amount of interpersonal tension? One reason is that unlike any of the other three sets of preferences (Sensing vs. iNtuition, Thinking vs. Feeling, Extraversion vs. Introversion), the Judging-Perceiving preference is difficult to hide on a day-to-day basis. An Introvert could, for example, develop sufficient skills to fool you into thinking he or she was an Extravert. You could, at times, mistake a Sensor who was theorizing about something as an iNtuitive, or mistake a schmaltzy-talking Thinker for a Feeler. But the J-P preference is the one you will find easiest to detect as you begin Typewatching. That is because this is the preference that most affects how we interact with others.

Take, for example, these three "P" statements:

- "I saw the new Fellini movie."
- "That Fellini movie is getting a lot of press."
- "The Fellini movie just opened at the Paramount."

You'll notice that in each statement, there's no judgment—you don't know how the speaker feels or thinks about Federico Fellini, nor is there any evaluation of the movie. They are simply statements describing the situation or calling for more data about the situation, with no implied judgment.

Now here are three "J" statements:

- "The Fellini movie was beautifully filmed, although it was too long."
- "I think Fedrico Fellini should win an Oscar for his new movie."
- "Don't miss Fellini's new movie."

In each statement you are aware of the speaker's opinion of Fellini and his new movie, and where the speaker stands on the subject. Those three statements have considerably more closure and definition than the first three and, insofar as they reveal both something about the speaker's opinion—at least when it comes to the new Fellini film—something about the speaker. *(What* exactly it leads you to think about the speaker will depend on *your* type and your feeling about Fellini and his current work.)

The above statements about Fellini, of course, are pretty tame compared with the major and minor issues we face each day. Whether at work, play, or home, most of us are faced with a never-ending array of information and decisions that involve other people, from family to friends to strangers on the street. And those data and decisions—regardless of how important or trivial the issue—are a source of constant friction between Ps and Js, who all the while retain a mysterious attraction to one another.

For example, Judgers run Perceivers up the wall with their continued need for closure—to have an opinion, a plan, and a schedule for nearly everything. Perceivers, meanwhile, drive Judgers to drink with their ability to be spontaneous and easygoing about *everything* short of life-and-death issues, and sometimes even about those. Neither preference, Perceiving or Judging, is right or wrong or more desirable. Indeed, we need both types in our world. Js need Ps to inspire them to relax, not make a major issue of everything; and Ps need Js to help them become reasonably organized and to follow through on things.

WAKE ME WHEN IT'S OVER

P: "When a group I'm in is trying to make a decision, I wish I could just leave the room and come back when it's over."

It's hard to describe the extent of the problems resulting from J-P conflicts. Not long ago a Judger who had been through one of our seminars went home to practice Perceiving-type behavior. Rather than simply make a decision, he thought he would "collect some information" and respond accordingly. That evening he called to his wife in the living room, "Would you like some peaches for an evening snack?" To which his Perceiver wife responded, "We haven't had peaches in a long time." (This was a *perception,* of course, not a *judgment.*) This bugged the J in the kitchen, who wanted a decision on his offer. "Tell me something I don't already know!" he responded, somewhat sar- castically. He closed the refrigerator door and walked away, saying to himself, "Let her get her own peaches." Without a doubt, within the next ten minutes or so, his wife wondered, "Where are my peaches?"

It was a classic J-P communication—or, more precisely, mis- communication: the Judger was looking for a *judgment*—a deci- sion, a direction, a sign—and the Perceiver shared only her *perception,* albeit one with an implied yes. (If she didn't want peaches, she might have responded, "We've had peaches a lot lately.") These kinds of frustrations plague us daily.

Ps tend to find Js obnoxious, opinionated, and close-minded, while Js find Ps unbelievably flaky and unfocused. In the busi- ness world, for example, it is the Js who write the books on time management—and use them to beat the Ps over the head. ("Why can't you stick to the game plan?") Outside the work- place, it is the Js who write the diet books so that Ps can become frustrated trying to follow a structured, organized plan, and end up putting on weight rather than losing it. ("It's a simple diet. Just eat exactly what it says.") In general, Js get things organized so that Ps can foul up the Js' grand schemes. Both Js and Ps, of course, wonder why the other insists on making the day so difficult.

Our favorite J story involves a young boy during a flash flood, sitting in his house watching everything wash down the street— furniture, cars, bicycles—with the exception of a red hat, which gets to the corner of the house and turns around, passing by the house, back and forth, back and forth. After a few minutes of this, the kid is simply overwhelmed. He runs to his mother, saying, "You've got to see this! Everything is washing down the street except this red hat. It gets to the end of the house and turns and comes back again!" The mother responds, "Relax, dear, that's your father. He said he'd cut the grass today, come hell or high water!" That may be extreme, perhaps, but it's an example of a Judger's not responding to new data, merely stick- ing to a rigid, preset schedule.

FILE IT UNDER "P"

I'm an ENFP, but even Ps have to have some order. Last vacation, I spent a week organizing my files! I wanted to brag about it so I called up my ISFJ friend. He rushed over, shuffled through the drawers for a while and emerged unimpressed. "Just as I thought," he said, "you P'd all over your files."

Js, we're fond of saying, aren't beyond making great time going in the wrong direction.

Not that Perceivers are always a joy either. Ps have poor concepts of time, they're often late as a result of always responding to "new information," but they're just as likely to be early. A Perceiver may show up early for a meeting and find no one there. The new information ("The room is empty. I must be early") leads to new action ("I'll go get a cup of coffee"). In the process, the P runs into someone else (more new information), and gets into an engaging conversation, only to realize that the meeting started twenty minutes ago. Now, the P is late.

Thanks to constant new information, it is possible to lose a P somewhere between the front door and the car.

It comes down to a balancing act. A preference for too much J or P without the other is dangerous, a strength maximized into a liability. Judgers need Perceivers because they provide alternatives and excitement and the playful or childlike part of life. And Perceivers need Judgers because they provide the necessary follow-through to any project, from making breakfast to making a business work. In Transactional Analysis terms—a theory of psychological behavior popular in the 1970s, based on Eric Berne's best-selling book *Games People Play*—the J in each of us is the critical parent and the P is the natural child, and within any given person it is healthy to be able to activate both parent and child.

Four Typewatching Rules for Js and Ps

1. Perceivers *must* generate alternatives. This is their true nature. No matter the subject, they can generate new options.
2. Judgers, after listening to the Ps' alternatives, take charge. Ps will be grateful for this, as it helps them focus on what they want or don't want.
3. It is the nature of Js to moan. They must complain immediately if something interrupts their schedule or changes their plans.
4. The "hit-and-run" method—in which you introduce a new idea to a J, then leave the room for a few minutes—allows the J necessary time to moan without getting into a needless interpersonal conflict.

Everything Is Relative

You now have determined your type, at least tentatively, in Chapter Two, which gave you some indication of your four preferences; and you've read the above descriptions, which either confirmed your feelings or helped you make adjustments. You should therefore have a good idea of your four Typewatching letters, which, combined, constitute your "type." It's important to keep in mind that there are no "good" or "bad" types. Each has its own strengths and weaknesses. It literally takes all types to make a world. You can see all sixteen types on the table on the following page.

It is also important to remember that in Typewatching, there are no absolutes and everything is relative. If your two best friends are both Extraverts, but one is socially gregarious while the other is a bit more tentative, the tentative friend may seem an Introvert by comparison. So it is perfectly possible to have accurate Typewatching skills and still be uncertain about a particular call; it's important to keep in mind that behavior is rela-

		SENSING TYPES		INTUITIVE TYPES			
		WITH THINKING	WITH FEELING	WITH FEELING	WITH THINKING		
INTROVERTS	JUDGING	ISTJ	ISFJ	INFJ	INTJ	JUDGING	INTROVERTS
	PERCEPTIVE	ISTP	ISFP	INFP	INTP	PERCEPTIVE	
EXTRAVERTS	PERCEPTIVE	ESTP	ESFP	ENFP	ENTP	PERCEPTIVE	EXTRAVERTS
	JUDGING	ESTJ	ESFJ	ENFJ	ENTJ	JUDGING	

tive. One Typewatching expert has put it this way: "An Extravert is like every other Extravert, like some other Extraverts, and like no other Extraverts." Which is to say that while Extraverts are fairly predictable in their behavior, every now and then you'll meet someone who doesn't fit the mold. The same is true for Introverts and all the other Typewatching preferences.

The relative nature of preferences is best illustrated by the graph on page 46, which shows your results upon answering all 126 questions. That form illustrates how preferences are expressed as a matter of degree. For each pair of preferences— Extraversion versus Introversion, Sensing versus iNtuition, and so on—an individual's scores are shown first by a number in the boxes (showing the raw scores for each of the eight preferences), then by a line drawn on a graph (showing the strength of the preference).

Take, for example, Janet's preference strengths, which we've charted on page 46. Janet scored (5) for Extraversion, which we consider only a "slight" preference, while scoring (13) for iNtuition, making her a "moderate" N. Her Feeling score (25) and Perceiving score (41) show "clear" and "very clear" preferences, respectively.

Otto, in contrast, scored the maximum points for Extraversion, iNtuition, and Feeling—making him very strong for those preferences—and an almost insignificant preference for Judging.

While both of us prefer Extraversion, Otto's extreme preference makes Janet look like an Introvert by comparison. But that simply isn't the case: she *is* an Extravert. So even if all four of our letters were identical, we would still be very different people, behaviorally, if the *strengths* of those preferences were significantly different.

According to the *Myers-Briggs Type Indicator Manual* (Consulting Psychologists Press, 1985), preference strengths (the numbers plotted on the graph of the report form) of 1–9 are considered to be "slight," 11–19 are "moderate," 21–31 are "clear," and 33+ are "very clear."

What happens when your preference is "slight"? In Typewatching terms, low scores indicate, among other things, that

JANET'S PREFERENCE STRENGTHS

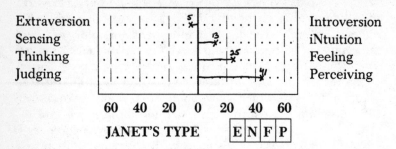

	60	40	20	0	20	40	60	
Extraversion					5				Introversion
Sensing					13				iNtuition
Thinking					25				Feeling
Judging						4			Perceiving

JANET'S TYPE | E | N | F | P |

you may give mixed signals to the outer world, showing both behavior preferences. This is particularly true in the cases of Extraversion and Introversion, Judging and Perceiving, the four preference alternatives that are most readily visible to others. In the cases of Sensing and iNtuition, Thinking and Feeling, a "slight" score may give mixed signals only to yourself. The resulting inner conflict can create tension; we've observed it manifested in the form of headaches, stomachaches, anxiety, and the general frustration that comes with not having a clear preference.

But having slight preferences doesn't mean that you'll suffer such maladies. Some people actually find the flexibility of being able to call upon, say, both Extraversion and Introversion with relative ease, a decided advantage. The important thing to remember about Typewatching scores is that they only show trends; they are not definitive statements. At best, they will open the door for a lifelong pursuit of self-discovery.

Too Much of a Good Thing Can Lead to Trouble

In Typewatching, your strength maximized becomes your liability. As with drinking, eating, or certain other things, too much of a good thing can lead to trouble. With Typewatching, if you have any one preference too strongly or too clearly defined, it may be more a curse than a blessing. For example, Extraversion is great (as is Introversion; remember that in Typewatching there are no good or bad types). But too much Extraversion may result entirely in outward focus, with no time or interest in reflection, meditation, or introspection. The same is true for too much Introversion, too much Sensing, or too much of any preference. Strong Introverts may find the constant inward-looking to be powerful and stimulating, but they also may find themselves procrastinating and having a great deal of difficulty interacting with others. This imbalance is also troublesome in the Judging or Perceiving preferences. If you are a strong Judging type, your life likely is driven by compulsions and you have trouble relaxing, just "taking things as they come." If you go overboard as a Perceiver, each day is a series of exciting starts, with precious few finishes.

Type Development Is a Lifelong Process

The development of your four preferences, and coming to terms with your nonpreferences, continues throughout life. While your four-letter type probably remains the same your entire life, the strength of your four preferences may vary considerably. In your twenties, for example, you may be a very strong Extravert, with high social needs. By your forties, while still an Extravert, your preference may have moderated because of different needs; indeed, this may be a rather Introverted time of your life. It does not mean that you have become an Introvert, however. It simply means that in your maturing process, you are beginning to respect some of the gifts of your non-preference—in other words, you find that there are certain qualities of Introversion that appeal to you. The same is true for each of the other three sets of preferences.

There is a tendency for some people to assume that scores close to the middle ("slight" and "moderate") show a good balance of preferences. (Perhaps this is confused with being "centered.") This is simply not the case. Observations over the years suggest that the clear preferences create fewer internal stresses.

What about those with "very clear" preferences? It's important to keep in mind that people who score, say, no points for Sensing and the maximum number for iNtuitive, can still have a capacity for Sensing, detail-oriented behavior—balancing a checkbook, for example. They do so, however, only long enough to accomplish the task at hand, at which point they revert to iNtuition, their preference for dealing with information gathering. For those with very clear preferences, it takes a lot of energy to use their "nonpreference."

It's important not to feel boxed in by your type. Despite the relative pigeonholing of Typewatching, each of the sixteen types still encompasses a wide range of behavior, styles, values, and tastes. Still, you will find that understanding your type and others' provides some strong insights on how to interact with those whose preferences are different—or even the same.

In Chapter Ten we'll provide profiles of each of the sixteen possible types. Meanwhile, we'll next describe an important Typewatching shortcut. Then, we'll help you expand your skills by giving practical applications for Typewatching in nearly any aspect of life.

4

A Typewatching Shortcut: The Four Temperaments

"Ready. Fire. Aim."

In the beginning, it can be difficult enough trying to understand each of the eight letters one at a time, let alone all four at once. Even if you understand, for example, what it means to say that someone is "Extraverted, iNtuitive, Feeling, and Perceiving," you still may not fully comprehend all of what it means to be "ENFP."

Fortunately, there are several shortcuts you can employ to make Typewatching easier to learn and use. One shortcut we believe to be particularly useful is to pick any two letters of an individual's four-letter type, noting that three other types also include those two letters. You will discover that just knowing those two letters will give you a world of information about all four types, on the basis of which you can make some pretty accurate predictions.

Take Extraversion and Judging, for example. The four types that share these two preferences are: *ESTJ, ESFJ, ENFJ,* and *ENTJ.* All four types, though different in many respects, have a lot in common. All EJs, for example, tend to "open mouth, engage brain," that is, talk without thinking. EJs' motto may be "Ready. Fire. Aim." They are argumentative, somewhat abrasive, up front in their position on most issues—and freely impose same on anyone within range. They have a habit of complaining first, regardless of whether the issue at hand merits the complaint.

To take another example, look at the four types that share Introversion and iNtuition: *IN*TJ, *IN*FJ, *IN*FP, and *IN*TP. Most INs would rather speculate as to why Rome is burning than actually fight the fire. They are speculative, reflective, introspective, conceptual, and highly abstract in orientation.

Now look at the four types that share Feeling and Perceiving: IS*FP*, IN*FP*, ES*FP* and EN*FP*. You should never have a party without an FP. They are fun, easy-going, responsive, and enjoy making other people happy.

We could go on, but you get the idea. You can do this with *any* two letters.

There is another two-letter-combination shortcut to Typewatching that is less random than the one described above. These combinations are called "Temperaments" and are the creation of David Keirsey and Marilyn Bates, authors of *Please Understand Me,* another book about type. Temperaments are useful because they afford the widest base of accurate behavioral predictions. So even if we don't understand how all four letters fit together, the two-letter Temperament helps us predict such things as how people teach, learn, lead others, entertain, manage money, and relate to others.

According to Keirsey and Bates, the S-N difference is the first key to determining your Temperament. The reason, they say, is that differences in how people gather information from the world are the most basic of human differences. Without some understanding of "where someone is coming from" (as far as information-gathering goes), communication is extremely difficult, as each individual believes his or her own data are *the* data. If I see a tree and you see a forest, each of us believes we're right —and we are—and distrusts the other's information-gathering process. A tree is a tree is a tree to a Sensor; for an iNtuitive, a tree is part of a system, an organic whole called a "forest." The tree therefore prompts images of the forest—when viewed by an iNtuitive. Is a cup half empty or half full? Sensors and iNtuitives each see it differently: iNtuitives, who see possibilities in everything, will be more optimistic about the glass's contents; Sensors, who focus only on what's actually there, not on what could be there, are less inclined to see the potential. Before either type begins to make a decision (Thinking or Feeling), and regardless of whether it's expressed internally or externally (Introvert or Extravert), the data must first be gathered.

So the first letter of a Temperament is either S or N, the information-gathering function. The second letter of a Temperament is determined in part by what the first letter is.

iNtuitives: If you are an iNtuitive, your preference for gathering data is abstract and conceptual. The second most important preference in reading your Temperament, according to Keirsey and Bates, is *how you prefer to evaluate the data you have gathered:* objectively (Thinking) or subjectively (Feeling). For iNtuitives, then, the two basic Temperament groups are: NF and NT.

Sensors: If, however, you are a Sensor—your preference for gathering information is concrete and tactile—the next most important preference is not how you evaluate the data but *what you do with them:* do you organize them (Judging) or continue to take them in, perhaps even seeking more (Perceiving). Thus, for Sensors, the two Temperament groups are: SJ and SP.

It isn't really necessary that you understand the theory behind this method of organizing types. Even Keirsey recognizes that the theory may not be logical. But we believe it to be behaviorially sound, and our longtime Typewatching experiences bear this out.

Accordingly, each of the sixteen types falls into one of these four Temperaments:

NF	**NT**	**SJ**	**SP**
ENFJ INFJ	ENTJ INTJ	ESTJ ISTJ	ESFP ISFP
ENFP INFP	ENTP INTP	ESFJ ISFJ	ESTP ISTP

We're not saying that when you've seen one NF—or NT, SJ, or SP—you've seen 'em all. There still are sixteen distinct types, each with the differences we discuss throughout this book. Temperaments, however, do provide us with some genuine insights and useful tools for developing Typewatching skills.

BEHAVING SWIMMINGLY

We have a swimming pool so we entertain a lot in the summer. Our SP guests always grab all the pool toys, head right for the water, and invent a new game.

The NFs sprawl on the lounge chairs and talk earnestly about life and people.

The NTs dangle their feet in the water, rib each other, and critique the issues and people in their professions.

And the SJs always, always find some work to do, like hanging up towels, husking corn, scrubbing the grill, or pulling weeds from the garden.

Styles of the Four Temperaments

Keeping in mind their limitations, let's take a look at the different styles of each of the four Temperaments:

The NF Temperament

NFs look at the world and see possibilities (iNtuition), then translate those possibilities inter- and intrapersonally (Feeling). They eat, sleep, think, breathe, move, and love people. Representing about 12 percent of the U.S. population,* they are the idealists of life and they tend to serve causes that advance human interests: teaching, humanities, counseling, religion, and family medicine, among others. As idealistic do-gooders, NFs articulate and champion various causes—they create anti-drunk-driving campaigns and peace movements and collect money to protect endangered species. But their sensitivity leads them to personalize any form of criticism, often resulting in their needlessly feeling hurt. Overall, NFs feel that the most

* Keirsey, David, and Bates, Marilyn, *Please Understand Me* (Del Mar, Calif.: Prometheus Nemesis Book Company, 1978), p. 60.

important thing is to be in harmony with themselves and with others. Everything else will naturally fall into place.

According to Keirsey, NFs' quest in life is for *identity*. This quest leads them forever to ask "Who am I?" (As fate would have it, the SJs, as you'll see, are inclined to provide an answer—something like "You're an *airhead*, that's who you are." For the NF, that simply fosters the next quest: "Who *am* I, now that I know that I'm an airhead?" And life goes on.)

The NF's strengths—which, when maximized, become liabilities—include:

▪ a phenomenal capacity for working with people and drawing out their best;
▪ being articulate and persuasive;
▪ a strong desire to help others;
▪ the ability to affirm others freely and easily.

Here, briefly, are some of the positive and negative ways the NF role plays out:

▪ **Management.** NF managers are positive, affirming idealists whom others may like, but whose warm style makes it difficult for others to disagree with them. NF managers often have difficulty being firm supervisors and tend to give workers too much leeway.
▪ **Mating.** As mates, NFs are often teddy bears who, out of a deep need to give and receive affection as well as to avoid conflict may inadvertently reduce a relationship to "a hug a day keeps problems away." Unfortunately, there's more to relationships than hugs and kisses.
▪ **Parenting.** They provide unlimited warmth and affection, but their ongoing quest for self-identity creates a confusing role model to a child trying to grow up. NF parents defend their children against all odds and in all situations.
▪ **Teaching.** The beauty of NF teachers is their ability to make each individual student feel important and cared about. They make superb teachers, albeit a bit idealistic at times. Successful learning, in NFs' eyes, is a product of students feeling happy and understood.

- **Learning.** NF students like to please their teachers but, perhaps more than SFs, take criticism too personally.
- **Money.** This is one of the least important things to NFs. Ultimately, money is to be used for, but not at the expense of, their ideals.

HAVE A NICE DAY!

To an NT: *"Have an interesting day."*
To an NF: *"Have an inspiring day."*
To an SJ: *"Have a productive day."*
To an SP: *"Have fun today!"*

The NT Temperament

NTs gather data consisting largely of abstractions and possibilities (iNtuition), which they filter through their objective decision-making process (Thinking). Their driving force, in their never-ending quest for competence, is to theorize and intellectualize everything. Driven to try to understand the universe, they ask "Why?" (or "Why not?") of everything: *Why* does this rule exist? *Why* can't we do it differently? NTs are enthusiastic pursuers of adventures who, in their enthusiasm, may take risks that unintentionally imperil people close to them.

NTs—who represent about 12 percent of the U.S. population*—learn by challenging any authority or source. They have their own standards and benchmarks for what is "competent," against which they measure themselves and everybody else. They are always testing the system. Relentless in their pursuit of excellence, they can be very critical of their own and others' shortcomings, and impatient when confronted with them. They are frequently perceived by others—often incorrectly—as aloof, intellectual snobs.

* *Please Understand Me,* p. 47.

The NT's strengths—which, again when maximized, become liabilities—include:

- an ability to readily see the big picture;
- a talent for conceptualization and systems planning;
- insight into the internal logic and underlying principles of systems and organizations;
- the ability to speak and write clearly and precisely.

Here, briefly, are some of the positive and negative ways the NT role plays out:

- **Management.** They are the strategic planners and researchers, although they can get lost in their strategies and overlook day-to-day business.
- **Mating.** NT mates intellectualize feelings and emotions, and are more interested in theorizing a relationship than nurturing and experiencing it.
- **Parenting.** With their high standards and desire to inspire independence in children, they become role models who may seem impossible to live up to. They demand intellectual prowess of their children and enthusiastically (sometimes overenthusiastically) surround their children with learning "opportunities."
- **Teaching.** NTs' conceptual clarity and precision of language can be exciting to students, although it can also be intimidating at times. They love it when students challenge them, allowing both parties to learn from the engagement.
- **Learning.** As one who learns by discussing, the NT is initially fun to have in any classroom, but over the long haul can become tiresome as a consequence of working any given point to death.
- **Money.** NTs cover the financial waterfront—they tend to have well-designed financial plans but can still lose their shirts because they like high-risk ventures.

The SJ Temperament

SJs' information-gathering process is practical and realistic (Sensing), to which they prefer to give organization and structure (Judging). SJs yearn to belong to meaningful institutions and, as such, are the bill payers of life. They are the foundations and backbone of society—America, Motherhood, and a Hot Lunch for Orphans. They are trustworthy, loyal, helpful, brave, clean, and reverent. They are stabilizing traditionalists who, as about 38 percent of the U.S. population,* represent the largest single Temperament group. As Judgers, their tendency is to organize—people, furniture, schedules, organizations, and on and on. Just as people are integral to the NF, and conceptualization integral to the NT, SJs' lives revolve around procedure. They have a procedure for everything, from making breakfast to making love.

The SJ's strengths—which, when maximized, become liabilities—include:

- administration
- dependability
- the ability to take charge
- always knowing who's in charge

Here, briefly, are some of the positive and negative ways the SJ role plays out:

■ **Management.** SJs make phenomenal administrators of systems that require precision and organization. They have a tendency to do what needs to be done today, often to the neglect of what must be done tomorrow.

■ **Mating.** Home and hearth are cornerstones of SJs' relationships. An SJ's relationship roles are clearly defined and must not vary. Rituals and traditions are a stabilizing factor, but the rigidity with which they are carried out may become tedious.

■ **Parenting.** SJs make clear who is the parent and who is the child—and what is expected of each. Though sometimes overly rigid, they provide the structure and boundaries many children need. Such definition, though, can be confining, especially to a child of a different type.

■ **Teaching.** Punctuality and neatness can at times be as impor-

---

* *Please Understand Me,* p. 39.

tant as content, whether the subject at hand is an assignment, a student's appearance, or the condition of someone's locker.

■ **Learning.** SJ students respond well to teachers who are organized and deliver what they promise. Their rigidity may make them less than open to learning new things.

■ **Money.** SJs are the money (and moneyed) people of the world —the bankers, accountants, lawyers, and stockbrokers—who conservatively guard society's trust funds.

Fashion Temperaments

Who are the flashy dressers? Who is always color coordinated? How you dress has a lot to do with Temperaments, according to Sharon Summer and Sharon Jackson, marriage and family counselors at the Creative Development Center in Placentia, California.

Idealistic
NF

—Has a flair for combining styles, textures, and colors
—Is often innovative, a trendsetter
—Enjoys creating "unique" look
—If saves clothes, may do so because to throw them away is to throw away a statement about self
—Likes soft lines and colors

Fashion Image: Making a unique statement, flair, creating a personalized look

Inventive
NT

—Chooses clothes for comfort and utility, out of habit
—Does not pay much attention to conventional practices
—Considers price and durability

—Keeps clothes for years; when they wear out considers it a personal offense

—May wear what is easiest to get to, what is closest at hand

Fashion Image: Not a high priority, except as required by a job

Traditional
SJ

—Prefers a classic look

—Buys clothes of quality, durability, value, longevity

—Takes methodical care of clothing

—May purchase a planned, coordinated outfit of related garments

—Keeps clothes for years and cannot throw them away when they are not yet worn out

—Will adhere to a prescribed color plan

Fashion Image: Wants a classic, long-lasting look

Adventurous
SP

—Chooses clothes for *impact*

—Prefers action-oriented garments that allow flexibility of movement

—May tend toward "casual" dressing

—Chooses brands and labels that *others* will recognize

—Can be bold, dashing, daring in style

—Can artfully intertwine bargains with designer labels

Fashion Image: Making an impact on others

The SP Temperament

SPs' data collection is practical and realistic (Sensing), to which they bring spontaneity and flexibility (Perceiving), which makes them the original "now" generation. Their Sensing grounds them in the reality of the moment, and their Perceiving keeps them open for other ways of dealing with that reality. The only thing an SP can be sure of is the moment; a "long-range plan" is a contradiction in terms. Their quest is for action, leading them to "act now, pay later." About 35 percent of the U.S. public,* they are attracted to careers that have immediate, tangible rewards: firefighting, emergency medicine, mechanics, farming, carpentry, and anything involving technical skills. Although they are frequently misunderstood because of their somewhat hedonistic, live-for-now nature, they make excellent negotiators and troubleshooters.

The SP's strengths—which, when maximized, become liabilities—include:

- practicality
- adept problem-solving skills, particularly at hands-on tasks
- resourcefulness
- a special sense of immediate needs

Here, briefly, are some of the positive and negative ways the SP role plays out:

- **Management.** When a crisis needs solving, SP managers are geniuses at generating solutions. But they are not above intentionally creating crises to solve, just to give them a sense of purpose.
- **Mating.** Life with an SP can be a thrill a minute and a surprise a minute, which can be intense to a partner whose type demands predictability. Planning and structure are always low priorities.
- **Parenting.** Their proclivity for life in the here and now means that SPs may forget promises made yesterday and neglect a vision for their child's future—but deliver very handsomely on immediate expectations.
- **Teaching.** SPs are best when teaching practical, hands-on skills, such as industrial arts, vocational-technical skills, and elementary-school subjects, tending to shy away from areas that

* *Please Understand Me,* p. 39.

are more theoretical or abstract. Lesson plans are the banes of their existence.

▪ **Learning.** Because they tend to dismiss the relevancy of theo-

---

"WOULD YOU LIKE A PIECE OF PIE?"

SPs ask themselves:	*"Am I hungry?"*
SJs ask themselves:	*"Is it time for dessert?*
NTs ask themselves:	*"Am I in control?"*
NFs ask themselves:	*"Will it make me feel good?"*

---

retical courses, SP students often shun intellectual pursuits. They learn best those subjects that seem practical and immediately rewarding.

▪ **Money.** SPs are the original high rollers, tending to win big and lose big. Money, like almost everything else, is something "of the moment." Budgets and financial plans are therefore out of the question.

As we said at the outset, Temperaments are a shortcut. Once you understand the basic characteristics of, say, an SP, you can then add on other preferences to get a fuller grasp of an individual's type. An Extraverted-Thinking SP (an ESTP) is very different from an Introverted-Feeling SP (an ISFP), although both share many SP traits, including the love of the immediate, hands-on experience, avoidance of theory and planning in favor of the reality of daily life, and disdain for rituals, procedures, and regulations. The ESTPs' Extraversion and Thinking cause them to be more outgoing, often the life of the party; they are very engaging, "up" types, although they can be unintentionally abrasive. ISFPs, in contrast, are typically shy and retiring. Although they are very sensitive to people's needs and feelings, they can be so self-effacing that they often negate their own positive qualities. Yet, in spite of their differences, because of their SP bond—their Temperament—ESTPs have more in common behaviorally with ISFPs (with whom they share two preferences) than with ESTJs (with whom they share three).

As you can see, Temperaments are an easy, albeit limited,

way of observing and cataloging Typewatching behavior. While providing an incomplete picture when compared to using all four of an individual's preferences, Temperaments can serve as handy references. For those interested in delving deeper into the subject of Temperaments, we can recommend no better source than Keirsey and Bates's book.

Now that you understand the basic concepts behind Typewatching, let's get into how it can be put to use on a day-to-day basis.

5

The ABCs of Determining Someone's Type

"Whoa, this isn't the same person I've known in the office."

Typewatching, as we've said, is as much art as science. And like any art—be it music, painting, sculpture, or speaking a foreign language—it requires equal parts perspiration and inspiration. We hope we've provided the inspiration. Now it's time to start doing. The remaining chapters of this book will describe how Typewatching fits into many aspects of daily life: the workplace, relationships, home life, parenting, and learning, among other things.

Fortunately, as we've also said, Typewatching is something most of us have done instinctively, in the form of name-calling, all our lives. But as name-calling, it was probably put more to destructive than to constructive use. The challenge to the kind of name-calling we describe—Typewatching—is to accentuate the positive, or at least give equal time to it, to learn to celebrate differences rather than mock them. Whatever your type, you will find it rewarding to convert your name-calling energies into a positive and constructive activity.

Before we begin learning how to "type" others, however, a few words about the process of becoming a Typewatcher. It takes practice, to be sure, but also patience. In the beginning, an individual's four letters become evident one letter at a time; sometimes one or more of an individual's letters may be very difficult to discern. Moreover, sometimes those letters can change. You might look at your boss, for example, and decide after a bit of observation and analysis that she is *definitely* a Judger. After all, she is superorganized, makes endless lists, is always on time, and doesn't like it when you don't do things her way. That sounds an awful lot like a J. Then one day you are invited to her house for dinner. In this "new" environment she seems quite different, taking on the characteristics of a different type. Dinner is late, her home is messier than you'd have expected (considering the organization of her desk at work), and she is not ruffled by the fact that there's not enough white wine or that one of the couples she invited to dinner canceled at the last minute. Such a relatively laid-back attitude is typical of Perceiver-type behavior. "Whoa," you think to yourself, "this isn't the same person I've known in the office." Suddenly, you're not sure what type your boss is.

This isn't uncommon, and it doesn't mean that you mistyped her or that you aren't a good Typewatcher. It merely means that you had access to only some of the information that made up this person's type. With the new data you might retype her —as a P, as less of a J, or as someone who prefers equal amounts of each, and behaves according to the situation.

It's also important to remember, as we stated earlier, that behavior is relative. Although your preference may be for Extraversion, you may *seem* like an Introvert compared to a spouse, child, or friend whose Extraversion preference is stronger than yours. Two "Extraverts" can behave very differently.

The point is that your perception of another person's type shouldn't be cast in stone. Someone may be quiet and withdrawn with family but loud and aggressive with friends, for example, or a tough nut in the office but a teddy bear at home. Or the other way around. To be a good Typewatcher, then, you must be flexible, to allow room for new information about an individual's personality. (This will come much more naturally to Perceivers than to Judgers, but everyone should be capable of doing this.) Look at it this way: You wouldn't want someone to misjudge *your* type at a time when you weren't "being yourself."

Begin with the Obvious

While there's no fixed order to the Typewatching process, it's best to start with those characteristics most readily visible to the observing eye. That's usually the Judging-Perceiving preference, although it can sometimes be the Extraversion - Introversion preference. The other two pairs of preferences, Sensing-iNtuitive and Thinking-Feeling, are much more difficult to observe for beginners. Therefore, we will start with the obvious preferences and as we become more proficient, tackle the tougher ones.

When beginning to Typewatch, ironically, it's hardest to start with people you already know well—a mate, an older child, a parent, or some other family member—because you know so much about them and in such detail that you will find it difficult to see the broad general outlines of their personalities. Typing strangers can be difficult, too, although the fact that they are "clean slates" to you makes it easier to identify the preferences as they emerge under your watchful eye.

Spotting Extraverts and Introverts

Imagine for a moment that you are on an airplane, sitting in the middle of three seats. On your left is an individual who clearly wants to engage you in conversation, even though you are not receptive to her overtures. By the time the FASTEN SEAT BELTS sign goes off, you already know about where she is going, what she will do when she gets there, what her husband does, and how her son is doing in school (poorly) and why. (In the process, you manage to reveal only your name.) She seems oblivious to your stifled yawns. It would be safe to assume this person's preference is for Extraversion.

Meanwhile, on your right is an individual you find intriguing —there is something about the way he looks, perhaps, or what he's reading. You try to start up a conversation by asking, "Are you traveling on business?" To which he smiles and replies only "Yes," and continues reading. Undeterred, you try again: "Do you get to the Coast often?" Again, a pleasant but brief answer: "No, not much. How about you?" He avoids having to talk at length by asking questions, thereby putting the onus on you to carry the conversation. After a few minutes of listening and responding to your friendly chatter, he lays down his book, excuses himself, and closes his eyes. The message is clear: This Introvert wishes to be left alone.

As you can see, the Extravert-Introvert preference is relatively easy to spot. Still, you could have been fooled: the man on your right could have just spent the entire day lecturing and consulting, and might have been an Extravert who was simply "burned out."

Another difference between Extraverts and Introverts, aside from their outgoingness, is their differences in energy levels: Extraverts' energy tends to *increase* and become even more enthusiastic as a conversation develops, while Introverts' energy tends to *decrease* and drain out of them, leaving them feeling depleted, although they may not let on that this is happening.

Expressive or Reserved?—E-I Differences

- Extraverts speak more loudly than Introverts; indeed, Introverts often want to "hush" Extraverts, although they don't necessarily do so.
- Similarly, Extraverts tend to speak more rapidly; Introverts tend to hesitate, thinking before speaking.
- While Introverts often understate a point, Extraverts often overstate and repeat their points.
- Extraverts use more nonverbal communication—hand-waving, facial movements, and the like—while Introverts often appear more aloof and reserved.

Spotting Judgers and Perceivers

Perhaps the easiest preference to spot is the last letter of the four-letter type—the J-P preference.

GONE, BUT NOT FORGOTTEN

ENFP: "Nothing is ever lost. Another P has it and can't find it, or a J has filed it."

Let's return, for a moment, to your airplane seat. After lunch is served, the woman on your left opens her briefcase. It is very orderly—pens and pencils are neatly lined up, papers are organized in well-marked file folders, and tickets, glasses, and everything else seem to have their place. Instead of taking out work, however, she spends the next few minutes *re*organizing everything, putting the file folders in a new order, realigning the pens and pencils, doing a systematic overhaul of the whole interior of her briefcase. It would certainly appear that this person's preference is for Judging.

CAVEAT EMPTOR

Supermarkets are cleverly designed for both Judgers and Perceivers. The aisles are organized, the cans are neatly stacked, and there is a directory on the wall, appealing to Js. For the Ps, at the end of the aisles, and especially, at the cash register, there is a variety of impulse purchases, often several products thrown together into a single basket labeled SPECIAL BARGAINS.

At about the same time, the man on your right opens *his* briefcase, and things couldn't look more different. As he pops the latch, the briefcase bursts open and the remnants of an old sandwich fall into his lap. As it does, it reveals an amazing array of things: papers in no apparent order, a pair of socks, pencils with no lead, and a half-written business letter, among many other things. He rummages through, seemingly oblivious to the disarray, pulls out an agenda for his upcoming meeting, which he reviews and stuffs in his pocket. One could determine, with reasonable certainty, that this man's preference is for Perceiving.

Here, too, you could be fooled. In spotting Js and Ps, it's important to keep in mind that Perceivers, because of their adaptive, flexible nature, are capable of appearing like Judgers —though Judgers are less able to exist within the flexible world of Perceivers.

Rigid or Flexible?—J-P Differences

▪ While Judgers tend to remain more focused on a task or topic, Perceivers more easily move from subject to subject, sometimes to the point of appearing scattered.
▪ Judgers have a built-in time clock, whereas Perceivers don't have this innate sense of schedule.
▪ Perceivers are capable of generating alternatives to any situation, while Judgers tend to get locked into one method.
▪ Judgers, as their name suggests, tend to offer decisive opinions on most topics, while Perceivers are less likely to do so, often preferring to answer a question with another question.

Identifying Sensors and iNtuitives: A Tougher Job

Unlike the E-I and J-P preferences, the Sensing-iNtuitive preference is more difficult to observe in action. The reason is that

---

QUESTIONS AND ANSWERS

Judger: "The problem with you Ps is that you always answer a question with another question."
Perceiver: "Is that bad?"

Sensing and iNtuition—the preferences within the information-gathering function—are the processes by which we filter incoming information. Unlike Extraversion, Introversion, Judging, and Perceiving, whose "results" are more readily visible in the form of words and behavior, Sensing and iNtuition take place "inside" and are much more subtle.

ARE WE THERE YET?

We once took a flight with two friends, a Sensor and an iNtuitive. Both were white-knuckle fliers on a fairly rough flight. After a couple of hours, upon breaking through the clouds and spotting the runway just ahead, the iNtuitive, associating "seeing the runway" with "being on the ground," sighed, "Ah, we're there." The Sensor, recognizing that you're not "on the ground" until wheels touch pavement, looked askance at the iNtuitive and said, "We're not there yet!" This is a typical S-N distinction: As we stated earlier, iNtuitives typically see a cup as "half full" and brimming with possibilities, while Sensors see it as "half empty" and less full of potential.

Sensors may be the easier of the two to spot. Their tendency to take things literally can be a giveaway. (However, since iNtuitives tend to be wordsmiths and often like to twist, play with, and juggle words, they might give a literal answer to a question simply for the fun of it.) Try asking someone, "How was your day?" While an iNtuitive more likely would give a general, conceptual answer—"I spent the day trying to whip my staff into shape," for example—the Sensor is more inclined to give you a detailed blow-by-blow description of the process: "I called a staff meeting at nine-fifteen to discuss some organizational problems. We met for about an hour and a half, at which time I talked privately with my two top salespeople, negotiating a revised commission schedule, which we'll put into place next month. . . ." Of course, if the Sensor is an Introvert, he or she may not be so talkative. Indeed, Introverts can make it difficult to spot any of their preferences—except perhaps Introversion

—by being so inward. Rest assured that they will eventually reveal themselves, but it may take a bit more time.

Remember that Sensors are the here-and-now people: they

"EXCUSE ME, WHERE IS THE REST ROOM?"

Sensor: "Go through the green double doors and turn im-mediately left. You'll pass a staircase and a sign that says "Caution: Doors Open Outward." Three doors past that is the director's office. The rest room will be the next door on your right."

iNtuitive: "Go through the doors and turn left. It's down the hall. You can't miss it."

---

are grounded in the present reality, while the iNtuitives' focus is more general and oriented toward the future or the past. The question "How ya doing?" directed to a Sensor might be answered matter-of-factly as "Fine" (or "Tired" or "I have a headache"), while an iNtuitive might see many other levels of meaning in the question. In response, an iNtuitive is as likely to proffer a philosophical dissertation on his or her life's goals and objectives as to give the simple reply, "Not too bad."

Forest or Trees?—S-N Differences

- iNtuitives tend to look for the meaning of an event or an experience, while Sensors tend to examine its various components.
- Sensors like to understand a process by looking at it sequentially, while iNtuitives randomly gather information and fit it into a theoretical model.
- Sensors focus on "what is" and find "what can be" unsettling; iNtuitives focus on "what can be" and find "what is" depressing.
- Sensors are impatient with fanciful schemes; iNtuitives are impatient with many details.

Spotting Thinkers and Feelers—Toughest of All

The decision-making function is the most difficult preference to discern. The Thinking and Feeling processes—the means by which we critique, evaluate, and decide about the information we have gathered (through Sensing or iNtuition)—is a very personal one. It can be difficult to tell at any given moment whether someone's opinion is an objective or a subjective one.

In general, Feelers are pleasers. Let's return one more time to our two fellow airplane-seatmates. The Introverted gentleman on your right, you may recall, was pleasant and friendly as he spurned your conversational overtures. He did nothing to offend and seemed almost apologetic in declaring his boundaries. His striving for harmony, even with strangers, suggests that he has a preference for Feeling.

The Extraverted woman on your left—who talked incessantly, telling you her life story in the opening few minutes—made several statements which, on first blush, sounded rather harsh. In describing her son's problems at school, for example, she told of how she refused to let him transfer into a different math class—one where he knew the teacher, who understood his special needs. "I explained to him that the challenging teacher was good for him," she explained. "In the long run, it would help him to cope with difficult people in the real world." Decisions based on reason, without reference to how they will make people feel, suggest a preference for Thinking.

(At one point in the conversation, should he feel comfortable to express his opinion, the Introverted man on your right might lean over and say to the woman, in true Feeling fashion, "Don't you think he'd learn better if he was comfortable and felt understood? I've always felt that people perform better when they're happy.")

In general, Thinkers are capable of looking at situations objectively, often making statements that may sound a bit uncaring and unfeeling to others. Feelers often become embroiled in interpersonal issues to which they may not even be a party; they often feel a need—indeed, a responsibility—to ensure that fairness and others' feelings are considered, defending the underdog whenever possible.

Head or Heart?—T-F Differences

▪ Thinkers seek objective clarity, while Feelers seek harmony with people.

▪ Feelers are usually situational and subjective; Thinkers tend to apply their decisions more uniformly and consistently.

▪ Thinkers look at the cause and effect of a decision, while Feelers show more concern for how people will feel about it.

▪ Both have feelings, but Feelers prefer to experience them while Thinkers prefer to understand them.

Why Fs Are Underpaid

There's good reason, according to interviews and observations made by Susan Scanlon, editor of *The Type Reporter:*

ESFJ: "I've always believed that my accomplishments should be acknowledged and rewarded without my having to ask."

ESTJ: "I look forward to asking for a raise. It's fun. I love going in there and telling them why I deserve more."

ESFP: "I think I have two things going for me when it comes to negotiating salary: I focus on details so I give detailed breakdowns of my costs, and I enjoy a chance to negotiate anything."

ESTP: "I used to go through a big, long process to decide how to charge. Now I just make up a number. You get a feeling for what number people grimace at and what number they'll think is too cheap. Then you just pick one in the middle."

ENFP: "I hate money. I hate thinking about it. I hate

talking about it. If I feel I'm being underpaid, I'd rather change jobs than ask for more."

ENTP: "Almost all the Fs I know think poor is pure and rich is evil. I don't know too many Ts who believe that. I constantly go around putting a value on my time."

ENFJ: "I always cringe when people ask me what my daily rate is. It's never a simple question; every doubt of my self-worth flashes before my eyes."

ENTJ: "I don't expect supervisors to know how good I am, so I send them periodic updates and make appointments to meet with them and discuss my performance."

ISFP: "Sometimes I find myself negotiating against myself. If I see the other person wince at what I ask for, I try to take care of them."

ISTP: "I wouldn't leave a salary figure up to them. I'd figure out first what I wanted and be prepared to be totally in command of the direction of the discussion."

INFJ: "I know I could make more money as a consultant, but I'm still in the government because I can't be bothered with selling myself. I need a structure to support me."

INTJ: "I have a high sense of ethics, but I'm not going to be taken advantage of."

ISFJ: "I'm always surprised when someone looks you right in the eye and tells you how much they charge."

ISTJ: "I'm not concerned with what the other person will think of me. I'm more concerned with what they'll think of the data."

INFP: "I keep asking myself 'Can they afford it?' and 'Am I really worth it?' I have to remind myself that the work is valuable and I'm just the vessel the work flows through."

INTP: "I don't consider negotiating a game, I consider it a point of clarification. You work together to define the conditions and the logical consequences of taking a job."

A Few Tips for Determining Others' Types

There are three more important things about Typewatching to keep in mind:

Typewatching can be addictive. The more you Typewatch, the more Typewatching you may want to do. Some people "type" strangers on the street, historical figures, pets, and even inanimate objects like companies and cities. (After a considerable amount of observation, for example, we believe that San Francisco is an ENFP city: it is a gregarious, warm, accepting town that embraces life-styles that are many and varied. Even its unofficial theme song, "I Left My Heart in San Francisco," has a classic ENFP title. Washington, D.C., by contrast, is largely an ISTJ city in its tradition, its need for rules and regulations, and its enduring provinciality.) To the uninitiated, such fanatical behavior can seem overdone, even obnoxious. Moreover, a lot of people don't like to be "figured out"; they find it to be some kind of invasion of their privacy and individualism. (These are often the same people who are quick to label others.) You should respect others' rights to be left out of the Typewatching process—or at least not to be informed of your conclusions about them.

It isn't necessary for someone to have taken a formal personality test for you to observe his or her type. While the Myers-Briggs Type Indicator can determine an individual's type with particular accuracy, your own ongoing observations can still be useful. Remember, though, that your determination of someone's type is made through your own Typewatching "glasses." That is, what you observe is affected in part by your own type and experiences. We might see someone as one type and you might see that same person as another type, and we might both be right, given what aspects we've seen of that person and "where we're coming from," behaviorally. As such, any determination of type can and should leave room for adjustment.

Typewatching is only an explanation. It is never an excuse. We can't emphasize this enough. We've seen it happen among both neophyte and experienced Typewatchers. One person will say, "Gee, it doesn't matter if I'm late, because I'm a Perceiver and Ps are always late." Or "There's no need to tell him how I'm feeling because he's a Thinker and probably wouldn't understand anyway." Suffice it to say, this is no way to further understanding and communication among people.

Enough prologue. Let's go into the workplace to see how Typewatching can be put to practical use.

6

Typewatching from 9 to 5

"Somehow I'd like a little more margin for error."

The art of Typewatching can be used in almost any workplace, in almost any way. Typewatching has been applied to a wide range of organizational activities, including goal-setting, time management, hiring and firing, conflict resolutions, and team-building. There are many other applications, but, at least for openers, we'll look at some of these issues, recognizing that they represent only examples of the possibilities.

How the Types Set Goals

Goal-setting is one way to keep organizations focused and successful. It is also important for establishing the general criteria by which the productivity and value of an employee's performance is ultimately measured. It is indeed a crucial area of the work world, whether it is a two-person office or a behemoth bureaucracy. As one might suspect, different personality types approach goal-setting in very different ways. To start, let's look at the process of goal-setting in terms of Extraverts and Introverts.

Extravert-Introvert Goal-Setting

Extraverted managers need to do their thinking out loud;
hence, the goals they commit to are very much in the public
domain. Exactly how the goals are shaped and explained depends, of course, on the kind of Extravert. Extraverted-Judgers
determine early on what the goals should be, make them clear
to all, and impose them on everyone—often before they've
been agreed upon by key members of the group; remember
that Judgers are not beyond "making good time going in the
wrong direction." Extraverted-Perceivers, no matter what the
goal, want to argue about it for a while. Sometimes it can be
very frustrating for subordinates in such situations to get a clear
picture of exactly what the EP's goals are. For EPs, goals can
change overnight—or even midsentence—as they continue to
refine things verbally and get feedback from others.

Clearly, this can be problematic. A case in point is an army
general with whom we consulted. One morning, staring out the
window, the Extraverted officer said, "I wonder what would
happen if we moved that ditch about six feet back." To his
amazement a few hours later, he looked out the window again
to find a cadre of troops busily filling in and digging out. He said,
"What the hell are they doing?" (He didn't even remember
wondering out loud.) To which the general's chief of staff replied, "General, you said you wanted the ditch moved."

An Introvert, on the other hand, would rather collect information about possible goals, then go somewhere and sift
through the data alone, gradually working toward a conclusion
about what's feasible. Only when a decision has been made will
the Introvert begin to share it with others; but the process of
getting to the decision is a contemplative, inward one. Clearly,
decision making by committee is not an Introvert's long suit. In
fact, if pitted against an army of Extraverts, Introverts will
almost surely do battle. The more the Extraverts push, the more
likely the Introverts are to clam up. The result: We lose the
Introvert's most significant contribution—the ability to reflect,

listen, and contribute clarity of thought and speech. Great ideas get lost in the process. The fact is, Introverts don't know what they think about something until they have time to think about it.

Effective goal-setting, then, should give Extraverts the opportunity to verbalize—and reverbalize—their ideas, Introverts the time to reflect by themselves on what has been discussed.

Introverts may tire of the Extraverts' aggressiveness in goal-setting. They become bored with the apparent redundancy of Extraverts' verbalizations and feel imposed upon. They would prefer to start meeting the goal instead of talking about it. One helpful technique is to ask Extraverts to put their ideas into writing, however sketchily, before a meeting, which provides the Introverts a chance to peruse the goals on their own.

Extraverts, in turn, must be clear to the Introvert about exactly what they'd like feedback on. It would be better to say, "Let me know what you think about items one, three, four, six, eight, nine, and fifteen," than to simply say, "Let me know what you think." Extraverts tend to assume that Introverts' silence means consent, which isn't necessarily true. With these techniques, both parties will be ready and willing to share their thoughts and strive for consensus.

Sensor-iNtuitive Goal-Setting

How do Sensors and iNtuitives fit into the goal-setting process? Let's start with the Sensors. More than anything, they want practical, down-to-earth goals; they want to emerge with something tangible, something that isn't pie-in-the-sky. Toward this end, Sensors often nitpick—they want translations of things that seem visionary; they don't want the big picture, they want specifics. They don't want some elusive goal; they must have the day-by-day description of where things are going and where things should ultimately be. Overall, Sensors hone in on the vital details and bring clarity to the goal-setting process.

For Sensors, the goal-setting process is much like that classic formula for giving a speech: "Tell 'em what you're gonna tell 'em; tell 'em; and tell 'em what you told 'em." Effective goal-setting for Sensors must run a similar course: The Sensor must know what's going to be accomplished with the goal; then the goal must be set; then there must be some tangible evidence that the goal can be reached. Without these components, goal-setting for a Sensor will be an exercise in futility.

Of course, iNtuitives prefer not to bother themselves with such minutia. They want to look at the future in terms of far-reaching impact. The nitty-gritty of goal-setting, in fact, seems dull. What's exciting is to fantasize about where they want to be a year or two down the pike. As we said earlier, iNtuitives always reach for the "there and then"; the "here and now" is much too mundane.

In goal-setting, as in any activity that involves brainstorming, iNtuitives see many possibilities. They are less fearful of the unknown and more willing to explore new paths. They can quickly develop a "big picture" of any situation, though it may not be very realistic. Ns see the interrelatedness of various aspects—how all the pieces fit together. This can be a real asset in goal-setting, in which the whole is truly greater than the sum of its parts. Unfortunately, since iNtuitives aren't always as aware as they should be of the details and scheduling realities of their organizations, their grand schemes sometimes turn out to be more theoretical than practical.

ONE STEP AT A TIME

An N supervisor was complaining that one of the new workers could not learn a routine task. Suspecting that the new man was an S, someone suggested that he would learn if he was shown move by move. The N was aghast, saying that he never explains things that way—it's too insulting.

We said earlier that the numbers favor Sensors about three to one among Americans: There are simply more of them wherever you go. Because they are into *doing,* you'll find them successfully involved with the practical hands-on aspects of the corporate and military world. It's when they are removed from the hands-on aspects of work—often courtesy of promotions—that problems begin. When Sensors succeed at jobs for which Sensing skills are particularly useful—for example, a line manager who is terrific at keeping things moving—they are often pulled out of the ranks and put on some kind of career advancement track—an MBA program, for example. Typically, this new environment calls for iNtuitive skills, the ability to look at the "big picture" and into the future instead of at specific details in the here and now. This pattern holds particularly true for the military, where almost everything takes place "here and now." In the military, exceptionally competent officers are pulled from action-oriented work and sent for a year of leadership training, only to be returned at year's end to practical down-to-earth management positions. While in leadership training, they are told about the far-reaching nature of what they will be doing as managers. The curriculum of such places is iNtuitive theory, yet most of the positions available to them after this training involve nuts-and-bolts Sensing-oriented management. As a result, such programs—and this is true of civilian graduate schools too—set up a Sensor for frustration, disappointment, and career debilitation.

Thinker-Feeler Goal-Setting

It is the Thinker who strives for the most objective, concise descriptions of what the goals will be. Thinkers, particularly iNtuitive-Thinkers, are word nitpickers, so if they are involved in the goal-setting process, they can spend an inordinate amount of time working, reworking, and sometimes overworking, the wording of the goal description. While this may produce an effective and excellent document, Thinkers often don't understand why everyone else doesn't appreciate their perfectionism—or, even worse, why they are sometimes criticized for taking so long to find that perfect word.

For Feelers, if a goal is to be considered worthwhile, it must be people-oriented, a criterion that Thinkers, particularly Thinking-Judging types, see as a mushy, wishy-washy waste of time. But Feelers can play a major role in goal-setting. They tend to focus in on the professional growth needs of the people within the organization, from the hourly workers to the board of directors. They often moderate the unduly harsh deadlines or procedures for reaching a goal in order to take into account employees' capabilities and needs. Their persuasiveness makes them well suited to "sell" the goals to the rest of the organization. More often than not, the goals they sell have to do with people-oriented issues.

Judger-Perceiver Goal-Setting

Extraverts, Introverts, Sensors, iNtuitives, Feelers, and Thinkers notwithstanding, it's the Judging-Perceiving difference where goal-setting differences are most visible. The reason: Js want to establish agreement on a goal as quickly as possible—wrap it up, put a neat bow on it, package it for the whole world—so that they can get on with implementing it. Further, an Extraverted-Judger will gladly impose goals on everybody within earshot, and then some; Introverted-Judgers, in contrast, are less voluble once the issues have been resolved, but no less eager to resolve them. One of the frustrations of Perceivers in goal-setting is that as soon as an idea emerges about which there is general agreement—or even for which one individual has made a good case—the Judgers are quick to consider the matter closed, denying others the chance to evaluate it or hear other sides of the issue. And once Judgers are on a roll in goal-setting, they are likely to plunge into action, assuming that everything is settled and everyone has come on board.

On the flip side of this behavior is the Perceiver, constantly redefining goals, even after everything seems to have been settled. Ps aren't comfortable with things being "decided"; they'll want to reopen, discuss, rework, argue for the sake of arguing. (This is especially true for Extraverted Ps.) It's not out of the question for the P to "revisit it one more time just to make sure" no matter how long something has been discussed. Such behavior is anathema to Js, and can ultimately reduce both sides to tears: Ps get intimidated and argumentative; Js, frustrated and impatient. In the process, the whole goal-setting process can come to a screeching halt.

SWEET REVENGE

An MBTI trainer divided her group into Js and Ps. She asked each group to "design a new library wing" while the other group watched. The Js went first. Someone had a bag of jelly beans and in five minutes they had laid out a floor plan in jelly beans.

Then it was the Ps turn. They complained about the assignment briefly, then they ate the jelly beans.

Preference Imbalance: A Recipe for Disaster

An ENFJ we worked with illustrates what happens when one preference is imposed too strongly on the goal-setting process. The individual, a presidential appointee in Washington, D.C., in good Judger style determined by himself what he thought were effective goals for his agency. Not surprisingly, they were largely ENFJ-type goals, calling for everyone to work harmoniously toward self-fulfillment through achievement of the Common Good. The problem was that not everyone else in the agency shared these values and few were committed to achieving them. Moreover, people hired to train employees toward reaching the goals were severely resisted. In the end, the ENFJ felt rejected and thought his staff didn't like him. In fact, they simply disliked the way he imposed his goals. Things might have gone differently had the ENFJ made better use of the Perceiving mode during the goal-setting process: gathering more information, getting others' reactions, trying to reach a consensus before imposing his own goals on others.

As our ENFJ illustrates, goal-setting comes easy to Js—often to the dismay of their subordinates of whatever type. Sticking to and achieving the goals is even easier—regardless of whether

the goal remains relevant over the long term. Ps, by their nature, often feel they have not yet collected enough data to
establish a firm goal. True to their nature, Perceivers recognize
that "more data" is always needed: it's hard to set a goal when
you know that new information, still unknown, could render a
plan invalid. Thus, while Judgers can get to the wrong goal with
dispatch, Perceivers may never even get around to defining a
goal.

Preference Balance: A Recipe for Success

Ultimately, successful goal-setting can be enhanced by bringing
together a group that reflects a cross section of the various
preferences. That's easier said than done, of course, but there
are ways to increase the chances of success of any group.

One thing Typewatchers can do to facilitate the goal-setting
process is to determine the group's prevailing type by simple
count. How many Extraverts versus how many Introverts? How
many Sensors versus iNtuitives? Thinkers versus Feelers? Judgers versus Perceivers? So, if there are five Extraverts and two
Introverts, the "group type" can be said to be predominantly
Extraverted. The same determination needs to be made for the
other three sets of preferences. Ultimately you will end up with
a four-letter "group type." You may then want to read the
appropriate typological profile in Chapter Ten, viewing the
group as the "person" in question. The profile may provide
insight into how a group may perform as a unit.

This process can help everyone become aware of the group's
natural strengths and blind spots. If a group is more Introverted
than Extraverted, for example, it will be necessary, after achieving some commonality of goal, to make sure the goal is effectively communicated to employees once it has been agreed
upon.

Goal-setting Tips

Here are some other tips on how each type can do its bit for balanced and effective goal-setting:

■ **Extraverts: Put it in writing.** This will appeal to Introverts, who prefer to be able to reflect on something before having to discuss it. To this end, it would be most helpful to hand out such written material as far in advance as possible.

■ **Extraverts: Practice your listening skills.** Make sure everyone has the chance to voice his or her opinion. Extraverts will tend to dominate discussion time; Introverts may take longer to let their thoughts be known. Having a "gatekeeper" who can keep track of how often and for how long each participant speaks (or doesn't speak) may ensure that all members are able to have their say. Extraverts should remember that silence doesn't constitute consensus. When we consult with organizations, we ask Extraverts to make a contract with themselves to give Introverts sufficient time for reflection before pressing them for a decision.

■ **Introverts: Give Extraverts "thinking space."** Extraverts tend to think out loud: they clarify their ideas by sharing them with others, refining them as they speak. We often ask Introverts to make a contract with themselves to allow Extraverts to do their thinking out loud, and not assume that the first things out of their mouths are intended as "finished products."

■ **Sensors: Don't immediately dismiss "fanciful" ideas.** Sensors need to be willing to listen to plans and schemes that sound "pie-in-the-sky" or too futuristic or remote in time. By rejecting such proposals without a fair hearing, they may limit growth and creativity.

■ **Sensors: Try to see the "big picture."** It's important for Sensors to move beyond a focus on individual pieces of the puzzle and on to an understanding of how the pieces fit together into a whole. Sensors must learn how decisions made in one part of an organization may affect another, or how any single decision fits into the larger scheme.

■ **iNtuitives: Pay attention to pitfalls.** Most iNtuitives don't like to attend to the practical realities of their schemes. They jump to the envisioned end and ignore the reasons it may not be possible to get there in real life. It's important for them to find the patience to hear the Sensors out, for the Sensors may have important things to say about the feasibility of goals.

■ **iNtuitives: Don't ignore the present.** It isn't uncommon for iNtuitives to become so wrapped up in their ideas and plans for the future that they forget about situations that require immediate attention today.

■ **Thinkers: Consider the "people" side of the equation.** Thinkers are so determined to reason their way to goals and problem-solving that they ignore the human element (which can be unmoved by the arguments of reason). Instead of being single-mindedly task-oriented, Thinkers must remember to focus on how people will be affected by the goals they are proposing.

■ **Feelers: Don't be afraid to bite the bullet.** Sometimes life is not harmonious and confrontation must take place. Feelers must realize that the world will not come to an end if they take an unpopular stand and that growth and positive change often result from healthy disagreement.

■ **Feelers: Don't take things personally.** Criticism of a goal or ideal shouldn't be seen as a personal attack. Feelers need to recognize that while others may disagree with them, such disagreement doesn't necessarily constitute dislike or personal criticism. Feelers need to be more objective.

■ **Judgers: Listen to alternatives.** It is easy for Judgers to dismiss new options or ways of doing things. Js "know" they are right and may find it difficult to entertain another view. Moreover, Judgers need to set aside sufficient time when goal-setting to allow all the options to be heard and considered.

■ **Perceivers: Focus on closure.** It is easy for Ps to keep considering new information. There are times when a firm decision is necessary on the basis of the available information, however incomplete. Moreover, Perceivers need to pay more attention to deadlines and other time constraints.

Making Goals Work

It may be helpful, upon completion of goal-setting, to review the goals in light of how they reflect the overall group type. If the group is heavily weighted toward Extraverts, iNtuitives, Feelers, and Perceivers, are the resulting goals correspondingly expansive, intrapersonally oriented, with room for flexibility and development? If not, perhaps these are not the right goals for this group. After all, having set the goals, the group must live with them. The goals must be compatible with the people who will strive to meet them. Whatever the goals, they must be reachable. If not, it is an invitation to frustration.

This is not to say that those in the minority should be ignored. If our Extraverted, iNtuitive, Feeling, Perceiving group comes up with ENFP goals, will there be room for Introverts to operate within that system? Will the objective advice of Thinkers be heeded? What about Judgers—will their schedules be followed? Will the systems they set up be undermined by the relatively laid-back nature of Ps? Matching the goals of an organization with the overall organization type is often deceptively easy. In the process, it is easy to become blind to the contribution that could be made by those who are of different types.

Goal-setting Traps

We know a group of six dentists who went into business together some time ago. They were all ISTJs—Introverts, Sensors, Thinkers, and Judgers. Their explicit, agreed-upon mandate was to provide excellent dental care for those in their community. They hung out their shingle, and after two years all six found that the business was not doing well. They couldn't figure it out. How could they miss? They were all professionals, well trained, with the appropriate credentials and experience. A careful examination of their business in light of their type and collective goals found that no one was thinking about the future, about the big picture, about communicating with the public, about the interpersonal aspects of their practice, and about how to ensure flexibility and open-endedness in their operation—in short, they were ignoring the Extraverted, iNtuitive, Feeling, Perceiving parts of their dental practice. There was no one making sure the dentists were speaking before Rotary clubs and PTAs (Extraverted), they weren't forecasting the community's changing dental needs (iNtuition), they weren't doing those nice things that make people like, or at least tolerate, their dentists, from handing out toys to kids to sending thank-you notes to adults (Feeling), and their rigidness didn't let them explore how they got in the dilemma (Judging). They had set their goals in concrete and charged ahead. Worse still, they were so set in their ways that they were unable to respond constructively to their dilemma and simply got deeper and deeper into trouble.

We were brought into the action and the first thing we showed them was how similar they were typologically. In many ways it was a classic case of a strength (of all four identical preferences) becoming a liability. It was too much of a good thing. Next, it was a matter of finding ways to attack the problem. Among other things, they decided that if one of them "played Extravert"—going to meetings, giving speeches, and so on—that person needn't put in as many hours in the office. In other words, such Extraverted activity was to be considered as much a part of doing business as filling teeth. We found similar appropriate activities for each of the other three missing preferences, sometimes hiring others to perform those duties; the important thing was what got done, not who did it.

Ultimately the goal-setting process is a reflection of an organization's type. Organizations whose goal-setting is determined largely by Judging types often turn into the slow-gain, solid, steady, Fortune 500 types—Ford, AT&T, Exxon, and most government agencies, for example. P-type goal-setting often leads to organizations that are high-risk, rapid turnover, innovative, and sensitive to changing markets and trends—for example, most Silicon Valley computer firms are started by high-risk P-type entrepreneurs. Success for them depends on their ability to follow through with J-type management and organizational skills. The "new" Chrysler Corporation is a good example of

P-style goal-setting, as described by its president, Lee Iacocca, in his best-selling autobiography: after going through severe financial straits, it made a number of entrepreneurial-like high-risk moves, including firing dead wood, letting employees try new approaches, selling assets to obtain cash, and several other unorthodox (for a major auto-maker) maneuvers—all of which were very short-term. Once the firm was stabilized (which happened amazingly quickly) the goal-setting process changed from short-term to mid- and long-term.

Typewatching and Time Management

As with goal-setting, our personality types influence how we look at and manage time. To show how this works in practice, we often separate those attending our seminars into groups according to one letter of their type and ask them questions related to their perceptions of "time." For example, we ask:

- *Extraverts and Introverts to describe what they would do if they suddenly inherited a bunch of free time.* Es will spend the time in external activities—parties, phone calls, shopping, and other activities that provide a lot of stimulation; Is will gravitate toward things like reading, going for walks, hobbies, and other more contemplative activities.
- *Sensors and iNtuitives to "describe time."* (Information-gathering is a process of describing things, not evaluating it.) Sensors will be quite literal and precise in their descriptions of time; iNtuitives will be more general and abstract.
- *Thinkers and Feelers to "define time."* (Decision making calls for the process of defining and putting limits around the data we've gathered.) Thinkers will be more objective, sounding like dictionaries, while Feelers will be more subjective and personal about what time means.
- *Judgers and Perceivers "what to do with time."* Judgers, predictably, will organize time and use it for some kind of measurable accomplishment. Perceivers will be more open-ended about time and will want to spend the time in activities for which they will be less accountable—like playing.

From seminar to seminar, the answers to these questions remain predictably consistent and true to type. And each type always seems to be surprised by the answers given by its opposite type. Extraverts, for example, find Introverts' choices for use of free time boring. Introverts find Extraverts' choices exhausting.

Below are the answers given by participants at one typical seminar. They are uncensored, showing the order, variety, and breadth of answers given. For example, Extraverts and Introverts responded as to what they would do with free time as follows:

What Extraverts and Introverts Would Do with Free Time

Extraverts	Introverts
city lights	go sailing
metro tour	take a walk
yacht	take photo lessons
furs/jewels	sit and be quiet by myself
shopping mall	travel
paintings/sculptors	study the manual, literature
swim	visit a museum
kites	go to the theater
Yosemite	meditate
hike	
car	
plane	
guitar	
read	
animals	
wild hot movies	
red shoes	
parakeet	
string quartet	
long purple skirt	

Extraverts (cont.)

Japanese dinner
fan
handsome man
champagne
ice cream
candles
good conversation
walk on the beach
lollipops
ballet
balloons
flowers
tattoo-butterfly, rose on tush
lace undies
poetry
potpourri (strawberry)
party

Note the sheer volume of the Extraverts' response—an indisputably Extraverted answer. That the words are rambling and redundant further demonstrates how true to type these answers were. Introverts, looking at the Extraverts' list, commented that it seemed tiring and boring—to them it was simply overkill. This is a crucial E-I issue when it comes to time: what excites Extraverts drains Introverts. (Es' and Is' use of time was demonstrated in the process of actually making the lists. The Introverts made their list quickly and sat quietly until the exercise was over; the Extraverts would still be making their list if we hadn't stopped them.)

How Sensors and iNtuitives Describe Time

Sensors and iNtuitives described "time" like this:

Sensors	iNtuitives
minute	infinite
hour	forever
seconds	eternal
short	circular
long	waves
sad	fleeting
happy	short
enough	linear
not enough	forward
no time	flowing
quiet	measured
meeting	intangible
fiscal year	internal
calendar year	external
right	abstract
time of day	cosmic
time to listen	finite
relax	defined
wasted	tic toc
party	constraint
time ticking away	
year	
productive	
sleep	
wake-up	
decade	
night	
day	
century	

Sensors (cont.)
bad
past (ancient)
season
future
holiday
time to go
vacation
good
reflective
free
class
clock
calendar
schedule

Two things are worth pointing out about these lists. The first is how specific most of the Sensing words are, compared to the more abstract nature of the iNtuitives' words. Second, of the sixty-three words used on the two lists, only a single word—*short*—appears on both. You may find it truly amazing that two groups doing the same assignment would use two completely different sets of words, but they are simply being true to their types. If you were to put the lists together, both groups would probably agree that they constitute a much more comprehensive description of time.

How Thinkers and Feelers Define Time

Thinkers and Feelers, asked to "define time," responded in somewhat different forms. While the Feeling types produced a list, the objective Thinkers, true to type, produced a unified statement.

Thinkers	Feelers
the dimensions we used to establish checkpoints involving past, present, and future	Chronos/Kairos
	collective moments of awareness
divided into measurable units	meeting point of people, events, situations
not reusable	passing of history
always goes in a forward direction (fast)	a way of defining/ interpreting human experiences
	measuring milestones along their/your/mine/our life journey
	that which we never have enough of
	what flies when you're having fun

Again, the differences between the two lists are sharp. The objective Thinkers want to "establish checkpoints," while the subjective Feelers see "milestones" in "life's journey." The word *people* never even appears in the Thinkers' list. It simply wouldn't occur to a Thinker to include such "schmaltzy" terminology when concocting a hard-and-fast definition.

What Judgers and Perceivers Do with Time

And Judgers and Perceivers, asked to answer what to do with time, responded this way:

Judgers	Perceivers
plan it	find out how much we have
fill it up	play
make each moment meaningful	brainstorm the possibilities
deadline	check out any limitations
organize it	have fun
use it	

Perceivers (cont.)

get coffee
treasure the idea of choice
investigate the concept of
   time

Around the office or at home, how we use time is crucial. For the Judgers, once they know what's scheduled, they know how much free time they have. For the Perceivers, it's all "free"—so be careful what you schedule. (Indeed, Ps are often so unstructured that when we asked this question to a group of Ps at a Fortune 100 company, they simply wrote "It depends."

Clearly, such differences in perception of time have implications for how the workday takes shape, whether it is structured time or free time. Typological differences concerning time perception can lead to a variety of disagreements—the Introvert may resent the Extravert's constant interruptions, for example, or the Sensor may disagree with the iNtuitive about whether an hour's worth of work really can be accomplished in twenty minutes—and can have a definite impact on productivity. When a Judger overorganizes Perceivers' unscheduled time (which the Ps may well need), it can stifle productivity. Judgers, for their part, find too much unstructured time frustrating, and its mere existence can lessen their productivity.

Procrastination and Type: No One Is Immune

Minimizing procrastination, the domain of no one type, is another key element of time management. Everyone procrastinates sometime. While it is often thought that only Perceivers —laid-back, flexible, unscheduled types—procrastinate, there are ways and times in which all types can procrastinate:

▪ **Extraverts:** Extraverts procrastinate when it comes time to be quiet, reflective, and introspective. They *know* there is a need for such things but would rather put it off to tomorrow.

■ **Introverts:** Introverts procrastinate when it comes time to get up before a group to share information, or when asked to work (or play) as part of a larger group.

■ **Sensors:** Sensors procrastinate when it comes time to engage in fantasy and fanciful thinking, or in thinking about the future. They would rather be doing what is "at hand," here and now.

■ **iNtuitives:** For iNtuitives, procrastination comes when it is time to engage in projects that involve Sensing-type detail. April 15, for example, is the bane of every iNtuitive's existence.

■ **Thinkers:** Thinkers procrastinate when it comes to the inter-personal aspects of life. They may be slow to say, "I'm sorry," when it was appropriate to do so. To facilitate the process and to oil the wheels of relationships, Thinkers should remember that "schmaltz" is not a sign of weakness.

■ **Feelers:** Feelers procrastinate when it comes time to tackle jobs that involve little interaction or, even worse, negative in-teraction with people, especially anything even remotely con-frontational. Feelers want to be involved—positively—with people and will put off anything that calls them away from this priority.

■ **Judgers:** Judgers procrastinate when it comes time for fun, leisure, and relaxation. They always think, "I'll relax *after* I finish this project." There are an endless number of projects, of course, and relaxation time never comes.

■ **Perceivers:** Perceivers procrastinate when it comes time to make a final decision about something. There is always some-thing else to know, more information to be gathered and ex-amined.

Time-management Tips

Whatever the time-related problem, regardless of whether it involves supervisor or subordinate, here are some suggestions for making the best use of time, both at work and at home:

■ **Extraverts: Avoid having to share everything.** It is natural for Extraverts to run down the hall or into another office on the spur of the moment to discuss and get feedback on whatever has just occurred to them. A better use of time may require scheduling such interactions and limiting their duration. In general, Extraverts can become easily distracted by the "outside" world. Time management may require restricting activities and focus.

▪ **Introverts: Don't stay inside.** Introverts must walk a fine line between the constant bombardments of the "Extraverted world"—phones, meetings, and unexpected emergencies—and their own longing to retreat within themselves, to the inner world where they prefer to dwell. They must know when to emerge from their Introversion to do what must be done.

▪ **Sensors: Remember that there's more to time than minutes and seconds.** It is important for Sensors to try to see beyond the exactness of time. They do well with their own realities—those minutes and seconds—but fall short when what is required is a sense of history or a vision of the future. Nor are they random about time when dealing with others. They can be real nitpickers.

▪ **iNtuitives: Be realistic.** An important question for iNtuitives to ask themselves is "Can I really do all I have set out to do in the time I have to do it?" Most iNtuitives have an unrealistic sense of what can be accomplished in a given amount of time.

▪ **Thinkers: Consider others' time.** No matter how clearly one sees time as objective and linear, others may see time in different ways. It is easy for Thinkers to negate the human and subjective elements of time, forcing others to conform to their rationale. They should learn to take into account the needs of the other people who will inevitably be part of a routine, project, or event, allowing space for their schedules.

▪ **Feelers: Define your boundaries.** Feelers sometimes have a difficult time setting aside blocks of time for their own work, responding instead to whoever is needy. While Thinkers more readily impose themselves on others, Feelers become the imposed-upon, often assuming others' guilt, problems, and responsibilities. Feelers must learn how to say no without feeling guilty.

▪ **Judgers: Keep in mind that time is not always of the essence.** Judgers naturally work well with schedules and time managing.

There is a danger, however, of executing something too quickly just to reach completion. This can lead to stress and inferior work, and may possibly jeopardize the project at hand. In the long haul, if it means a project must be redone, going too fast could actually slow rather than speed a project. When a Judger feels a strong need for completion, it may help to get another's input, particularly that of a Perceiver.

▪ **Perceivers: Try to focus.** Perceivers are easily distracted and can flit from one project to another. Ironically, they often see this as time-saving behavior—after all, they are tackling several projects at once. The result, of course, may be many projects left uncompleted. Perceivers may have to limit themselves arbitrarily to "only" two or three projects at a time.

Hiring: The Attraction (and Distraction) of Opposites

One truism of Typewatching we've found over the years is that "Type begets type." This, of course, is just another way of stating that old adage "Birds of a feather flock together." Whether choosing a friend, a church, or a job, we tend to find people and organizations that resemble us.

Working or living closely with someone who is your four-letter opposite can keep you very busy, behaviorially speaking. On the one hand, your relationship spans the full gamut of preferences: Extraversion, Introversion, Sensing, iNtuition, and all the rest. On the other hand, every time you face each other you are each looking at the part of your personality that you don't prefer. (More on this in Chapter Seven.) In the supervisor-subordinate relationship, as with marriage and parenting, four-letter opposites allow us the maximum growth potential but also present the greatest amount of difficulty. If you're more alike, however, which is usually the case in organizations, there can be other problems.

The fact is, managers tend to hire people similar to their own personality types, although this will be instantly denied by all self-respecting equal-opportunity supervisors who think they hire rationally and objectively. It's understandable that in the hiring process, you would choose someone whose personality you like, who thinks like you, who responds enthusiastically to your ideas, and with whom you feel "in sync"—in other words, someone who is "your type." Indeed, the types hired or promoted, for example, tend to be more similar than different, at least at certain organizational levels. Sixty percent of the upper management of any organization tend to be Thinking-Judgers; the higher you go in the organization, the more likely that is to be true. But, as you'll see, too much similarity of type can, indeed, cause blind spots because certain preferences—and their strengths—won't be represented.

Variety is truly the spice of life, and nowhere is this truer than in organizations. An individual who is different from the organizational mainstream can make a powerful contribution to the organization. Yet over the long haul that person will be seen as a maverick, an outsider, someone with "different chemistry." Inevitably, that person will be pressured to "shape up." It isn't an accident that everyone at IBM wears a long-sleeved white shirt and a dark suit and everyone in the U.S. Army wears khaki. In both institutions, people are expected to dress alike because they are expected to behave alike. As a result, both organizations tend to draw similar types of individuals. It's no surprise, then, to learn that people in the army and at IBM are both overwhelmingly the same type—in this case, ISTJ.

One reason for solving blind spots is that it allows us to avoid the paranoia that comes when people who are different criticize us. Because "type begets type" in an organization, it is only natural that when you complete, say, an action paper for a superior, you will first run it by various colleagues to whom you have gravitated within the organization—usually someone of a type similar to yours. It is natural to run something first by those who will be looking at it with the same glasses you wear, metaphorically speaking: they are more likely to understand and approve of your effort. Later, when the paper is presented to a superior of a different type, who will criticize it based on a different preference and view of the world, it will cause you less stress because you will already have received approval from those who "understand" you.

Without such an appreciation of how different types view the same piece of work, it is easy to attribute criticism to a wide range of other misleading factors: race, sex, age, politics, superiority, fashion, whatever. Often such misunderstood criticism provides "proof" that one of your critic's primary roles in the organization is to "screw up my day." An abundance of different types—combined with some basic Typewatching skills—provides an organization's employees with a full complement of "glasses" through which things can be seen, reducing needless paranoia and increasing understanding and productivity.

What's the ideal mix? Ideally, there should be enough similarities among types to maintain peace, and enough differences to allow for challenge and stimulation.

WHY TJS ARE NATURAL MANAGERS

It's no accident that 60 percent of the world's managers are Thinking-Judgers. Even in systems that are overwhelmingly Feeling, TJs rise to the top; in the clergy, for example, most bishops are TJs. The reason is that important decisions—those that involve people's lives, money, and careers—must be handled objectively. The Thinking-Judging dimension allows for organization and carry-through when it's needed most. While personal involvement may seem appropriate, in the end, what's needed is for someone to remain cool, calm, and objective.

Too Much of a Good Thing Is a Bad Thing

Organizational blind spots due to similarity of types and lack of a complementary vision plague many firms. NASA may have lost seven astronauts to a fiery, premature death because the organization is overwhelmingly Judging—more than 80 percent at the agency's top decision-making level, according to three studies of NASA personnel conducted by a government agency, a major university, and ourselves. As a result, even though the data said convincingly not to launch the space shuttle *Challenger,* the Js' strong need to stay on schedule (regardless of whether there were any political or organizational pressures to do so) ruled in the end, with tragic results. Had there been more Ps involved at that level, they might have persuaded the Js to be more responsive to additional data, less absolutely committed to maintaining the schedule. (This example is a bit oversimplified, of course. The *Challenger* investigation showed clearly that the folks at NASA and related organizations did carefully consider other data. Ultimately, however, "staying on schedule" proved to be an overriding concern.)

And so it goes with each of the four sets of preferences. A marketing firm made up entirely of Extraverts isn't as likely to stop and listen to an Introverted client's needs. An abundance of Sensors in an organization can become so grounded in reality that the organization becomes blind to its own future; while its bills may get paid exactly on time, it may still fail because of its inability to keep up with changing markets. An organization overloaded with Feelers will overlook rational data, while a firm with too many Thinkers will rely too much on data, overlooking the human side of the equation.

One good example of this last situation—too much T and not enough F—can be seen in the great "New Coke" debacle of 1986. Coca-Cola had spent millions to launch the new product, conducting taste tests that determined that their new product was well liked. With great fanfare and hype, New Coke was launched—only to fall quickly from grace. What happened? The answer is simple: Amid all the marketing tests and surveys, it seems that no one bothered to ask whether anyone was tired of "old" Coke. In fact, they weren't. The result was that the objective, T-oriented marketing folks created a new product that everyone liked—but no one wanted.

Another argument for diversity of types is that workers in an organization with disproportionately similar types are generally incapable of building on each others' strengths and learning from each others' weaknesses. An overwhelmingly P organization, for example, is great at exploring new possibilities, at thinking about alternative products, at being flexible, and at putting out the organizational brushfires of the moment. But good luck trying to keep them on schedule.

It doesn't matter where the typological lopsidedness occurs. When you have too many of one type, you lose something of value to your organization.

The Building Blocks of Creativity

A few years ago we conducted an experiment involving a group of engineers at one company. We had four groups compete with one another in what is called the Reddy-Kroeger Lego Man exercise. (You probably know Lego as those children's colorful plastic blocks that snap together.) Each group was given an hour to assemble its Lego blocks. The goal was to replicate, as precisely as possible, a Lego Man model sitting on a table in the center of the room. A few simple rules were to be followed, and it was made clear to each group that what counted was the actual time used to construct the replica.

While all four groups had an hour to accomplish the task, they could use whatever time they needed to plan the construction —twenty minutes, thirty minutes, even fifty-nine minutes— before building. All that counted was actual construction time. As you may have guessed, we assembled the groups according to type: Table One had six Sensing-Perceivers, Table Two had mostly iNtuitive-Thinking-Perceivers, Table Three were Sensing-Judgers, and Table Four had primarily Thinking-Judgers. Exactly why we chose those particular combinations of preferences isn't as important as the fact that each team consisted of like-minded people.

While participants were told that assembly time was all that counted, we did actually keep track of each group's planning time and that proved to be very significant. Table Four, the predominantly TJ group, won. They put the model together in four minutes, having spent twenty-six minutes planning. And when the exercise was over, one ISTJ refused to speak to the rest of the members of the group—she felt she had been excluded from the process and that her contribution had been demeaned—to which one of the TJs said he felt bad about that, but that's what happens when winning and losing is the name of the game.

The next best group was Table Two, the NTPs. They spent nine minutes assembling, although they spent the longest amount of time—thirty-one minutes—planning; they made one error.

The third best group was the SJs—they spent seventeen minutes in planning and fifteen minutes assembling.

Finally came the SPs. SPs are the ones most into action, so much so that they didn't want to waste much time planning. In fact, they spent only four minutes planning; it took them thirty minutes to construct, including the time it took to correct one error. What was interesting was that members of the group that came in last were very happy with themselves, even though they had taken the longest. They explained that their total time —four minutes planning plus thirty minutes assembling—was only four minutes slower than the number-one group's.

The discussion that followed was lively, enlightening, and very true to type. Everyone, it seemed, defended their own approach, regardless of whether they "won" or "lost." The SPs, the group that came in last, loved the way they did it; among other things, everybody in that group was speaking to one another and, indeed, if we gave them the same assignment again, they likely wouldn't change a thing. Meanwhile, the TJs, the winners, were very divisive and had alienated one of their members.

What's the point? First of all, it was clear that each group behaved remarkably true to type. Second, by not having a mixture of types, each group displayed blind spots, tunneling their respective strengths into weaknesses: the action-oriented, flexible SPs spent too little time planning, opting instead to "get it done," right or wrong. The get-it-done-at-all-costs TJs alienated people in favor of results. The conceptual NTPs spent most of their time in redesigning their design, never quite executing it. And the procedure-oriented SJs struggled too long determining how it should be done before getting it together.

Problem Client or Problem Staff?

Another reason for deviating from one's own type in hiring is that with a more representative selection of all preferences, we can better anticipate the variables of the outside world—everything from unexpected events in the marketplace to customer and client relations to a host of other issues and mini-crises faced regularly by any organization. Even to understand the cross section of humanity that constitutes "the outside world" requires, ideally, the entire range of psychological types.

For example, it isn't uncommon to have one "problem client" with whom no one can get along except one particular employee, who seems to "understand" that client. The two develop a special relationship, to the amazement (and, usually, relief) of the rest of the organization. Those two individuals likely share several letters, enough, at least, to make their personality styles far more similar than different. Having a ready supply of different types on staff provides maximum flexibility for dealing with the wide range of types any organization is likely to encounter.

We can't overstate the need for diversity in an organization. While it's always tempting to have an organization full of like-minded individuals, in the long run, it will hinder more than help.

Typewatching and Conflict Resolution

Typewatching's value can't be better demonstrated than when it comes to resolving disputes. Despite the amount of conflict that rages in many organizations—admittedly sometimes a product of the very diversity of people advocated above—most organizations don't do a very good job of extinguishing these everyday brush fires. Make no mistake: There is nothing wrong with conflict. Avoiding it usually means avoiding progress.

What's important is making sure that conflict improves rather than destroys the organization.

It's no secret that one person's "hearty discussion" is another's "fight." And, in many ways, that is a reflection of our preferences and our types. Moreover, it can be said that no type deals well, effectively, or easily with conflict.

Our experience tells us that all types face real stress dealing with conflict, and therefore a Typewatching approach to conflict resolution could be one of the most important things you'll take away from reading this book.

Extraverts vs. Introverts

A conflict to Extraverts is something to be examined out in the open. They talk more than they listen, and not necessarily to those with whom they are in dispute. ("Let me tell you what that son of a gun just did to me.") Indeed, Extraverts can get quite assertive when conflicts arise. And the more they talk, the louder and more excited they get. So what starts as a relatively minor irritation can turn into a full-blown argument in no time.

Introverts internalize a disagreement so they can reflect on what took place. They rehearse and rework dialogue inside their heads, engaging in both hindsight and anticipation of what's to come. ("I wish I had told her she wasn't listening to my point of view. Maybe next time I'll be able to tell her what I really think.") Clearly, one danger for the Introvert is that such internal reflection often resolves the problem—internally—and nothing happens externally. Another danger is that the Introvert may, consciously or unconsciously, store the experience for future reference. So when another person next encounters the Introvert, that person may suffer the fallout of a dispute he or she never even knew happened.

Sensors vs. iNtuitives

As we've said previously, arguments often start with differing perceptions. The Sensor hears *literally* what's said, while the iNtuitive hears *figuratively* what was meant or what he thought was meant—and things can go downhill steadily from that point. "Don't tell me what I heard or what I said," says the Sensor with an abruptness and self-righteousness almost certain to generate a fight. The iNtuitive responds, "I know what I heard and I know that I'm right." And off we go.

The only real conflict to a Sensor is that which is actual and immediate. Pending situations aren't of concern, nor are those that are "out of sight, out of mind." The danger for a Sensor is that because they are too single in their focus there may be a lot going on about which they aren't even aware. ("How should I know you're angry if you don't tell me?") Sensors work best when fighting specific battles, as opposed to trying to win a larger war. A Sensor who is perennially angry at a supervisor will prefer to settle the immediate dispute of the moment rather than overhaul their overall relationship. It would be more constructive if the Sensor could see the bigger picture: the relationship between the immediate irritation and the total relationship.

The danger with an iNtuitive is that, as with everything else, conflict is a matter of conceptualization—everything is in the mind. Their iNtuitive skills allow them easily to see the links between causes and effects involved in a conflict, putting people, programs, and other parts of a system into proper perspective. Their strength is in being able to construct a blueprint for settling a dispute. Their weakness is that the blueprint may not include a provision for implementation. It is iNtuitive to say "I think we have a problem here. To resolve it, we should put things in proper perspective. Let's examine the communication flow with the West Coast office." Such words are red flags to Sensors. "I am angry now," says the Sensor. "I don't care how anybody else fits into the picture."

An amusing illustration of the difference in perception comes from the comic strip *Peanuts.* It shows Lucy, a Sensor, saying to Linus, an iNtuitive, "You get out of life exactly what you put into it, nothing more and nothing less, exactly what you put into it." While Linus examines that rather thoughtfully, Snoopy (also an iNtuitive) walks away, reflecting, "Somehow I'd like a little more margin for error." That's typical of iNtuitives: they'd prefer to avoid the exact—in favor of some extrapolation from the facts to a larger vision.

Thinkers vs. Feelers

You might expect Thinking types to be particularly competent at dealing with conflict because they are more objective than subjective. They have a reputation for being adept at firing, disciplining, and handling all those other unpleasant personnel issues. But in reality, Thinking types *shun* conflict: they bury it, avoid it, and run away from it just as much as Feeling types. ("Let's not get excited. If we remain calm and rational, we can work it out.") And while they may not personalize things as much—they seek neither conflict nor harmony; they merely seek clarity and justice—they are no more skilled than Feeling types at handling conflict.

Thinking types in general have a fear of that which gets sticky or interpersonal, so a T, seeing that your feelings are hurt or that a conflict is getting abrasive, may not always know what to do about it and may be intimidated by the emotion that's being demonstrated by another person. Often the result is that fear takes over and the T can become quite clumsy dealing with an interpersonal conflict.

Feelers personalize everything, especially conflicts. Harsh words spoken about anything translate personally to the Feeler. "We've really screwed up as an organization" means, to the Feeler, "I've done something wrong." A statement by a supervisor that "We're not meeting our deadlines" will automatically translate to a Feeler as "I'm goofing up," even if the Feeler is always on time. Even seemingly neutral words can be interpreted as inflammatory. "Let's examine our relationship" can bring fear and trembling to a Feeler, who may infer that something is wrong, even if nothing is. Moreover, it will be assumed that he or she is part of the problem, which may not even exist.

A good example of the T-F differences with conflict grew out of a workshop we conducted in which we asked a group of four Feelers and four Thinkers to define "conflict." Here are the answers, exactly as they were written:

Thinkers defined conflict as "any discussion, conversation, or debate when win/lose is the only perceivable possible outcome."

Feelers reported that "conflict exists when we have four sets of opinions/feelings, ideas/experiences, and we're trying to reach consensus."

As stated earlier, Feelers tend to personalize the issues. Their strength is their ability to identify with another's difficulty. This strength, when maximized, is that they translate everything through their own personal experience, as they did in the above definition. In general, Feelers' approach to conflict is to smother it. "There, there. We're all on the same team, aren't we?" Their preference is to resolve conflicts by sweeping them under the rug—which doesn't resolve anything.

Judgers vs. Perceivers

The minute something enters the Judger's world, it must be aggressively dealt with. Often, if it involves changing a schedule or adding new or conflicting data, it is quickly rejected. (Some people call this "bitching.") As a result, even the most innocuous dilemma can turn out sounding like a conflict.

Judgers strive for control, and they do this during conflicts. Their motto: "Stay on top, be in charge, and, above all, don't lose your cool." A classic J approach is to look around for someone else to blame. (This is especially true of Thinking-Judgers.) Js often sound more abrasive on points of disagreement than they really may feel. They sound so closed, so right, and so unwilling to negotiate.

Perceivers always seek alternatives. They can be sources of unending frustration to those of different types, especially to Js. When a Perceiver generates an alternative, he or she frequently has no intent of ever following through on it—it's just part of the Perceiving process—and Judgers end up becoming frustrated and angry over what is, in effect, argument for the sake of argument or merely alternative for the sake of alternative: "Let's take a look at *all* our options."

Another problem is that Perceivers don't always say exactly what they mean. In typological terms, Ps, as their name implies, usually share their *perceptions* instead of their *judgments* and think they sound more definite than they actually do—particularly as far as Js are concerned—because they need to hear very definite and concise statements. We witnessed this phenomenon not long ago in a conversation between a Judger and her Perceiver supervisor. In preparing a mailing the J was stuffing envelopes with an amount of paper that made the envelopes bulge. Her supervisor thought a larger envelope should have been used. The P supervisor approached her worker and shared her perception: "Isn't that envelope too small?" The J employee replied with a simple no and went on with her work. The supervisor then had to confront what she considered to be the employee's poor judgment. Had the supervisor originally shared a *judgment* instead of a *perception*—"I think the envelope is too small. Please use a bigger one"—it would have made the process smoother and quicker, and would have minimized the potential for conflict over this issue, however trivial. (The supervisor could easily resolve the problem by telling her employee, "I shared a perception and not a judgment. What I really meant to say was . . .")

A further impediment to conflict resolution is that Judgers are so sure they're right, they have no tolerance for any shades of meaning. "I know I'm right," says the J, "and because I know I'm right, you must be wrong." If you're also a J, of course, you're equally convinced you're right and *bingo,* there's nowhere to go. Ps, on the other hand, get so busy in a conflict—searching for new data, opening up alternatives, and trying to figure out how the J came to that conclusion with incomplete data—that by the fifth or sixth sentence into an argument a P may not even recall what the argument is about. Needless to say, that can be frustrating to others, especially to a J.

The Five Key Steps to Resolving Conflicts

In any kind of conflict, whether at home (as we'll see in Chapter Seven) or at work, there are five basic steps to ensure that parties involved get a proper perspective on the issue at hand, which will go a long way toward finding a solution. The five steps require answering some basic questions:

1. The Issue: What are the issues involved in the conflict? List them clearly.
2. The Basis: Are they typologically based? Can you pinpoint the issue to a letter preference and sort it more objectively?
3. The Cause: How did the impasse originate? What of its history can you recall? Can you pinpoint that typologically?
4. The Solution: Can each party involved identify with the other's point of view?
5. The Contract: Finally, are there compromises or contracts that can be negotiated around modifying the problematic situation?

The Five Steps: A Case in Point

Let's see how this works in real life. We once had a case involving two Judgers at a federal agency some years ago. There was an ESTJ male manager, the supervisor of an INTJ female. As an ESTJ male, he was a traditional-minded individual who thought that on account of both his maleness and his managerial role he was supposed to give the orders. ESTJs bring to the world a confidence in knowing the answers to everything; the questions are often irrelevant. His female subordinate disagreed. As an INTJ, the most independent of the sixteen types, she could always come up with a better way of doing things.

It was inevitable that the INTJ female would resent having to take her ESTJ boss's orders. She was convinced she could do the job better than this man who was imposing a bunch of "stupid archaic procedures" on her. For the ESTJ, the procedures weren't stupid, they were tried-and-true techniques that kept the system oiled. It was a case of the SJ's "Don't fix what isn't broken" versus the NT's "Change for the sake of change produces learning."

The conflict escalated to a point where they were hardly speaking, and yet the nature of their work and the system demanded that they work closely with each other.

Otto was called in to mediate and it was then that he imposed the five-step process on this situation.

1. The Issue: It was presented to Otto as supervisor-subordinate tension resulting from sexism. An additional part of the conflict was that he, the boss, was trying to thwart her career development, and that she, the subordinate, was trying to undermine her boss's authority.

2. The Basis: Knowing the sharp differences that can exist between an ESTJ and an INTJ—both types that frequently think they're right and are not always open to negotiation—the first thing he had each party do was to read their own individual typological portraits and underline what they thought was accurate about themselves. The ESTJ found a great deal of accuracy in reading about his type and underlined appropriately; the INTJ, too, found much that was accurate. Otto then had them swap their underlined portraits and read about each other.

3. The Cause: Having examined the basis at some depth, we discovered some underlying causes. To their amazement, the specifics of their conflict were covered in the general statements they had read and underlined about themselves. Their typological differences had been translated into sexual differences: he got blamed for being a "bossy male chauvinist pig" while she got blamed for being a "tough broad" who didn't know how to take orders. Both of them had to reckon with the knowledge that society is not comfortable with T women, ESTJ males least of all because they are such macho traditionalists.

Seeing conflict as a matter of typological rather than individual differences can depersonalize—and defuse—conflict.

4. The Solution: Ultimately, as the two began to understand those differences and put things into a Typewatching perspective, they were able to work at least eight hours a day with each other in a fashion that was far more constructive than destructive.

5. The Contract: They agreed that she would make a genuine attempt to meet some minimal organizational procedures while he would give her some space to work independently without breathing down her neck. Moreover, once a month, they would check in with Otto to make sure they were staying on course.

The plan was successful. The two never got to be best friends, but they at least reached the point where they could bury the hatchet somewhere else than in each other's back. They were able to deal more objectively and less personally with their differences.

When the Boss Is Too Nice: Another Case History

Some organizational conflicts don't result from sharp differences and rigid, dictatorial management styles. Even fierce loyalty can cause problems, especially when it reaches the point where subordinates are unable to criticize their boss.

Consider a case we encountered in a nonprofit organization dealing with minority education headed by an INFP female. She had come to the job with high credentials and a winning track record. She inherited an organization of career professionals who represented many years of service and expertise in the field. The organization's corporate culture was to be open, frank, and direct.

Because of her natural interpersonal skills, she was able to garner a loyal following among her troops. They had high respect for her personally and professionally. As any new leader would, she began to make changes in the system, some of which led to differences between the old guard and the new leadership.

For many in the organization, it was a dilemma: they liked her immensely, but disagreed with new ideas. For her, it was a dilemma too: she wanted openness about their disagreements, but as an INFP, took such criticism personally. By the time we were called onto the scene, it had accelerated to the point that despite the continued loyalty and mutual praise, both sides were frozen, and virtually nothing was being accomplished.

Here's how we approached the situation.

1. The Issue: The boss's management style conflicted with the rest of the organization's working style, and all of it was couched in genuineness and compassion—for each other as well as for the program.

2. The Basis: After several days of interviewing the boss and her staff, we found that there clearly was a typological issue. The INFP's style appeared flexible and easygoing. She was more reflective than assertive but, as a Feeling type, tended to interpret her staff's different points of view as personal criticism. Moreover, her positive attitude toward the staff was one of appreciation and constant affirmation, which discouraged open disagreement.

3. The Cause: The boss wanted openness but her behavior discouraged it. The staff wanted to be open, but because of their affection and loyalty to her, "didn't want to hurt her."

4. The Solution: We asked them to do a number of things, one of which was to participate in role reversal in order for each party to hear what the other was saying. We asked the boss to recall and repeat what she heard from her staff ("I disagree with changing Program B," for example); we asked the staff to mimic both verbally and behaviorally her responses (slumped shoulders and a frown, while saying, "I appreciate your disagreement, but . . ."). It was clear that the boss was giving mixed signals that were frustrating her staff. As always, we also asked everyone to read everyone else's type profiles and give feedback, especially where significant to the problem.

5. The Contract: Every time the staff received a mixed signal, they were to call it to the boss's attention. The boss promised that she would immediately let them know if her feelings were hurt; otherwise they could assume that they could continue to disagree with her.

The air became much clearer after that. The loyalty continued—as did the confrontation—but with much more effective results.

Tips for Resolving Conflicts

Here are some things we've found particularly useful over the years.

Extraverts: Stop, look, and listen. Extraverts always think they can talk their way through—and out of—most conflicts. The very thing they find most difficult is what may be needed most: listening to the other person's point of view.

Introverts: Express yourself. As difficult as it often is, and sometimes seemingly redundant, it still is imperative to tell your side of the story—and maybe even tell it again until the other person has heard it. When conflict is concerned, a little overkill can help. Make sure you get a hearing.

Sensors: There's more to conflicts than just the facts. Sometimes, though it seems a waste of energy and may appear to cloud the issue, it is important to look at extenuating circumstances. If someone always disagrees with you no matter what you say, there may be issues involved that need attention other than just the situation of the moment.

iNtuitives: Stick to the issues. When conflict arises, iNtuitives want to relate it to the total picture. That's not always appropriate or helpful. It clouds the specifics and complicates resolution. Sometimes it helps just to settle a simple dispute, which then allows you to deal with the bigger issue.

Thinkers: Allow some genuine expressions of emotions. Thinkers become unglued when others cry at work; they act similarly when people hug or express warmth. But these emotions—at work or anywhere else—are integral with conflict resolution. Even if you're unable to express these things yourself, you should allow others the freedom to do so.

Feelers: Be direct and confrontive. The world won't come to

an end if you say something you really mean, even if it's negative. What sounds harsh to you as you say it probably won't be
received as harshly by other types; they'll probably even appreciate and respect your frankness. If you are given to expressing
a lot of emotion, don't apologize or feel guilty for doing so.
Being upfront about your feelings facilitates moving to constructive resolution.

MIXED MESSAGES

*We have one F and one T supervising our production
shop. When asked how things were going, the T said he
often had to reprimand one man who did not follow instructions. The F then said, "Yeah, and every time you yell
at him, I have to go over and make up for it."*

Judgers: You're not always right. It may be difficult to believe
this, but you must if you want a conflict ever to be resolved.
Judgers see the world as black and white, right and wrong, and
have difficulty accepting opposing points of view. It's hard to
negotiate with someone who thinks he or she is always right.

Perceivers: Take a clear position. Perceivers can often argue
both sides because they truly see both sides of an argument.
Sometimes it comes in the form of playing devil's advocate.
While flexible and adaptive, that's not always helpful to resolving a problem. It may even intensify the dispute. If you really
feel strongly about something, better to take a stand and defend
it.

Typewatching and Team Building

So far we've provided some insights into typologically managing time, setting goals, understanding subordinate-superior situations, and resolving conflict. Given that, we're now ready to
build a team.

Typewatching and team building go hand in hand. We've
already said that the ideal team often never comes to pass

because we tend to pick types that are more similar to than different from ourselves. No doubt the ideal working group would comprise all sixteen types. We would have a smattering of Extraverts, Introverts, Sensors, iNtuitives, Thinkers, Feelers, Judgers, and Perceivers—and we would put them together in such a way that they would not only understand their differences but could also draw on them. But in reality, we tend to do what is most comfortable for us, and that means hiring and working with people typologically similar to ourselves. The result is groups in which the preferences don't balance each other —lopsided groups, in other words. As we've already pointed out, these groups have tunnel vision, blind spots, and too much uniformity at the expense of creativity.

Asking the Right Questions

So, how does one go about team-building typologically? Do we just take a smattering of each type and throw them together and hope for the best? Before we can discuss that, we must first ask three basic questions:

▪ **What do we really want to accomplish in this organization?** You likely have a statement of mission somewhere. Dust it off and take a look; some objectives are listed there. How rigid are they? How literal? How figurative? How objective? You must look for the kind of team you need to accomplish what it is your mission statement says you're all about (unless, of course, you're a strong P and wish to redefine the mission before you build your team).

▪ **What typological preferences are natural for that mission statement?** Is it a mission for hardheaded, directed people, who must make tough decisions quickly with only a minimum of data? Are customer relations important, requiring employees with human sensitivity? How much creativity comes into play? How much planning and how much actual doing?

Given the answers to the first two questions, the third is,

▪ **What are our blind spots?** No matter what the mission statement, no matter what the makeup of your organization, no matter what you're doing well, what kinds of preferences are missing? How can you put together a team that will overcome those blind spots for the greatest good for the greatest number in the organization (including the stockholders)?

The answers to such questions can serve as a solid frame of reference, not only in the nitty-gritty of the organization's day-to-day life but also in moving it toward accomplishing what it is supposed to be doing over the longer term. The secret to success is to build a team that is tailor-made for the task.

A case in point can be found in a government agency (which shall remain nameless) that we worked with in Oklahoma. The group's twelve key people compared their types to the agency's mission statement. The top-ranking executive was an Introvert and disliked those parts of the mission that involved community interaction—speaking before the Rotary Club, issuing news releases, and sitting on community boards and agencies, for example. By the same token, her deputy, an Extravert, was excited by many of these things and would have preferred to do them, but his job description had different demands. There was a similar phenomenon in both the finance and administration departments. A top person was a type less than compatible with the demands of his or her position, and there was an underling who was more typologically suited to the job, but who was assigned to a different task.

We tried to align individuals' missions with their types, instead of with seemingly arbitrary personnel practices. This required a three-day retreat. Much of the time was spent just getting Introverts and Extraverts to trust each other: would the Introverted boss trust an Extraverted subordinate who, by interacting with the public, will gain most of the recognition? It took a great deal on each person's part to understand a "team" concept. It also took a great deal of group effort to transcend organizational rules and regulations in favor of personality strengths and weaknesses.

A Healthy Balance: A Case Study

As you look at the three questions —and the answers you get
when asking them—you can see how Typewatching can help
with team-building. Let's say, for example, that your department's mission is to provide marketing and sales in a Fortune
500 company. And let's say the overwhelming number of people in your shop are ESTJs—Extraverts, Sensors, Thinkers, and
Judgers. It is a good organization: people are productive, happy,
and get along; you meet deadlines. You feel confident you have
the right team for the job.

But look further. Your market and your company have strong
needs for Introversion (reflecting on how you're doing), iNtuition (long-range planning), Feeling (consideration of customers' needs), and Perception (flexibility to changing market conditions)—INFP. In your hardheaded J-ness and S-ness you may
feel that there's no need to change—things are going along
swimmingly. And in your objectivity (your T-ness) you may not
really care about how the clients really feel. After all, they're
getting what they paid for—effective marketing plans and dis-
tribution—and on time. You've delivered the goods.

Still, with the benefit of Typewatching, you can see that trouble is afoot. The more you understand Typewatching, the better
you will be able to put together a team that most dynamically
meets your mission statement—in both its immediate and its
long-range implications.

A Typological Organizational Chart

Sometimes, finding type-related problems in an organization
can be done best by looking at a standard organizational chart,
but with individual types substituted for (or added to) names
and titles. We've used this technique with extremely positive
results.

Consider, for example, the organizational chart on page 119,

F IS FOR FEEDBACK

I'm a T with an F supervisor. It drives me crazy when he says, "I think that's a good idea, now go out and ask everyone else what they think about it."

---

which illustrates a county government we worked with in the South. We were called in for two reasons: There was some general interest in Typewatching; and there were some specific communication problems among the four branches of the organization, between the support staff and the branches, and between top management and the branch chiefs.

After everyone had been typed and had a basic understanding of Typewatching, we charted the organization and, together, began to diagnose the issues.

There were several key problems. For one thing, the chief executive and the deputy, both women, were Introverted-Thinking-Judgers. The four branch chiefs, all males, were four-letter opposites: ENFP versus ISTJ, and ESFJ versus INTP.

The problem, as you might guess, is that the four-letter opposites of the branch chiefs led to a great deal of arguing. For example, every practical, bottom-line-oriented thing the ISTJ wanted to do was quickly shot down and called dull by the ENFP. Further, the INTP wanted to conceptualize about where the organization should be ten to twenty years hence, while the ESFJ felt they weren't paying enough attention to the day-to-day interpersonal dynamics of the office. As a result of such arguing, staff meetings were loud and vociferous. The two Introverted women at the top exercised their prerogative and simply stopped calling staff meetings; as Thinking-Judgers, they felt the meetings lacked productivity and were therefore useless. The four male branch chiefs assumed this was done because the two women managers couldn't take the heat.

So much for the folks at the top. Within the branches themselves there were several typological issues at work. Note, for example, the inordinate number of Judgers, especially Thinking-Judgers. Note, also, that one branch was all Extraverted, including the branch chief. The sheer noise level from that

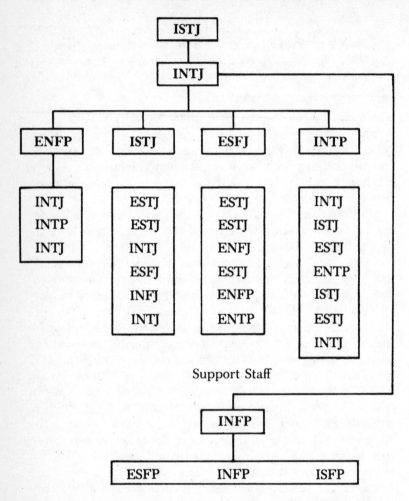

Support Staff

portion of the office was most distracting to the rest of the organization.

And finally there is the support staff, all four of whom were Feeling-Perceivers. It is their preference to have harmony, happiness, and a good time, and they have a strong desire to satisfy others. So every time someone brought in something to be worked on—usually needed "yesterday"—the FP support staffers would stop whatever they were working on and devote attention to the new assignment. Inevitably, this happened several times a day, so that at day's end, there was a sizable pile of uncompleted work, with the most recent work in the typewriter. Further, as deadline pressures mounted, the FPs would meet at the Coke machine for a little release. (During the two days we worked with them, the FPs found excuses to put on two office parties.)

Looking at the organizational chart, the group came up with three basic solutions:

1. The four branch chiefs arranged a half-hour meeting before weekly staff meetings to air their differences privately without involving everyone else.
2. The Judgers within the branches took turns organizing the work for the FP support staff. The Js would set the parameters for the work—everything to be done that day had to be submitted by ten o'clock A.M., for example, or it would be done the next day. The Js loved doing this, and the support staff were less stressed (and spent less time at the Coke machine).
3. The Extravert-heavy branch became more sensitive to noise and worked consciously to limit their gregariousness to coffee breaks and lunchtime.

The whole group, in their newfound typological awareness, began Typewatching on a regular basis. As they came to speak the language with ease, they found new applications and were much more constructive in how they dealt with the problems that confronted them.

Some Tried-and-True Tips

Having worked with a host of organizations of varying sizes and types—from the Institute for Educational Leadership to Exxon to the U.S. Army—we have identified several easy and effective ways to implement Typewatching techniques in the workplace. Some of our favorites:

Why Extraverts Go into Sales
(And Why Introverts Should)

Extraverts seem to be naturals at sales. They are outgoing, gregarious, and effective at making contacts and letting the world know about their product. Conversely, Introverts tend to undersell themselves. But sales trainers tell us that the key thing in sales is "closure"—making the deal. If that's true, we believe Introverts have the advantage.

Consider, for example, an Extraverted salesperson with an Extraverted customer. The salesperson's poor listening and constant talking may get in the way of closing the deal. And an Introverted customer hardly has a chance with an E salesperson. The customer's point of view will be overlooked and he or she will be subject to the E's overkill.

Now consider these situations with an Introverted salesperson. Extraverted customers will sell themselves. They talk themselves into the product and only need well-timed encouragement and someone to listen to them. And Introverted customers will relate to the Introverted salesperson and will appreciate not being pressured; customers can respond to the reflective moments as a chance to come to their own conclusions. What's important is a sense of timing and support from the salesperson, not a gregarious push.

It takes Extraverts to advertise something, letting the world know it exists. But Introverts are better suited to swoop in for the kill.

■ Encourage everyone, from the CEO on down, to display their four-letter types—on their desks, their name badges, and anywhere else they normally display certificates, credentials, or other identifying information. This presents a model of openness and affords the opportunity for conversation about Typewatching. Imagine a typical scene: An outsider stopping by your desk and asking, "What do all the scrambled letters mean?" provides you with the chance to explain a bit of your Typewatching knowledge and share your enthusiasm about this positive way of describing differences.

▪ Have personnel—again, from the top down—exchange profiles of themselves. Have each person underline or highlight those parts of the profile in Chapter Ten that he or she feels are accurate—perhaps even noting things that *aren't* accurate— and share that underlined or highlighted profile with key supervisors, co-workers, and subordinates. This exercise will generate a tremendous amount of constructive discussion among individuals as to what each thought of the other's profile.

▪ Before meeting with an individual to whom you find it hard to relate, read his or her portrait. (If you don't know that person's exact four letters, make an educated guess.) Try to find some explanation within the portrait that might explain the difficulty you've been having. Locate the typological differences between you and the other person and try to figure out how each of you has translated those differences into personal issues. Then depersonalize—and defuse.

JUST SAY NO

I'm an ENTJ and when I go to my ENTP boss for advice, he often tells me things that I just can't do, given my nature or other constraints. It used to anger me until I realized that he was brainstorming, and not giving directives. I can listen to him much more easily now and pick out the best of his ideas. But I have to keep reminding myself, "I don't have to put all these ideas into action."

▪ Develop a central type table like the one in Chapter Three— some form of bulletin board displaying the sixteen personality types. (One office we know put sixteen cork squares together, one for each type.) Have each person in the office tack his or her name in the appropriate square. Be careful, though: Do not violate confidentiality by placing others' names on the board;

the individuals must put their own names up. The board can serve as a good reminder of an office's typological makeup, and may provide some insight when sticky situations arise.

All these suggestions are based upon openness. Where issues of confidentiality exist—in which others haven't yet shared their four-letter types—an individual's permission will be necessary before you can talk about, reference, or otherwise disclose their type. If some choose not to disclose their type, that is their right. But you can still use your Typewatching skills to determine what you *think* they are.

Whatever the case, Typewatching's magic will usually make relationships go more smoothly. That's true in the workplace, to be sure, but also at home. Which is where we're going next: home, to see how Typewatching works with spouses, lovers, and family members.

7

Friends, Lovers, and Type

"At last, someone who will help me get my life in order."

We won't get into a discussion here about the difficulty of having an intimate relationship. That's a given, whether the relationship is the product of a match made in heaven or a shotgun wedding. Indeed, nothing—not even Typewatching—will eliminate the hard work involved in any intimate relationship. But with a little bit of effort, and some basic Typewatching skills, you can greatly enhance your understanding and appreciation of each other; some couples and families even experience a celebration of growth and life using Typewatching skills. It's happened to those who have been together for a few months, and those well past their silver anniversaries. We're not promising miracle cures, but we've seen good things happen in case after case—and have used it in our own marriage to our advantage.

We've already mentioned the phenomenal attractions of opposites. There isn't a more powerful source of love and hate in relationships than that attraction. You've seen it all the time, probably experienced it yourself: two people attracted to each other because each has what the other lacks. "Ah," says the spontaneous, disorganized Perceiver individual when meeting a potential life partner who appears to be organized and scheduled, "someone who will help me get my life in order." "Great," says the organized, scheduled Judger about the same encounter, "someone who will help me loosen up and be spontaneous."

You know the inevitable result: Several years (or months or weeks) down the road, the J is admonishing the P to "please get organized!" while the P is begging the J to "try and loosen up." What was once a major source of attraction is now a major source of heartache.

The goal, then, is for both members of a relationship to ask themselves, "What can I do to keep (or regain) that which was originally so attractive, so as to keep (or regain) excitement in the relationship?" That's a primary role of Typewatching in relationships.

HIDE AND SEEK

I'm an ENFP and my husband is an ISTJ. He says that the inside of my mind is like a swirling cloud where everything in my life is all moving around at the same time and everything is connected. His, on the other hand, is like a long corridor with many different rooms and they all have doors; each door has a different name on it, such as RELATIONSHIPS, WORK, KIDS, HOUSE, RECREATION, PRAYER, THINGS TO BE DONE, *etc. When we have a conversation and I keep changing subjects (which I don't see as changing subjects because it's all related to me), he has to keep running up and down the corridor trying to find the right room—and as soon as he gets the door open, he discovers I'm in another room.*

As we did in the workplace, let's examine some of the types to see the roles they typically play in relationships.

How Extraverts and Introverts Play the Dating Game

For openers, let's start with Extraverts because they are easy and fun to get along with—for a while, at least. They are easy in that you can count on them to do the talking, make the date, instigate the come-on, be the aggressor. They're fun in that they'll fill the time and provide the entertainment, whether it's a night on the town or an evening of talk. Extraverts can converse with amazing facility. In fact, when "conversing" with an Introvert, they can spend the evening answering their own questions and at the conclusion, thank the Introvert for a wonderful time.

One Introverted couple described "an ideal date" as dinner for two, low lights, soft sounds—and *no* talking. "The time together speaks to us and for us," they said.

Not that Introverts are wallflowers. But for them, one party or event in an evening is enough. Extraverts aren't above trying to be everywhere at once.

The fact is, Introverts are generally attracted to Extraverts. They find Extraverts easy to be with simply because of their social gregariousness; if necessary, Extraverts can carry on entire conversations seemingly by themselves. Extraverts can play to a wide and varied "audience" all through a date: ushers, waiters, hostesses, and anyone else in earshot. Another Introvert, cynically describing a relationship with a strong Extravert, put it even more bluntly: "I don't need to show up for a date. He might not even miss me, but would thank me for a good time."

As dates, as well as everywhere else, Extraverts shoot from the lip.

You can see how easy in some ways it is to be with an Extravert, as well as the obvious drawbacks. If we were to sum it all up—particularly in the early-stage game of Getting to Know You—you could say that "Extraverts are nice to have around when there is a conversation going on in which nothing needs to be said." That's a typical Introvert view of Extraverts, and in fact it's what often takes place on casual introductory dates. That's why Extraverts perform well in such situations. From the Extravert's point of view, of course, it could be said that "Introverts are nice to have around when you want to be alone." That's a perfect arrangement for many Extraverts: to be alone and still have company.

How Sensors and iNtuitives Play the Dating Game

Now on to the information-gathering function—Sensors and iNtuitives. In the dating game, these two preferences are at once a source of attraction and excitement and a cause for confusion.

Sensors, as a rule, are very realistic about dates. They see the other person for what he or she is. Remember: They are well grounded in objective reality, seeing clearly the good and bad qualities and the here and now. They're not necessarily impressed with a lot of phony-baloney or potential. For iNtuitives, on the other hand, most of the date takes place in the mind. Their imaginations are rich; indeed, their perceptions of the date often are more exciting than what actually transpires. Sensors fantasize, too, but after the fact. After an initial encounter, for example, they'll imagine what the next encounter will be like—they can imagine all sorts of exciting things, but it is all grounded in reality, in extrapolations from what did in fact transpire on the preceding date. For iNtuitives, facts only ruin their fantasies.

For Sensors, who are by definition tuned into their senses, an exciting date is one that involves all those senses—the two people, ideally *look* good, *smell* nice, *taste* good food, *hear* nice music, *feel* cozy, and so on. It's through the five senses that the dating experience happens. For iNtuitives, it is their sense of potentiality rather than reality through which they experience a date; in some ways, the date is far more fantasy than fact. Indeed, the excitement the iNtuitive brings to the date is courtesy of an enthusiastic imagination, which creates a vision of what the date could be like.

Sensors and iNtuitives approach dates very differently. While for a Sensor, the date doesn't begin until the two parties get together, for an iNtuitive, the "date" may begin as soon as the arrangements are made, however many weeks in advance that may be. The resulting fantasies of what could happen may reach the point of obsession. Even second dates are revealing. The Sensor's expectations depend on the actual experiences of the first date. If the Sensor had a good time, he or she will be excited about the next encounter. For an iNtuitive, the real experience once again plays second fiddle to the imagination. Even a great first date won't live up to the iNtuitive's fantasies. Similarly, an iNtuitive's description of the first date might be so embellished that a Sensor might take offense, considering it to be something less than truthful. The Sensor might wonder, "Was *I* on that date?" In reality, the iNtuitive's rich imagination may be becoming confused with reality.

One problem is that on a date, Sensors may have trouble following the iNtuitives' many trains of thought. A Sensing friend once described her date with an iNtuitive like this: "He was like a fly, never landing anywhere, for any appreciable time. Just one, uninterrupted string of baloney. It was fun, but tiring." Another Sensor put it like this: "It was 'Earth to Donna, Earth to Donna,' all evening long."

In the dating dance, good conversation is usually a key ingredient for success. First dates tend to be conversation-intensive, allowing tastes, personalities, and images to emerge. Sensors are more comfortable talking about concrete things: people they've known, events they've experienced, things they've seen, places they've been—and the specifics on all of the above. In contrast, iNtuitives are excited by conversations that involve their dreams, visions, beliefs, and less tangible subjects in general.

One big conversational problem is details: Sensors and iNtuitives have very different styles. An iNtuitive male told us of his irritation at his Sensing mate, who would constantly interrupt his storytelling to correct some insignificant (to him) fact. "I remember in July when we were at Sam's Fish Place," he would

say. "I ordered a Scotch and soda and they gave me cream soda
and—"

She interrupted, "It wasn't cream soda, it was lime soda. And
it was last August."

"Who cares?" thought the iNtuitive.

For the Sensor, it was important that the facts be correct
before the story continued. For the iNtuitive, the details
weren't as important as the flow of the story, and the interruptions were distracting and annoying.

JUST THE FACTS

*I'm an N and my wife is an S. One day I came bounding
into the house shouting, "You're going to be able to go to the
conference with me! And afterward we can visit your parents!" She just kept on washing pants and gave no response.
Finally I stopped. "Let me start over," I said. "In the lobby
at Eastern Airlines there is a big poster advertising that you
can fly anywhere in the system for one price. It means we
can both go to the conference in Stanford and on to your
parents in Portland for about $1,500."*

*"That's wonderful!" she cried. "Why didn't you say that
in the first place."*

Clearly, the degree to which any conversation takes place has
a lot to do with whether the individuals are Introverts or Extraverts. While two Extraverts can effortlessly pass the time
with nonstop chatter, two Introverts may spend painful hours
uncomfortably trying to initiate and maintain a workable conversation. An Introvert-Extravert match may be ideal: the Extravert has a captive audience while the Introvert loves to focus
on listening—and be relieved of the pressure of making clever
and witty responses.

Time is always a potential Sensing-iNtuitive problem. If a
movie starts at eight o'clock, the theater is twenty minutes
away, and it's seven-fifty, the Sensor will become frustrated at
the prospect of being at least ten minutes late. For the iNtuitive,
time is much more flexible. "Movies usually start late," they

think (or say). "Besides, there are usually previews before the main feature. And if we are late, we'll catch up. It's no big deal." In fact, it is.

How Thinkers and Feelers Play the Dating Game

In the course of the dating process, the decision-making function—Thinking and Feeling—provides the impetus for moving forward in—or perhaps out of—a relationship. In fact, we believe the decision-making preference to be the most significant one when it comes to intimacy.

That can be a problem because, as we mentioned earlier, this is the gender-related preference: there are more Thinking males than females and more Feeling females than males. So in just the luck of the draw, there will be more T men attracted to F females. As a "date" evolves into a more intimate experience, this preference will be the one that can prove most divisive. The irony is that while the T-male/F-female configuration is the most "normal" and predictable for heterosexual relations, it has the largest potential for causing difficulties in a relationship. Thinking types want to *understand* intimacy; for them, it is a state of being analyzed, mastered, and fine-tuned. Feeling types simply want to be intimate—hold the analysis, *please.* The result is that Ts may seem rather cold and aloof at times, as they "process" and "analyze" their feelings. And they may dislike being pushed to *experience* the intimacy their F partners are enjoying. Make no mistake: Ts can clearly feel emotions swirling inside them; it's just that they must intellectually come to grips with those emotions before they can share and express them.

Thinkers' need for understanding begins with the first date and continues throughout a relationship. At the beginning, for example, it is important for them to define both parties' expectations clearly: "Are we going to be just friends, or do we have expectations beyond that?" Of course, after both have decided to remain "friends," there is still much room for definition— some friends sleep together, for example, some don't. Even deciding to pursue a long-term relationship is less than clear-cut: What is "long-term"? Is it forever? How much freedom will we have? How will we measure our growth? And on and on.

For a Thinker, even "I love you" is subject to further discussion.

For Feelers, all this definition and clarification merely defeats the whole purpose. Even if it is only a one-time date, they feel, just "being together" is definition enough. The more you're together, the more the relationship defines itself. A Feeler is likely to respond to the Thinker's quest for definition with something like "You'll know it when it happens" or "Your heart will tell you." Both responses are entirely too mushy and vague for a Thinker.

For a Feeler, "I love you" speaks for itself. It needs no further discussion.

IF IT FEELS GOOD, DO IT

My husband, a Feeling type, was complaining because I take trips to New York for training. He pointed out that it was expensive and time-consuming, and I could get the same training here. Finally, I said: "I go to New York because it feels good."

"Oh," he said. "Then go ahead, and have a good time."

A completely different set of problems arises in those anomalous situations when you have a Thinking-type female or a Feeling-type male. Both violate stereotypical gender roles in the dating and relationship process. There's the T female, for example, whose Thinking preference leads her to objectify and analyze the dating experience and understand it—all of which violates her feminine scripting, which taught her to be reactive and emotional. Women (as everyone knows) are supposed to be soft and mushy, not cut-and-dried. For the T female, this internal split can cause a real struggle, both within herself and in her relationships with men—not to mention her friendships with Feeling-type women.

On the opposite side of the coin, of course, is the Feeling-type male, whose Feeling subjectivity calls for him to experience the moment and to be soft and caring in violation of all his masculine scripting, which demands that he be objective and "above it all." Here again, wires get crossed, circuits jammed, leading to extremely awkward situations. For both the T female and the F male, what can follow is what we call "compensatory behavior," in which F men become ultramacho—they'll appear less caring than they really feel, often to the point of being hostile—and T women become ultrafeminine—with everything from flowing handwriting to frilly frocks, sometimes even having more children, further "proving" their femininity. At less of an extreme, either individual can simply moderate their behavior: T women may temporarily set aside their feminist ideals, sweetly waiting hand and foot on their mates; F men, for their part, may firmly (but politely) take charge, mustering newfound logic and objective behavior.

It's important to interject here something that's been said before but is worth repeating: Feeling types do think, and Thinking types do feel. Typewatching labels merely describe what each type *prefers*. We can't emphasize this enough.

How Judgers and Perceivers Play the Dating Game

Ultimately, the Judging-Perceiving differential is the one that best allows Typewatching skills to pay off early in a relationship. It's considerably more difficult to disguise one's preference for Judging or Perceiving than for any other preferences. You can usually detect this preference even on the phone. Js want to "schedule" dates, for example, to plan the experience, keep things in order, be on time, and perform all those other "organizational" duties of a relationship. They like to take charge of a date—deciding where to go, what to do, when to do it—and, ultimately, a relationship. They're generally not comfortable making "rough" plans, figuring things out "at the appropriate time." They want to *know* what's going to happen, even if the plans change later on. Js are more goal-oriented during the dating part of a relationship. They like to know where things are going—not just on the date, but in the relationship in general. The problem, as we pointed out earlier, is that this can be very appealing to a P—for a while, at least. But some Ps feel trapped by this J scheduling, even in the early stages of a relationship. ("Why do you want me to meet your folks? We've only been dating for six weeks. Isn't that a bit serious?") Ps, you see, represent the easygoing, playful child in each of us. In dating, once again, that is very attractive, particularly early on. But it may cause problems over time. ("Listen, honey, we've been seeing each other for two years. Won't you *please* meet my folks? It's no big deal.")

Judgers and Perceivers can have particular problems when traveling. We knew a dating couple who took several trips together. The more relaxed and haphazard the Perceiving woman became, the more stressed and rigid her Judging male companion behaved. Among other things, his needs drove him to impose his obsession with time and schedules upon her; she became resentful. They later described it as "What started out as fun and a chance to discover each other soon became a disaster. We wondered if we ever wanted to see each other again."

SCHEDULES

An SJ: "I love schedules. I make them and I stick to them. I can tell you exactly where I'm going to be at six o'clock tonight."

An NJ: "I love schedules, too, but I don't stick to them. I always have a schedule but I'm always changing it."

The J-P differential can play a big role in how a date (or any other social event) unfolds. In conversation, for example, Ps are capable of discussing many subjects in a single breath, but not feeling strongly on any of them. Js are more likely to stay focused on a single topic, and to have a strong opinion about it. Problems can come when Ps feel attacked or otherwise offended by Js' strong opinions. The Ps, put on the defensive, can end up digging their heels in on a subject they had merely wanted to open up for discussion. Often to their own surprise, Ps in such situations hear themselves expressing a forceful opinion on a subject they'd never before had strong feelings about.

Wolves in Sheep's Clothing

The world of dating and relationships is unlike any other. It is a case of "Typewatcher beware." To make just the right impression during these crucial first encounters, it is not uncommon for individuals to overemphasize their *non*preferences, often to counteract insecurities about their natural behavior. Introverts, for example, may try to be more outgoing and appear more Extraverted; Extraverts, who have often been told that they talk too much, may clam up and listen more. Sensors may say and do iNtuitive things, and iNtuitives can become aware of tangible Sensing things to which they might not otherwise pay attention. Thinkers get very schmaltzy, and Feelers—who know they tend to get swept away emotionally—may don a hard shell, appearing tough, cool, and aloof. All of these defensive measures may be short-lived and can disappear once either party gains a modicum of security in the situation.

The important thing to remember about the dating process is that this is the one time people are least likely to show their true stripes. The irony, of course, is that it may be the one time they would most benefit from doing so. Ultimately, of course, the game can only last a while. Then both parties slip back into their respective preferences, both wondering what happened to the exciting relationship they once had. None of this behavior is right or wrong. It is merely a dynamic process, part of the dating and mating dances we instinctively perform from time to time. But it sure confuses even the best of us and gives even those with well-honed Typewatching skills a run for their money.

Beyond Dating:
Typewatching in Love and Marriage

We could write a book on this subject alone. In many respects, in fact, most Typewatching skills in this book relate in some way to intimate relationships, including those discussed in "Type-watching From Nine to Five." (A relationship, after all, is a sort of mini-business, in which goal-setting, time management, conflict resolution, and other organizational skills come into play. But we won't carry that analogy any farther.)

To look at how the eight preferences operate within a marriage, let's take a look at some dynamics leading up to a wedding—and the first year thereafter.

Extraverts and Introverts:
What's a "Small" Wedding?

This is a personal story involving our own wedding a few years ago. While we agreed that we both wanted a small wedding, we had some clear differences on what that meant. To Otto, the clear Extravert, that meant "only" the three hundred people he counted as close friends. For Janet, the more Introverted one, that was ludicrous; she wanted just ten or twenty people.

That was just for starters. As we dealt with the ceremony, receptions, and other aspects of the event, it soon became clear that we would need three separate occasions to accommodate all of our needs. Which is exactly what we did. We had an Introverted service one weekend, with ten very special friends, beginning with sunrise at the ocean with champagne and reflections of what brought us all to that point in time. The next weekend, we had the Extraverted-Introverted service, limited to forty selected friends and family, all of whom served as witnesses, signing documents, and all sharing parts in the garden ceremony. That afternoon was the Extraverted service, with 175 close friends (125 others couldn't make it) in a sharing-declaring-disclosing-imposing-eating-dancing-laughing-pray-ing extravaganza.

While we're not suggesting such varied affairs for anyone entering wedlock, our initial problem was typical. Who can't recall a bride or groom becoming stressed (or stressing out a loved one) because of Extraverted-Introverted differences? (How many Introverted couples have had to face Extraverted parents who declared, "Of course, we'll have a huge wedding!")

GET HIM TO THE CHURCH ON TIME

We've seen some particularly interesting things with some of our ENTP friends. A few years ago at our wedding, for example, one ENTP couple showed up a day early. Another ENTP gave us our present a year and a half later, although she purchased it a month before the wedding. As iNtuitive-Perceivers, ENTPs aren't particularly well grounded in specific, time-oriented details. They are always on to some new idea or distraction, and present-day reality isn't always as evident as it should be.

As we've pointed out earlier, E-I differences don't end after the honeymoon. They can plague marriages for decades. It doesn't require an extraordinary imagination to foresee the problems that can occur over the long term. The attraction of Extraverts is that they are very affirming and stroking. The bad news is that they overdo it—even when they are praising themselves, which they have a tendency to do regularly. Introverts may interpret such behavior as insecurity or insincerity. We have a very good friend who is an Extravert and married some forty years now to a strong Introvert. We remember sitting one night in their kitchen and the Extraverted husband said, "It's been a good marriage, we've had a lot of fun, the years have been great. If I had one complaint it would be that she does not tell me enough that she loves me."

The Introvert said absolutely nothing. We continued our conversation in the kitchen and some time passed until finally the Introvert looked at us and said, "Isn't talk cheap?" There we had a perfect example of the Extravert-Introvert contrast: One wants words, the other action. It was between these same two individuals, with whom we once took a long car trip, that the following conversation took place:

Extravert: "Look at those pretty farmhouses! Don't you like them?"
Introvert: (nods head)
Extravert: "Would you like to live in something like that?"
Introvert: (nods head)
Extravert: "How about it? We could retire there! Don't you like that idea?"
Introvert: (nods head)
Extravert (turning to us in the backseat): "Is there anyone else in the car, or am I having this conversation with myself?"

The Introvert felt miffed because, in fact, she had felt quite involved in the conversation, despite her nonverbal responses.

TUNING OUT

I'm the only Introvert in a houseful of Extraverts, but I still manage to sneak in some "I" time. I direct my eyes toward a TV program, while I actually do some thinking.

Another case in point involves an Extraverted mate coming home from work quite tired, ready to spend some time in front of the tube. Upon his arrival, his Introverted mate reminded him that they had committed themselves to attending a party that evening. The Extravert complained, but they got ready and went. Not surprisingly, the Extravert caught a second wind after a half hour at the party. He got wound up in the excitement and didn't want to leave. But the Introvert became increasingly drained as the evening wore on. While she liked the party, she clearly had her limits. Further, as she saw her husband's enthusiasm rise, she began to wonder, "What's the matter with me? When we were alone, he was exhausted."
But it wasn't she that lacked excitement, and the husband

would probably be the first to declare that. It was simply a matter of the events energizing the Extravert and, in the long haul, draining the Introvert. But without such an understanding, the marriage can become stressed and the Introvert, observing the situation, may unfairly blame herself as the cause of the problem.

Sensors and iNtuitives: Meeting the Parents

Making good first impressions—when meeting a mate's parents or anyone else—are very different for Sensors and iNtuitives. For Sensors, who prefer to be grounded in "what is," are keenly aware of appearances: every hair must be in place, colors must match, and styles must be up-to-date and appropriate for the occasion; even a hanging thread can keep a Sensor from having a good time. So, as a meeting approaches, it is important to Sensors to be on time and to have things happen with exactness and precision. Moreover, if the Sensor is also a Judger, then timeliness and respect for traditions is mandatory.

You can imagine the potential for mixed signals when a Sensor meets a mate's parents. If the parents are late, for example, it could be interpreted as "They don't want to meet me." If, for some reason, both parents were to leave the room together, the Sensor might imagine, "They disapprove. They're out there talking about me." It's not that Sensors are paranoid, it's just that as realists, they tend to view the unknown as more negative than positive.

Meanwhile, iNtuitives can have problems too. Exactness isn't as important to them as are general impressions. They may hope to impress a mate's parents with intelligence but, not being particularly conscious of time, may show up rather late, thereby marring the first meeting. Conversation can sometimes take on a life all its own as the iNtuitive's imagination carries him or her to a variety of subjects, not necessarily related to anything previously discussed. "I understand you're a junior in college," says a parent. "Funny you should mention that," responds the N. "Just last week we were studying the relativity of placement in college to placement in birth order, and there are some amazing correlations . . ."

Unfortunately, this is only the beginning of what could be

LABOR DAY

One of the members on our board is an INTJ. When his wife delivered their first child, he took a statistics book into the labor room because he figured he'd have "nothing to do for fifteen minutes at a stretch."

---

years of S-N communication differences. Consider the case of Manny and Helen who, along with their two-year-old, moved into their first new house a few years ago, even before it was completely built. Manny, in his iNtuition, saw the house as complete, despite the fact that there was still plaster dust, mud, and construction materials everywhere. Despite the mess, it was easy for him to imagine the finished product. Meanwhile, Helen, a Sensor, dealt daily with the reality of the situation and endured many inconveniences, from an unconnected washing machine to a living room carpet that wouldn't stay clean. Her complaints, however, were only brushed aside by Manny, who couldn't get excited about such "minor details." Years later, they wonder how the marriage survived the house.

And then there's our iNtuitive friend Jack, asked by his wife to fix a leaky faucet, who spent the next two weeks reading about faucets, and trying to understand the whole plumbing system, before his wife got impatient and called a plumber.

The stories could go on and on. The S-N differences, while very attractive, can be the source of serious communication problems.

Thinkers and Feelers: The First Anniversary

Picture the first wedding anniversary, the end of a fairly normal first year—whatever that means. Let's imagine a "traditional" configuration: a Thinking male and a Feeling female. For he thinks there are at least three possible responses to the anniversary celebration:

- "It's gone pretty effectively. Let's leave well enough alone. We'll go out to dinner and a movie afterward."
- "The year has gone pretty well. So we can improve what's already good, here are some questions to help guide our development. Let's spend the evening evaluating and celebrating."
- "Our anniversary conflicts with my bowling league play-offs, so we'll have to celebrate it on another date."

It's unfathomable to the Feeler that one can be so cold and objective about such a very special event. "Obviously," thinks the Feeler, "he doesn't care enough." Or, worse: "I've failed somehow to impress upon him the crucial nature of our first anniversary. It's my fault."

Feelers know that the first anniversary is the most important of all. (For Feelers, the first of almost anything is important—the first kiss, the first date, the first vacation, etc. Moreover, the Feeler little realizes that this level of importance will be attached to every anniversary.) The anniversary, for the Feeler, must be significant, experiential, schmaltzy, warm, expressive, and, above all, *meaningful.* If the Thinker fails to appreciate these dynamics or, worse, puts something of less importance ahead of this event, it will be interpreted as "You don't love me."

All of this can take on a different twist when the Thinker is a female and the Feeler is a male. Now all the female's objectivity gets translated as "unfeminine" and the male's subjectivity becomes "unmasculine." Without some Typewatching insight, accusations will inevitably fly, followed by threats to gender and guilt. The anniversary becomes a nightmare.

Having spent more than twenty-five years in the counseling business, we can report conclusively that first anniversaries, like wedding nights, can be traumatic.

Indeed, any special event can be stressful, from decisions about having children to vacations to major purchases. Consider, for example, Henry, a Thinker, and Irene, a Feeler, about to buy a car, their first major purchase as a married couple. To prepare, Henry took it upon himself to conduct exhaustive research on the subject—resale value, depreciation, and performance of various models. Among other things, he determined that certain colors (tan and white) were best—they showed dirt least, slowed rust, and reflected sunlight, making them cooler. Having done his homework, he presented it to Irene. "Honey, I've got it all figured out," he announced. "Here's the car model we should buy. The payments should be about $170 a month, and it should be one of these two colors. Now we can start looking."

Irene was crushed for a number of reasons, not the least of which was because she hadn't been included in the "homework." Although she couldn't fault Henry's research, she was disappointed at missing the opportunity to go shopping—to look at, sit in, and drive various models. In short, to *experience* each potential purchase. The biggest rub of all was the color. Of all the possibilities, tan and white were the least exciting for her. They were bland and did not express her personality; if anything, they left a negative impression.

Henry didn't understand any of this. Cars, he said, aren't personality statements; they're vehicles to transport people. At best, he believed, cars were poor investments and therefore must be made very wisely and objectively. And, he told Irene, "The color will grow on you as you come to appreciate the wisdom of this investment."

As is often the case in Thinking-Feeling disputes, the problem wasn't that either party was "right" or "wrong." It was a matter of each not being able to understand the other's perspective. Compounding the problem was the fact that they were both dealing with the same basic data; after all, she agreed with the homework he had done.

Obviously, the way through this mess was to pick and choose some areas of compromise: Could he give in on the color if she gave in on the model? Could he budge on price if she compromised on accessories? This is exactly how we resolved this. Fortunately, thanks to Henry's homework, we had a great deal of information with which to work.

The decision at hand could have been anything, but the problem—and its solution—would be the same: decisions are driven by our values. For Thinkers and Feelers, those values are arrived at very differently:

▪ **For Thinkers,** it's a very objective experience, one that shouldn't be embroiled in emotion; the more important the decision, the more objective you've got to be. The head must rule.

▪ **For Feelers,** it's a very subjective experience, one that must pay special attention to the people and issues involved; the more important the decision, the more carefully you must consider extenuating circumstances. The heart must rule.

SINGING THE BLUES

An ST said to an NF: "Look, if you want the walls painted blue, just say 'Paint the walls blue.' Don't tell me how blue walls make people feel wonderful."

Judgers and Perceivers: Making Your Presents Felt

Anniversaries, and many other gift-giving occasions, can be ripe for Judging-Perceiving misunderstandings. Remember the J

SENTIMENTAL ROCKS

I have what must be an NF rock collection. Family and friends pick up "just any" rock for me from places they visit. But my collection is purely sentimental. Recently, a well-meaning ST friend brought me a scientific book on rocks, which I read, wondering, "Who cares about this stuff?"

---

phrase "I don't like surprises"? Of course, the P would counter, "All the world's a surprise, and isn't it exciting!"

Consider a typical scenario. As a special day (a birthday,

Christmas, Valentine's Day, etc.) nears, the J approaches the P and says, "Here's a list of some of the things I'd like you to pick from." The J thought that the list would be very helpful and constructive. To the P, of course, the list stifles all creativity, and diminishes the thrill of the gift-giving experience.

For the P, the process is reversed. As the special day approaches, the P says, "Surprise me." That short sentence raises the hair on the back of the J's neck. "It would help if you would give me some guidance," the J responds. "Oh, no," responds the P. "Just give me anything." But that's simply too open-ended to a J. With so little guidance, the J heads out into the world, seeking closure; they want to wrap up the problem as soon as possible. As a result, the J might buy one of the first things he or she sees, instead of continuing to seek the "perfect gift." The P, no doubt, will be disappointed with the results: once again, it will be a necktie, sweater, or kitchen appliance.

NOW HEAR THIS

Some years ago, some Introverted colleagues were deliberating on what sort of birthday gift to get their Extraverted friend. Because their friend traveled a lot, they decided to get something for his car. They narrowed it down to one of two possibilities: a stereo tape player or a citizens band radio. Can you guess which gift these two Introverts chose? Of course, they picked the sterero tape player—it provided self-contained entertainment. They were minutes from making a purchase when it suddenly occurred to them that a better choice for an Extravert would be the CB radio, which would give him constant contact with the outside world. They did, and he did.

Focus on Attractions, Not Distractions

As you can see from the above scenarios, marriage (and the plans leading up to it) can be a breeding ground for a wide range of differences. Without understanding their typological roots, there is unlimited potential for disaster—or, at least, for some needless disputes. The beauty of Typewatching in relationships is that it enables you to see your differences as typological, not personal. It may also remind you of what you once found attractive in a mate, and now find merely annoying.

It is important to keep in mind that those differences, more often than not, were originally viewed as positive complements to your own traits—the organized J needing the spontaneity and relaxing nature of the P, for example. Although this is overlooked in the midst of a dispute, it would be counterproductive to try to make your mate "shape up"—to make the P as organized and structured as the J, to continue with the example given earlier. Even worse, if you were successful in changing this person, you would lose what was at the core of your original attraction. Part of your frustration may be that the other's contrasting style symbolizes a part of your personality that you at some point "chose" not to prefer. If you can see past the relationship's frustrations and recognize that they are grounded in typological differences, the potential for optimizing those differences is very exciting.

CEREAL DRAMA

An SJ woman and her NP husband can't agree on how to manage the cereal boxes. She doesn't think it's necessary to have three kinds of cereal open at the same time. "You should open one box and finish it," she says. "But I need choices," he replies.

The goal, then, is to accentuate the positive—to focus on the attractive nature of the differences instead of their irritating qualities. Using whatever appropriate means—given the individuals' types, there are at least sixteen possible approaches—Typewatching skills can unfreeze a frozen relationship, maintain a working one, make a good one even better, and bring calm to even the most turbulent interpersonal waters.

Two Basic Rules for Relationships

As we stated earlier, you can find Typewatching techniques applicable to relationships throughout this book, but here are two important rules for smoothing out the rougher edges of everyday living:

1. Compromise your differences. Given that differences exist, it may be appropriate to modify them to some extent. While it probably won't be necessary (or possible) for Extraverts to become Introverts, or Sensors to become iNtuitives, there is a wide range of middle ground. Moreover, the more you are able to use your nonpreferences, the fewer blind spots you—and your relationship—will have. Extraverts, for example, should consider building in time for listening, or other Introverted activities; Introverts might practice some direct verbal expressions—anything from affection to anger. Sensors might take time to dream positively about the future (despite whatever chores need immediate attention); iNtuitives might occasionally engage in some hands-on activities around the house, like fixing things (or calling the person who will). Ts might practice expressing some feelings; Fs might practice asserting their own needs ahead of their mate's. And Js might "plan" some spontaneity while Ps might complete at least one thing per day they had intended to put off until tomorrow.

2. Reserve some space for yourself. At the same time that you are (both) compromising, you should also try to reserve enough space for your deepest needs so you don't feel imposed upon. An Introvert, for example, should demand a reasonable amount of alone time without feeling guilty, and must also make sure that the time doesn't impose upon an Extraverted mate's needs. An Extravert mate might wish to go to a party during an Introvert's time alone, and should feel free to do so without any guilt over "abandoning" the Introvert. Late at night, a P might want to read a book, relax, or just go to bed early, while the J mate might feel the need to "tidy up" before retiring. The P should not be made to feel guilty about not helping, and the J should not be treated as a compulsive tidier.

Typewatching can yield not only tolerance but renewed affection for one's mate. That's why it is such a good technique to use in relationships.

Fighting Types

As a rule, we don't plan our conflicts and fights. When they erupt, it is usually a surprise and we most naturally fall back on our natural preferences:

- **Extraverts** talk louder and faster, and know that if they can "just say one more thing," the whole issue will be cleared up. They want to talk out problems *now;* if they can't, they may get frustrated, even panicky.
- **Introverts,** who are most often at a disadvantage when a fight breaks out, are at their best when they have time to think through, rehearse, and have some advance notion of the issues at hand. They may simply withdraw inside themselves when a fight takes them by surprise.
- **Sensors** like to argue the facts, the more specific the better. They are prone to sidetrack a bigger issue by focusing on smaller, less relevant issues.
- **iNtuitives** like to make broad generalizations, often inflating a specific incident into a sweeping pattern. They see the Sensors' emphasis on facts as nit-picking.
- **Thinkers** tend to get too analytical in a dispute, often missing the emotional side of things. Their logical analyses of arguments may have little to do with the hurt feelings involved. "Don't get emotional" is one T tactic during fights that usually causes more problems than it solves.
- **Feelers** tend to personalize everything, even things that weren't intended to be personal. They view disagreements as something to be avoided, and tend to "give in" before an issue is resolved, if only to reestablish harmony.
- **Judgers** "know" they're right. Because they tend to see things

in black and white (they demand that others do too), they see issues as being very simplistic in nature—it's either this or that, right or wrong, good or bad, and so on. It's hard to negotiate with someone who *knows* he's right.

■ **Perceivers,** who tend to see many options to everything, like to play both (or all) sides of an issue. Unlike with Judgers, few things are black and white to Perceivers. They have trouble settling a dispute because there are always more data to examine, hence more possible solutions.

The above notwithstanding, there are times during disputes when people fall into behavior more typically associated with their nonpreferences. Extraverts, for example, can clam up or may even run away, actually leave the room during an argument. Introverts, for their part, can mouth off and may lump together a whole range of pent-up issues ("And while we're on the subject, there's something else I've been meaning to tell you . . .") that are not particularly constructive to the situation at hand. Sensors, as things escalate, may become less grounded, envisioning horrendous things, while iNtuitives may begin liberally spouting facts, however inaccurate they may be.

Fair Fighting: The Five Key Steps

Rational thought flies out the window during such moments, often obscuring the issues and rendering effective communication all but impossible. One tactic we have seen work—and which has worked for us—at these times is for one party to call, loudly and clearly, "TIME OUT!" (It would be helpful to arrange a time-out signal to use in public that can be invoked without embarrassment to either party.) That temporarily stops the match and requires that both parties go to their separate corners, metaphorically speaking, until the emotion of the moment has subsided. It is then the task of each person to analyze the altercation that has taken place. While it is best to put this in writing, Extraverts in particular may prefer to answer the following questions in their heads:

1. The Issue: What are the issues involved in the conflict? List them clearly.

2. The Basis: Are they typologically based? Can you pinpoint the issue to a letter preference and sort it more objectively?

3. The Cause: Where did the argument go awry? What happened that made things reach the point where "Time out!" had to be called. Can you pinpoint that typologically?

4. The Solution: Can both people involved identify with the other's point of view?

5. The Contract: Finally, are there compromises or contracts that can be negotiated around modifying the problematic behaviors?

Let's take a case in point: an Extraverted-Perceiving woman —a mother who spends her days at home with her two children —and her Introverted-Judging husband. At the end of the day, he likes to come home to be alone—thinking, resting, recharging. She, having spent eight hours with toddlers, is more than ready to engage in adult conversation. But every night upon his arrival, he disappears behind the closed door of his study, then emerges for dinner, only to return to his solitude for the evening. His wife, clearly resentful and feeling neglected, becomes increasingly upset. When she asks him why he must do this, he explains, "I've worked all day with people and I want to be alone." Besides, he adds, "I can't change. I've always been like this." Over time, as he does emerge from his study, she becomes nagging and finds herself increasingly bothered by little things. When these "little things" finally reach a critical mass, she erupts in anger and a fight ensues.

Using the process we described above, the two people (once they have called "Time out!") might examine the issues like this:

1. The Issue: The principal issue is his need for "alone time" versus her need for adult company at the end of a day.

2. The Basis: There are two strong typological bases: his Introversion (needing to be alone after a day of talking) conflicting with her Extraversion (needing to talk after a day of being alone); and his rigid Judging position ("I can't change. I've always been like this").

3. The Cause: Things went awry when her resentment caused a

lot of "little things" to tip the scales. She lost focus on the principal issue, and became entangled in a web of frustration.
4. The Solution: After calling "Time out!" and analyzing the issues, it might become clear to both individuals that each has end-of-the-day needs and responsibilities that must be considered.
5. The Contract: He gets to spend an hour in his study entirely alone, after which he agrees to spend time with his wife and children. (After dinner, he could spend some additional time alone, but not every evening and only after the children have gone to bed.)

Clearly, not every fight is so easily defined—and so singularly focused—but the process is essentially the same.

Step Four, "The Solution," is crucial to resolving disputes. Fights smooth over remarkably once participants imagine themselves in each other's shoes. It's not that hard to do, and Typewatching makes it easier still by defusing the personal aspects. When this man and woman recognize that their end-of-the-day needs are related to their Introversion and Extraversion respectively, that puts the problem in more universal terms. Universalizing a situation often makes it easier for people to apologize to one another. And an "I'm sorry" can bring a fight to a very rapid conclusion.

As you've by now come to recognize, every person is more than the sum of his or her individual letters, to paraphrase an old axiom. When you combine the preferences into four-letter types, each letter takes on a new flavor. An Introverted-Judger fights differently from an Introverted-Perceiver, for example. An Extraverted-Feeler fights differently from an Introverted-Feeler, who fights differently from an Introverted-Thinker, and so on.

Two Simple Rules

Toward the elusive goal of raising fighting to a higher plane, here are two simple rules that can be helpful when fighting:

1. Let Feelers Think and Thinkers Feel. Years ago, in what was called "sensitivity training," we used a variation of that exercise: We would make two people who were struggling and fighting with each other take the other person's point of view. You'd be amazed at how quickly things get sorted out—sometimes with great laughter—when two people try to get into each other's moccasins.

Nowhere does wearing other people's moccasins work better than in T-F disputes. Consider the situation: While Thinkers are looking at things objectively, Feelers are looking at the same things subjectively. There's no worse way to try to resolve something. For Thinkers, it's important to understand that being able to analyze things objectively isn't always a solution; and Feelers need to realize that being objective may be what is necessary to solve a particular problem.

Consider the earlier case of Henry and Irene, in which they sparred over the decision to purchase a car. They could have used this role reversal effectively. For example, Henry could have "argued" the position that a car is a personal possession that should reflect one's tastes and values. And Irene could muster her most objective, defensible argument that a car is an investment that must be made carefully and rationally. Each of them needs a few moments to prepare their "scripts"; those few moments can also serve as a cooling-off period for a heated argument. Then, each side must present the point of view with the intent on winning. Both must grapple with the genuineness of the other's point of view.

Another helpful exercise for both parties is to "step outside" a situation as much as possible. (This is easier for Ts, whose objectivity facilitates such exercises.) For the Thinker, try to view the situation as a disinterested third party. Would the T's hard-nosed argument still make sense? As a disinterested third party, what warm and forgiving things could you imagine being said? Let the Feeler "step outside," too, imagining what things aren't being said because they sound cruel and harsh, which perhaps need to be said in order to get to the crux of the matter? Failure to say something as simple as "I am angry" or "I'm upset" may be impairing communication.

2. Don't Focus on "Winning." One problem is that Js and Ps have very different perceptions on "winning" and "losing" a fight. Invariably, in a P-J fight, Js, besides "knowing" they are right, tend to define the battle lines—the issues—early on. For their part, Ps tend to be angry about a number of things, unsure of what's *really* wrong. The result is that when the J begins to focus, the P often becomes focused too—on the fact that "the issue" (as defined by the J) is not the real issue (although the P still may not know what the real issue is). To overcome this dilemma it is necessary for the J to listen. One time-tested technique is to do what behavior trainers call "active listening": the J would be required to repeat, to the P's satisfaction, what the P has just said before the J would be allowed to respond. That forces the J really to listen to what's being said instead of judging the first words out of the P's mouth and forming a response without listening to the rest of the concern. (For Js, you see, life is actually an exercise in sentence completion: you need only begin a sentence with a few words—the J will immediately "know" the rest of the sentence.) The "active listening" exercise is good for the P, too, forcing the P to focus on a single thought and express it succinctly.

Keep in mind that you don't need typological opposites—a Judger and a Perceiver, for example—to conduct such exercises. Anyone of every type can take part.

Ultimately, it's a matter of working with our strengths, dealing with our weaknesses, then dealing with each other's preferences, strengths, and weaknesses.

The goal of Typewatching in fighting is not to avoid a fight. Tension and disagreement are a part of the human condition. It is out of the tension and disagreements of our relationships that we move to more intense levels of love, to increased understanding and forgiveness, and to higher levels of sharing and growth. Believe it or not, the ultimate flowering of a relationship is not possible without the struggle. Typewatching, then, provides an exercise that can help you fight constructively and lovingly.

Love, Sex, and Type: Turn-ons and Turn-offs

Typewatching can work as well with making love as with making war, helping to keep it in perspective too. We occasionally conduct workshops on love and relationships. We split up one particularly large group, dividing them according to their preferences. We then issue each group a large sheet of paper and ask the following questions:

- We ask a group of Extraverts and a group of Introverts, "How do you know when you're loved?"
- We ask groups of Sensors, iNtuitives, Thinkers, Feelers, Judgers, and Perceivers to make lists of sexual and intimacy "turn-ons" and "turn-offs."

The answers are comfortingly true to type. Here's a sampling:

Extraverts: Extraverts bring up the same two things as strong indicators that they are loved: noise and action. The "noise" can be in almost any form, but preferably in the form of words that provided feedback: verbal lovemaking during sex, words exchanged in the midst of laughter or tears, listening to their words when they speak, or *saying* just about anything to them, so long as words continue to be exchanged. In addition to the need to be verbally affirmed, Extraverts demand attention and responsiveness from mates—a trait that others can find very tiring. Although the action, too, can be in almost any form and often involves simply keeping the Extravert company, the need for such attentions is as constant as the need for verbal feedback. Without these, Extraverts report that they become restless or even fearful that the relationship is in trouble.

Introverts: They know they are loved when they are allowed quiet time and space. To express "I love you" to the Introverts is to give them space and place to be alone—to reflect, to sort out their lives, or simply to be quiet. Moreover, say the Introverts, not only is talk cheap, but the constant verbalizing of what should be obvious makes them distrustful. ("If our relationship's so good, why do you keep saying it?") Whereas Extraverts de-

How to Be an Enchanting Spouse (or Friend)

ESTP—
most un-predictable

Settle down

You love excitement, surprise, and variety, but that is not always comforting for a mate. Give more attention to "settling" events. Once in a while, be on time, hang around when things are boring, show respect for family traditions by doing things just the way they were done before.

ESFP—
most generous

Stay on track

You are very good at meeting the needs of many people at once, but that means that you may be sidetracked in so many directions, you don't meet the "routine" needs of your mate. An example is the parent who agrees at the last minute to take one kid to little league at six, and another to the gym at seven, while his or her mate is at home waiting for dinner that was scheduled for six.

ISTP—
most skillful with tools

Be impractical

Lots of exciting ideas for expressing affection pass through your mind, like building your spouse a coffee table, or entering "I love you" into the data disk. But you put the ideas down as being impractical or stupid or flighty. Don't argue with yourself, go ahead and act on your affectionate impulses sometimes.

ISFP—
most artistic

Use words

You think words are cheap and would rather express your affection in more tangible ways, like baking muffins (nothin' says lovin' like somethin' from the oven), or bringing home a huge bouquet. But once in a while use the written or spoken word. Stick a note in the muffin or on the flowers that says, "I love you, dummy."

ESTJ—
most hard-charging

Don't take it back

You like to show affection in a "macho" way, the slap on the back is a classic example, or saying something abrasive, like "You're all right for a———." Try not to give affection with one hand and take it back with the other; just come out and say, "I love you."

ESFJ—
most harmonizing

Show anger
Your desire to mother/smother means you may sweep problems under the carpet rather than face them. You reach too soon for the chicken soup; the world is not going to come to an end if you show anger. Don't be afraid to fight.

ISTJ—
most strong and silent

Praise good behavior
You tend not to praise good behavior because it's expected. But you should train yourself to add overt pats on the head and words of appreciation, for big or small things, to your list of things to do. And make it a rule to say "I love you" at least once a week. It's part of your duty toward your spouse.

ISFJ—
most loyal

Be more assertive
Your mate would probably like to tell you "I appreciate twenty years of loyalty, but I wish you'd get mad once in a while." Getting angry with you is like eating cotton candy; you bite into it and it disappears. That's not constructive for anyone. Try to be more assertive and less committed to duty at any price.

ENTJ—
most commandeering

Share your softness
You have the same temptation as the ESTJ, to give affection with one hand and take it back with the other, but you do it through sarcasm rather than macho remarks. Try to share your softness by itself, without caustic wit.

ENTP—
most inventive

Just *do* it!
You see that details in the house need attending to, but instead of doing them, you try to design a system that will attend to them. Then when your spouse confronts you with the unfinished work, you get one-upy and won't give in and do it. For the good of the marriage, don't worry about beating the system. Just do what needs to be done—right away.

INTJ—
most independent

Give a hand
You're very independent, but please don't demand the same thing from your mate. Give mates support and assistance. Don't let them sink three times to learn how to swim.

INTP— *most logical*	**Speak from the heart** When you try to use your Thinking to express your love, the meaning can get lost in translation. Share the fact that you *feel* love, not only *understand* it.
ENFJ— *most persuasive*	**Allow disagreement** You usually assume that your mate is in complete agreement, but if your mate raises a few normal questions, you overpersonalize it and get very hurt. Allow your mate some room to disagree.
ENFP— *most optimistic*	**Face today's problems** Rather than face a disagreeable part of the marriage, you'll seduce yourself and your spouse into a happier place. Don't escape so quickly into your imagination or the future. Try to solve your present problems.
INFJ— *most empathic*	**Show that you know** You're very aware of people's feelings; you seldom need an explanation of interpersonal dynamics, but you don't always do something about them. You know very well that your mate needs a stroke or an "I love you," but it's not your day to give strokes so you clam up. Push yourself to give when your mate needs it, not only when you feel "inspired."
INFP— *most non-directive*	**Offer advice** You have a great gift for helping people understand their feelings and feel better about themselves, but you have no confidence that you're being of any help. Don't be so tentative in offering advice, consolation, and appreciation to your mate.

scribe their constant need for affirmation through word and deed, Introverts declare that if a relationship demands too much, they soon grow tired of it and are unable to give their best.

To no one's surprise, the very thing each type needs, even demands, of their mates is the very thing that mates of the opposite type are least likely to deliver. Introverts want space; Extraverts invade space. Extraverts want verbal feedback; Introverts want to keep their thoughts to themselves. Failure to deliver on any of these expectations sets the stage for each to feel depressed, self-critical, and unloved.

Sensors: True to their name, Sensors are turned on by things that excite their tactile and sensory awareness. Touch is important, as is cleanliness. Smells, tastes, and the visual are very important too. Likewise, turn-offs include noises that interrupt, or touches, smells, tastes, or visuals that are too extreme. Sensors, especially Sensing-Judgers, seem to have less patience with turn-offs, and once turned off, are slower to get excited again.

iNtuitives: They are stimulated partly by the unknown. A little stimulation coupled with a lot of imagination is far more exciting than the reality itself. Another interesting observation, though iNtuitives can certainly be turned off, is that iNtuitive-Perceivers, given any chance at all, can usually transform a turn-off into a turn-on. ("I've never been crazy about redheads, but this redhead is attractive and funny; that's exciting." Remember that the iNtuitive's imagination is always richer than reality.)

Thinkers: They are quite clear about their turn-ons and turn-offs. The turn-ons include clearheadedness, objectivity, and the hunger to understand and improve the relationship, while any form of emotionality, schmaltz, or fluffiness turns them off, even, some Ts report, frightens them, if the emotionality reaches a pitch.

Feelers: Turn-ons include any opportunity to please their lovers or occasional epiphanic, deeply felt moments in which love, joy, or pleasure are experienced. Affirmation is also a turn-on to Feelers, even Introverted-Feelers. The absence of any of the conditions necessary for a turn-on is not only a turn-off but, in the long run, is a setup for self-punishment and feelings of failure as a lover. Of the eight preferences, Feelers, more than any others, can be turned off by a partner or an event, but can talk themselves into being turned on if they feel their mates are satisfied.

Judgers: They have the sharpest definitions of turn-ons and turn-offs. The best turn-ons are things that happen according to schedule—a schedule often more implicit than explicit. They report liking certain behaviors or words that set the event in motion and are then followed to the letter, yielding satisfaction for all. Interruption of a scheduled event is not only annoying but can ruin the moment altogether. Having set an agenda, the Judgers want no interruptions and no surprises. And though a Judger does like variations, they should be *planned* variations.

Perceivers: In dramatic contrast to Judgers, Perceivers note that their biggest turn-ons are the unplanned, the unusual, or perhaps even the risky—and certainly the surprising. The bigger the surprise, say Ps, the greater the turn-on. Turn-offs, predictably, are routines, schedules (overt or covert), or anything else that limits the room for surprise, exception, or variation.

It is too simple to say that the one's turn-ons are the other's turn-offs. In fact, at least initially, preferences opposite to one's preference are intriguing, exciting, and powerfully attractive. In the long run, however, once the initial excitement has subsided, people tend to revert to their own preferences.

So, as a relationship grows over time, there is almost a yearning for the security that one's own preference affords. Generally speaking, the biggest turn-ons in a long-term relationship are probably those that affirm and honor the desires of each of the partners, allowing both to feel entirely free to be themselves with each other. Probably the biggest turn-off is being made to feel ridiculous or inadequate for one's preferences, or, worst of all, being told to "shape up" and get turned on "the right way" —the way the other person prefers.

Putting It All Together

You're no doubt beginning to see how the themes central to each type's character play themselves out, both at work and at home. The benefit of examining these themes through Typewatching lenses is that:

■ It gives you the wisdom to know the difference between those parts of your personality and behavior that can (and probably should) be modified, and those parts that can't (and probably shouldn't).

■ It frees you to focus your energies where they can be most effective, relieving you of responsibility for changing those things over which you truly have no power.

■ Having increased your self-understanding, it provides you with a perspective through which to view others' differences in a positive light as well.

■ Finally, once you have reached such understanding, Typewatching enables you to reach the kind of compromises in your dealings with others that will allow enough space for everybody to be themselves.

In the end, everybody wins.

Next, we'll show how Typewatching can ease another major arena of personal stress: the parent-child relationship.

8

Parent-Child Typewatching

"Would you please look with your *eyes* instead of your *mouth*?"

We hear it time and time again: "Where was Typewatching when we were trying to understand our kids?"

It's a question that points up the universal applications of Typewatching. For anyone who has begun to put Typewatching principles to work, it doesn't take a degree in psychology to see how its potential for resolving disputes and teaching mutual respect can apply to the family—particularly to the never-ending dilemmas surrounding parenting. Even if you don't have kids, you did have parents. Typewatching skills, of course, can be used effectively by either party. We hope they will be.

You can probably imagine some of the more obvious dilemmas: the Introverted parent, whose Extraverted child has a telephone growing out of one ear and an insatiable appetite for parties, group study, and sleepovers; or the Extraverted parent, who feels a failure for not having instilled appropriate social skills into an Introverted child, who would rather stay at home and read than play outdoors with friends. Even the Extraverted parent worries about an Extraverted child who "depends too much on other people," failing to learn to be self-reliant.

But that's just the tip of the parenting iceberg. There is an endless array of Sensing-iNtuitive, Thinking-Feeling, and Judging-Perceiving parent-child differences (in addition to the obvious Extravert-Introvert difference), which most parents recognize but try to change rather than understand. How many times

SEEK AND YE SHALL FIND

As the mother, and only Introvert in a family of eight, I have always tried to provide nooks and crannies in which to be alone. They use them, but only to crowd in together in groups. Anyone who found me off alone somewhere would shout, "Hey, everybody, come on, Mom's alone here."

have you said—or considered saying—"Why can't you be like your brother (or sister)?" You may accept the idea of differences but still may not accept the differences themselves. Typewatching can help you deal affirmatively with those differences.

You probably have been Typewatching as a parent for years, if only to apply negative labels to behavior of which you don't approve. The Extraverted child may be called "bigmouth" or "insecure"; the Introverted child "shy" or, worse, "socially retarded." And so on.

You can catalog most any parenting problem as you proceed through the list of parent-child typological differences. Here are some of the biggest problem areas:

Introverts and Extraverts: Space Invaders

We've already covered a variety of Introvert-Extravert dilemmas, and most apply to the parenting process. In general, Extraverted parents seem to have a need to invade the space of other family members, including their Introverted children. This is where the royal *we* becomes more divisive than inclusive: "*We* are all watching TV now. Why aren't you watching with us?" The problem is that Extraverts, in their enthusiasm for certain activities, impose those activities on others without determining whether those individuals have other needs—like being alone. One of the great invasions of an Introvert's space is the classic well-meaning line "What are you *doing* up there in your room all alone? Come on down and play with the others!" Introverted children often wish not to be interrupted with "Am I bothering you?" or intruded upon with "That looks like fun.

What are you doing?" Introverts generally get frustrated with Extraverts' redundancy and restating of the obvious.

Moreover, Extraverts aren't great listeners, which can lead to many a disaster for a parent-child relationship. Extraverts may encourage Introverted children to engage in more social relationships and school activities than the children want, or before they are ready for such interactions. The first day of school can be an exciting adventure to an Extraverted child, but to an Introvert it can be intimidating at best, a nightmare at worst. It has been suggested that a simple but extremely effective technique is to walk the Introverted child through school the day before classes start, allowing the child to become acclimated at his or her own pace.

OFF TO A GOOD START

We moved to a new town when my ENFP was just starting high school. I'm an Introvert and was concerned about his finding new friends. I learned later that on the first day of school, he got up on a lunch table and said "Hi, I'm Leo Barry, how do you like me so far?"

That's a key thing to understand about Introverts: They need to do *everything* at their own pace, a pace that is internally directed. When the pace is dictated by others, problems can result.

When the tables are turned—an Introverted parent with an Extraverted child—the parent often fails to understand the Extravert's constant need for approval from others. There is a need for feedback on everything, from how well the kitchen was cleaned to the attractiveness of a particular item of clothing, no matter how many compliments have already been given on the subject. Needless to say, such feedback won't be readily forthcoming from an individual whose preference is to avoid redundancy.

Introverted parents are less likely to acknowledge the child's presence or give credence to the ramblings to which most children are prone. This sets the Extravert up to redouble his or her efforts, becoming louder, more insistent, or simply more "present" until sufficient acknowledgment is made—often in the form of irritation on the part of the parent. The oft-quoted phrase "Would you please look with your *eyes* instead of your *mouth*" belongs to Introverted parents and fails to recognize the close connection between the two for an Extravert.

For an Extraverted parent with an Introverted child, the most practical solution is to understand different spatial needs and negotiate accordingly. It's not unusual, for example, for Introverted children to fail to say hello when they come home, a practice that never fails to get the Extravert's goat. You won't believe how much this is a source of parent-child strife. This is an appropriate situation for negotiation: "I'll leave you alone if you simply acknowledge my presence when you come in the house," a parent might say. "Moreover, whenever I come home and say hello, you'll respond." If such a simple agreement can be worked out, the child won't feel invaded, and the parent won't feel avoided.

While Introverted parents serve as good sounding boards for Extraverted children, they're usually not as stroking and affirming as the child would like or need. The solution, once again, is negotiation: The child might try to minimize needless babbling, the parent might make an effort to be a bit more affirming, perhaps even provide a bit of seemingly unwarranted stroking. (For an Introvert, "unwarranted stroking" means complimenting the obvious, which, to them, falls into the dreaded category of redundancy.)

Sensors and iNtuitives: Where the Action Is

Sensing parents often are precise and specific with their directions, while iNtuitive children like to use those directions as a jumping-off place for myriad imaginative uses. The parent's request to "Please clean up your room" may sound simple enough, but to the iNtuitive kid, that's an open invitation to pick up the first object that needs to be put away and investigate its potential. The object may become a symbol of past and

Big Mac Attack

It's not uncommon for Extraverts to think out loud, much to the consternation and confusion of Introverts. A good example comes from a friend of ours, a very strong Introvert, who was driving down one of those many stretches of American highway that are loaded with fast-food outlets. In the backseat was his Extraverted son. As they drove along the conversation went something like this:

Extraverted Son: "Hey, there's a McDonald's!"
(Father pulls off the road and into the McDonald's parking lot.)
Extraverted Son: "Hey, why are we stopping here?"
Introverted Father: "Because you said, 'Hey, there's a McDonald's.'"
Extraverted Son: "Yes, and it's still there. And there's a Burger King over there, and a Wendy's down the street. They're all over the place."
Introverted Father: "I know that. I can read the signs. I don't need you to read them to me."
Extraverted Son: "Who's reading them to *you*? I'm reading them to *me!*"

future relationships (for an iNtuitive-Feeling child) or the first piece of an hour's worth of building (for an iNtuitive-Thinking child). Later on, of course, the Sensing parent comes upstairs, expecting to see progress, but finds that nothing has changed— or, worse, that the new activity has created more disorder. The parent might be better off recognizing the child's iNtuitiveness by making a more specific request—"Place your books on the shelf and toys in the box"—one that has less potential for imaginative distraction. This isn't to say that iNtuitive kids aren't capable of larger projects—indeed, larger projects that are never completed are attractive to iNtuitives. As the parent, you might ponder the question of whether "cleaning the room" is even appropriate for an iNtuitive, for whom the objects strewn

LOOKING OUT FOR NUMBER ONE

When my son Andy, an ENFP, came home from school, I asked him how he had done on his test. He said he got the second highest grade in the class. I congratulated him. Then his friend came over and reported that Andy had indeed gotten the second highest grade in the class, except that everyone else had gotten 100.

But Andy always looks on the bright side, and as far as he was concerned, life was still great.

about have meaning. A Sensor's "messy room" may be the iNtuitive's "dazzling array of possibilities."

(This, by the way, is helpful to know in general: Sensors are much better than iNtuitives at throwing things away. For iNtuitives, each object, however seemingly useless, spurs a host of memories and ideas and is therefore worth hanging on to—"It might come in handy someday." Sensors look at something and say "We haven't used this in years, let's get rid of it." The iNtuitive "knows" that it will be needed the day after it's discarded.)

The Sensing parent–iNtuitive child dilemma worsens when you have an *Extraverted*-Sensing parent and an *Introverted*-iNtuitive child. All of the child's iNtuitive imagination is worked through internal reflection and vision, with little need to translate that into meaningful activity—or any activity at all. The Extraverted-Sensing parent is among the most demanding action- and result-oriented types. Imagine the frustration on both sides when an E-S parent's Introverted-iNtuitive teenager talks about going to "college for college's sake"—for the pure experience of theorizing and learning about "new stuff." The parent is liable to respond: "I won't pay for something that you're not going to put to good use"—a good job, in other words. Sensors, you see, often have problems with learning something that isn't necessarily aimed at achieving specific results (like a job); they leave the iNtuitives to dabble in such theoretical playgrounds. One of the earliest of those playgrounds or laboratories is the iNtuitive's own room. When you order an iNtuitive child to clean up, you may be destroying "data" and "experiments" crucial to the child's intellectual interests of the moment.

With the situation in reverse—an iNtuitive parent with a Sensing child—the parent may often seem too general and vague to satisfy the Sensing child's need for specificity. It reminds us of the old joke in which the child asks a parent, "Where did I come from?" The parent, an iNtuitive, launches into the whole metaphorical birds-and-bees story, to which the child responds, "Gee, that was real interesting. But Mary came from Chicago, Billy came from Buffalo. Where did *I* come from?"

The situation isn't so funny when it becomes the model for all parent-child interactions and the child, always seeking specific answers and direction, but never getting anything but vague generalities, comes to feel that parents aren't particularly helpful for coping with the real world. Sensing children often grow up feeling "misunderstood." The solution to this problem requires striving for clarity and feedback in the communication process, checking continually to make sure parent and child understand each other, saying things like "Did that answer your question?" or "Tell me what you heard me say" or "What I think you're saying is . . ."

Thinkers and Feelers: Muddled Role Models

This differential, as we've stated earlier, has a gender bias: About two-thirds of American males are Thinkers and the same percentage of females are Feelers. The traditional role models, of course, support males—both fathers and sons—as the objective decision makers, with mothers and daughters being the guardians of more subjective values. When type and gender match accordingly, it reduces dramatically the number of potential parent-child problems. When they don't, however, the parent-child dilemma is heightened. The resulting problems are not short-lived, but can cause long-term role-model confusion and deep parental concern over behavior that is, in fact, typologically normal for the child.

HAPPY TO BE MAD

I'm a T and both of my parents are Fs. Fs don't like it when you're cool in an argument, so I learned to get mad and show feeling just to make them happy.

For example, a Thinking-type father—who is a role model for objective decision-making—may be frustrated when it seems like the Feeling-type son doesn't "follow in my footsteps." The F son may prefer such F-type activities as art and music (probably fife rather than drums!) and may "bruise" easily in disagreements with family or friends. The father assumes that his son won't "make it" in the rough-and-tumble world, when in fact the boy's sensitivity and talent could propel him to success in the long run. If the father pressures the son to do "male" things, the son may be terribly frustrated about having to prove himself on the football field when his real talents lie elsewhere.

EXCITEMENT

When our two daughters were waiting to be picked up for their first junior high dance, the F was chattering with excited anticipation while the T sat quietly in a rocker. We asked if she was looking forward to going and she replied, "Oh, yes. I'm just as excited as Jane is."

And then there are the problems that occur when Mom is a Feeler and Daughter is a Thinker. In true F style, Mom is the caretaker of the family's emotional needs. The T daughter, meanwhile, not only doesn't fit this role, she is repulsed by it. Even worse, she begins to question her own femininity, simultaneously struggling with the guilt her Feeling mother continually imposes upon her for not being "like the other girls." (Guilt, of course, is primarily an F issue.) Imagine the stress that occurs when the T daughter brings home a frog she wants to dissect for the sake of learning—or shuns home econ and English lit at school in favor of physics and trig. The F mother blames herself for her daughter's apparent confusion and raises the great maternal question "Where have I failed?" meanwhile instilling in her daughter role confusion, sexual ambiguity, and a potential lifetime of self-doubts. Other combinations—the F father and the T son, and the T mother and F daughter—present other frustrating role issues. F fathers with T children, for example, are often seen as "soft," even "wimpy," which can cause problems for some children, who may become embarrassed at not having a he-man dad.

THE WAY TO A MAN'S HEART

While driving home from picking up our T daughter, who works at a deli, my F spouse expressed to her his doubts about whether or not she really cared for him. From his vantage point she hardly ever acknowledged, hugged, or otherwise expressed affection toward him. She responded somewhat irritatedly by declaring, "Of course I love you. Why do you think I put extra meat on your sandwiches?"

Judgers and Perceivers: Shape Up or Ship Out

In whichever combination, the J-P difference, of all Typewatching contrasts, may be the source of the most day-to-day frustrations as well as some unexpected pleasures.

Let's look at the pleasures first. To Perceiving parents, Judging children seem so organized and "together" that it's assumed they must be in the fast lane on the road to success: they put their toys away, they get their homework done, they come home on time—all the things P parents wish they themselves could do but know they never will. To a Judging parent, the Perceiving child seems easygoing and playful, isn't unduly bothered by daily family "crises," and is able to cope more easily with the constant traumas associated with "growing up." To a J, this P personality may seem enviably stress-free.

DO IT NOW

Two of my married children took on the task of painting their homes last summer. The TJ couple began in February, asking questions about preparations, a good brand of paint, and when to begin. They measured the house, found out how many gallons would be needed, waited for a sale, and bought enough to complete the job. The SPs chose a color, bought a gallon, painted till it ran out, went for another . . .

That's the good news. Unfortunately, Js and Ps may also face a lifetime of personality clashes with each other.

To the J parent, P children seem unable to "get it together" and are a constant source of frustration because of their "uncontrollable" nature. Js, you may recall, love to control their environment, and a child is very much a part of that environment. No matter how hard the J tries, it seems as if the P child always comes up a day late and a dollar short:

- "Mom, I forgot to tell you I need a dozen cupcakes tomorrow morning for our class party."
- "Dad, I hope you don't need the car tonight, I have a big date I forgot to tell you about."
- "What mess? I *need* all these things on my desk."

Here is where the individuals' other letters become crucial to how such situations play themselves out. An *Introverted-Feeling*-Judging parent with a P child turns his or her feelings inward, feeling guilty about having been an inadequate parent who has produced a kid who is clearly not "up to snuff." Needless to say, this attitude, whether verbalized or not, can have dire consequences for a child's self-esteem. An *Extraverted-Thinking*-Judging parent, however, expresses this frustration in external ways, needlessly creating a kind of "boot camp" atmosphere designed to make the flaky kid shape up. In such cases, everyone suffers, including the other children in the family, who also must live in the boot camp. Both J parent and P child are only being true to their types, of course, but the process of coercion can make each become more entrenched in his or her own preferences: the J parent becomes more demanding about punctuality, for example, and the P child becomes more scattered trying to keep up with the new, tighter controls, forgetting things, perhaps, or simply being later than ever.

Let's reverse the situation—a Perceiving parent and a Judging child. To the P parent, a J child's stubbornness and rigidity may be interpreted as selfishness. It seems like "My Way" is the child's theme song, and the only way for the poor P parent to deal with such determination is by "selling out"—letting the kid get away with murder. (Odds are better than even that when you hear people complain about the lack of discipline of other people's kids, the parents being criticized are Perceivers.)

In real life, a Judging child sounds something like this:

- "You can't do it that way. It's *supposed* to be done like this."
- "I need to know the answer *right now!*"
- "Who rearranged the stuff in my room? Everything was where it's *supposed* to be."
- "You said we were having chicken tonight! Why did you *change* the menu?"

THE FAMILY NUDGE

Two IF parents had an ESTJ daughter and found that her assertiveness came in handy. Whenever they bought a product they weren't happy with, they'd send their daughter into the store to complain and get a refund, while they waited in the car.

One result can be fierce competition. The P parent, as a matter of principle, may impose his or her own system on the J child simply for the sake of being what he or she considers a responsible parent. The problem, however, is that such tactics have only short-term results. Though the P may win a particular battle, the child inevitably falls back into J patterns the next time; and the parent once again tends to go along. Unlike the J, for whom "parenting" (that new 1980s nonword) is a long-term, goal-oriented process, Ps approach parenting on an as-needed basis—parenting-by-crisis instead of parenting-by-objective.

Our bias, nevertheless, is that, overall, Ps have an easier time with the role of "parent." J parents typically try to "control away" the inevitable surprises of life with children by being more rigid; Ps, on the other hand, are better able to roll with the punches—whether the children are Ps or Js. Not that Ps don't have coping problems (as suggested above). Among other things, Ps tend to blame themselves when their families don't seem as well organized as other families.

WHY FPS MAKE MORE RESPONSIVE PARENTS

Given that children live in their own worlds, and given that each child needs space for his or her own development, Feeling-Perceivers make natural supporters, nurturers, and responders to a child's self-development. Judging parents, and especially Thinking-Judging parents, can get locked into a lifelong struggle of playing "shape up," especially with the child who is significantly different from the rest of the family. The beauty of Perceivers is their responsiveness to any situation. Feeling-Perceivers identify with the child's growth and development, creating a fairly free and constructive environment.

Improving the J-P Parenting Trap

Given the simultaneous attractions and frustrations of J-P differences, there are some things both parent and child can do to mitigate the potential problems. But first, it's important to point out that there are certain days when even the most perfect kids must test their parents, or the most easygoing of parents must impose parental authority—just because that's the way things are. It's not predictable or preventable, it's simply a fact of everyday life that no psychological test or system can predict, measure, or cure. But this, too, shall pass, even though that may be hard to believe during the misery of the moment. Remember Reinhold Niebuhr's prayer: "God grant me the courage to change the things I can change, the serenity to accept the things I cannot change, and the wisdom to know the difference." Typewatching skills provide us a frame of reference for understanding the difference.

So how much *can* you change, and how much *should* you accept? As a J parent, the question is: "How much can I roll with my P child's spontaneity, and how much should I impose my authority to meet my own needs and provide some structure for my child?" Recognize that, as a J, your need for closure and structure may inhibit you from even asking the question, or give you too rigid an answer: "The kid needs constant supervision and the benefits of my wisdom, of course. Therefore, I must maintain control." Perhaps a better technique—and one that speaks to Js' needs for structure—is to make a list of all the areas in which the child needs shaping up, from cleaning to punctuality to organization and all the rest. Sit down with the child and genuinely negotiate which demands the child can meet and which ones you can give way on. The danger, for a J, is to make each demand as important as the other, without recognizing the need for trade-offs. Without them, it becomes a vicious circle: you become more rigid and authoritative, the child's natural behavior becomes more disappointing, competition between you heats up, and on and on.

Despite their own natural inclinations, P parents too must instill some kind of structure and organization—to make sure that chores and duties are not only assigned but carried out, for example, or that planned events take place more or less as scheduled. The key for the P parent is not merely to envision a structure, but to see to it that some structure becomes a reality in everyday life.

Five Case Histories

Over the years, we've counseled many families, using Typewatching techniques to solve a variety of problems. Here are

BON VOYAGE

An NP friend of ours has an NP daughter who visits frequently from another city. When it's time for her to go, he has a tendency to get her to the airport within minutes, even seconds, of her departing flight. One time, determined to break this record, he managed to get his daughter in the car and off to the airport ahead of schedule. Racing to the airport, defying speed limits, he prided himself in his timeliness and declared, "We're going to get to the Newport News airport early."

"Newport News?" she said. "Didn't I tell you, we're flying out of Norfolk!"

five case histories we think are illustrative of the ways Typewatching can increase parent-child understanding:

Sally: An IN Among EJs

She was a firstborn INFP whose two parents and four younger siblings were all EJs. By the time Sally was eight, it was clear that she was "different" from the rest of the family: she was, in their eyes, unsociable, flaky, disorganized, moody, and pensive. Enjoying being alone, she spent a lot of time in her room and didn't see the need for the strict organization her parents demanded, or the need to be precisely on time for *everything*. As her EJ brothers and sisters came onto the scene, her differences became even more apparent. As an NF, she wanted to please; but as an IP, she could only fail to meet the demands of her EJ opposites.

When Sally was twenty-two, her father was introduced to Typewatching through some management training at work. He was sufficiently impressed to recognize that the insights of Typewatching could have a salutary effect on his family and he asked us to intervene. His first words on the subject were something like "We have had Sally, the messed-up one in the family, in different forms of therapy since she was eight." He also confessed that all previous efforts had been directed at "shaping her up" and making her more like the rest of the family.

In the meantime, Sally herself had become loaded with self-doubt: seeing how different she was from everyone else, she was convinced that *she* must be wrong. Despite her high IQ, she was failing in college and had gotten into various forms of "deviant" behavior—lying, cheating, and stealing, to name a few.

We started by helping everyone to see Sally's differences, and how they were made to seem even more extreme by the fact that the rest of the family was so uniform in type. We also began a process of reestablishing Sally's self-worth, through some private counseling aimed at getting her to see the strengths and beauties of her own type. In the process, we helped her to understand that some of her deviant behavior was her way of getting "strokes"—and overt strokes are very important to NFs.

Ultimately, the goal was to help both Sally and her family put their fourteen-year history of misunderstanding and name-calling on both sides in typological perspective. The challenge was to get everyone to accept their typological differences on more than the merely intellectual level.

Finally there came attempts at modifying attitudes and behavior. The EJs, for one, had to refrain from using deprecating terms to describe Sally's behavior and, moreover, to accept the legitimacy of that behavior. It may be okay, for example, that Sally had a different internal time clock, an odd definition of a "clean room," and different social family needs. Sally, for her part, had to reinvest in herself, acknowledging and accepting her positive attributes, and redirecting the negative deviant behavior into such positive behavior as simply telling the truth —and trusting that the family will accept it. Among other things, Sally came to recognize she did have an easy way with people: she was congenial and very accepting, and had a talent for motivating others.

Six years later the family is still working on such issues, but they've come a long way. Sally is a constructive member of the family and her EJ parents and siblings have learned to accept her contribution as valid rather than automatically discounting it. Moreover, Sally, too, has come to recognize the value of her contribution—she has become the family moderator, helping them to resolve disputes by teaching them better listening skills —at the same time that she has learned to incorporate more Extraverted activities and more structure into her life. She joins in on more activities and events, including the arguing (if only to tell them that they need to listen to each other), instead of staying alone in her room.

Linda: The Extraverted Child's Study Habits

An ENFP high school senior, Linda was brought to us by her IJ parents. The session began with her mother saying, "I opened the door to her bedroom last night and she had the phone to her ear, the radio on, and she was doing her homework. Those are bad study habits!"

To which we asked, "How are her grades?"

The mother responded, "That's totally irrelevant. Bad study habits are bad study habits, and we've got to help her."

The whole family had been through our Typewatching session at the Army War College and knew and respected typological differences, but clearly had not translated that knowledge into Linda's study habits. We asked them to list, based on their understanding of type, studying and learning "turn-ons" for ENFPs. We also had them list the same turn-ons for an Introverted-Judger. Together, they displayed an excellent understanding of how ENFPs would differ from IJs in study habits. For example, while Introverts like quiet for concentration, Extraverts prefer variety and action. And while Judgers like to get things settled and finished, Perceivers don't mind leaving things open for later change.

The dramatic differences between the lists spoke for themselves, and the fact that Linda was getting on the honor roll in high school underscored the validity of her approach for herself. The parents could begin to see that to impose their idea of proper study habits on their daughter could actually be detrimental.

We had the lists reproduced and asked them to attach them to the refrigerator door with magnets, as daily reminders of the different strokes necessary for different folks.

Rhonda: Coping with Intimacy

Her parents divorced when she was eleven. Prior to the divorce, Rhonda had exhibited all the characteristics of a Feeling type: she needed and gave many overt strokes, personalized criticism, tried to please, and was prone to a wide range of touchy-feely behavior. In most respects she was a happy, normal child.

When her parents split up, it came as a total surprise. There had been no obvious signs of tension at home. The divorce crushed her, and, in typical F style, she personalized the situation: she felt guilty that she may have caused her parents' separation. Moreover, she questioned her own self-worth.

We met her years later when, as a graduate student, she came to us, frustrated by her inability to maintain relationships, with friends as well as lovers. She acknowledged that she was suspicious of people—including her parents—and was afraid to relate in depth because, as she put it, "People hurt you." Taking the Myers-Briggs Type Indicator, she showed a slight preference for Thinking, a marked contrast to her description of her childhood behavior.

Through Typewatching, she was able to identify her dilemma as a T-F issue. In true F fashion, she was carrying guilt that didn't belong to her. A meeting with each parent helped her to see that she had had nothing to do with their divorce. The air was cleared around that, and the parents were able to reaffirm genuine affection for her—and even for each other.

None of this had been discussed over the years, and that was part of the problem. Simply clearing the air and relieving some of her guilt helped Rhonda to regain her self-worth. Her parents felt better too. They also had carried guilt about their contribution to her stress, and this opening up helped to unburden them.

But that was only half the problem; the issue of present and future relationships remained. Because most male-female relationships are modeled in some way after our parents' relationship, Rhonda agreed that staying open with her parents would be helpful to her building trusting, open, and intimate relationships.

Finally, she made a T-F contract with herself. When her objective side told her that she should be cautious of intimacy with an individual, she agreed to ask herself subjective questions about the situation: How do I feel about this person? Has the other person given any danger signals? What's the worst that can happen?

In this case, Typewatching wasn't an instant cure—she's still working out the difficulties from childhood—but it provided a positive framework through which she could understand the problem and begin to make constructive behavioral changes. Both Rhonda and her parents benefited.

Jonathan: "Greetings" from an Introverted Child

He was an Introvert in a family of Extraverts. His father had traveled all weekend, coming home the preceding Sunday night to the greetings, sociability, and activity of his Extraverted wife and daughter. Jonathan did not even emerge from his room, and still hadn't said hello after his father had been home for nearly three hours. Finally the father could stand it no longer and, in classic E style, marched up to Jonathan's room, abrasively demanding that his son acknowledge his father's presence, converse with him, and become involved in the family gathering.

It went downhill from there.

The next day happened to be the family's introduction to Typewatching, at which time they discovered the E-I difference. The father recognized that as an Extravert, *he* needed his son to be involved, *he* needed family activity, and *he* needed to be affirmed—"Greet me, I'm home"—but he also recognized that Introverts have many different needs in those areas.

The plan that resulted was an easy compromise: Jonathan

agreed to proffer a minimum of "Hello," perhaps more, if the Extraverts agreed that it was okay for him to be alone and not necessarily always join in their activities.

Amy: The Sensor Among iNtuitives

Her father, Don, an ENTP, came to us with a line we've heard many times: "I wish I had known about Typewatching years ago. I wouldn't have felt so guilty." Amy, a ten-year-old, first-born ESFJ, was the only Sensor in a family of five. There were two ENFP siblings, an ENTP father, and an INFJ mother. The guilt-inducing event occurred when Don was tutoring Amy in her arithmetic homework. The tension between them mounted —they had very different perceptions of the subject: while Amy saw math as a cut-and-dried process of adding, subtracting, multiplying, and dividing, Don tried to relate it to a larger conceptual world.

Finally, in exasperation and frustration, Don threw the math book at his daughter. Amy ran out of the room in tears, feeling scared by and estranged from her father—and full of self-doubt about her learning capabilities. It would be the last time Don would tutor his daughter—on any subject—and would lead to years of "math block" for Amy.

It wasn't until years later, when Amy was a postgraduate student, that we met Don at a Typewatching training session. When the discussion came around to the differences between Sensor and iNtuitive learning styles, the light bulbs flashed on. Don was not only able to "revisit" the situation in his mind but was compelled to discuss the whole affair with Amy. The result was that thirteen years after the incident, they had a discussion that not only relieved Don's guilt but also gave Amy new confidence in coping with math and healed an open wound in a father-daughter relationship.

We could go on. There's the story, for example, about the father and son who were four-letter opposites (ENTP son, ISFJ father). The son found boring every practical, down-to-earth activity—from coursework to career choices—the father wanted for him; and the father found his son's enthusiastic, inventive schemes to be harebrained and flaky. These conflicts were leading them to nowhere but trouble. Again, Typewatching skills helped them to "agree to disagree," recognizing that they would always have vastly different needs and interests, and to cope a little less destructively with those differences. The father agreed not to shoot down every new brainstorm the son had, and the son agreed to try to finish at least one project a week.

The point is one we've made all through this book. Our natural tendency is to try to make differences disappear, to make others as much like ourselves as possible. Nowhere is this tendency more evident than in parents, whose intentions are only honorable—we truly believe that—but who abuse their parental authority by compelling typologically uncomfortable or even impossible behavior from their children. Typewatching can help them honor their children's differences and accept what can't be changed—while also making true compromise and communication possible.

Of course, it's *not* possible to change your kids from one type to another. But that doesn't mean you shouldn't try from time to time to encourage more modified behavior. A Perceiving child, for example, might be encouraged to be "more J" in doing his or her homework; an Introverted child might be encouraged to be "more E" at the dinner table. One word of caution: J parents are more likely to want to "mold" their children. Thus, J parents need to be particularly clear in their own minds about their motives, and should ask themselves, "Am I trying to change my child because it's what I want, or because it will benefit my child in the long run?" P parents, for their part, tend to err in the opposite way: they are very accepting and adaptive to the child's behavior and therefore may be remiss in providing needed structure or discipline.

Coping with Older Parents

As we've stated frequently, Typewatching is a lifelong process, and its parent-child applications continue long after children are grown and married. In fact, they can be extremely useful during parents' later years, easing many of the difficult differences between active adults and their aging parents.

One of the problems during these years is that parent-child relationships often get reversed: parents become the needy ones who need nurturing and attention, while their children struggle with their newfound responsibilities. Making things even more difficult is that in their later years, people often dabble in their nonpreferences. We know one army general, a hard-charging Thinking-Judger who, upon retirement, dove headfirst into a variety of artsy-craftsy activities. Among other things, he and his wife rented a camper and toured the Southwest at a slow, leisurely, unscheduled pace. He submerged himself in watercolors and nature.

Such behavior can confound children, who must cope with these new realities while dealing with their own lives. Typewatching can help to put positive, constructive labels on such transitions, making things easier for both parties. In response to some troubling behavior on your parents' part, you might apply some of the skills you've already learned. Do your formerly gregarious parents suddenly seem withdrawn? It may be that they're "trying on" the Introverted side of their lives. Do they seem much more rigid or exacting? They may be fulfilling more Judging or Sensing needs—or merely experiencing these heretofore nonpreferred parts of their personalities. In either case, the Typewatching model can be very helpful. (In Chapter Ten we've included brief descriptions of how each of the sixteen types can behave in later years, which may serve as a point of reference.)

As Typewatching continues to grow in popularity—and as our society continues to gray—Typewatching awareness and skills will no doubt play a vital role in how we relate to older people.

Typewatching isn't a magic cure-all for all family problems—some problems simply transcend any behavioral system. Nor do we suggest that every little problem demands full-scale Typewatching skills—there are days (or weeks) when any of us gets out on the wrong side of the bed. Our experiences, however, have shown conclusively the beautiful, constructive results of parent-child Typewatching.

9

Typewatching Everywhere

"Have a cookie. You'll feel better."

If by now you've caught a mild case of Typewatching fever, we'd like to offer a few words that might bring your temperature back to normal. We do this because we've seen enthusiastic new Typewatchers attempt to translate the entire universe into Typewatching terms. They talk of Extraverted weeping-willow trees, Introverted goldfish, Sensing-Judging kittens, and iNtuitive-Feeling cars. It's fun stuff, and probably not without foundation, but after a while it begins to stretch the point.

Such behavior, however, is not as obnoxious as the next level of commitment: using Typewatching to excuse your bad behavior. It sounds something like this: "I meant to call you back, but I'm an Introvert, and we don't generally return phone calls." Or "I'd like to explain it to you, but you're a Sensor and you're limited in your comprehension." Or even "You obviously mistook me for someone who gives a damn. I'm a T." Again, while such statements may be true for the individual at hand, they don't allow much room for compromise or self-directed change, two things at the heart of our personal justification for Typewatching.

Having pointed out the risks—that we can overdo Typewatching, or use it as an excuse—we must concede that there aren't many areas of life to which Typewatching doesn't apply, so long as its basic message of respect for self and others is honored. One good source for pursuing Typewatching's many day-to-day possibilities is in *The Type Reporter* ($24 for four issues), a very readable lay newsletter that we highly recommend for neophytes and experts alike. (For a sample copy, write *The Type Reporter*, 524 North Paxton Street, Alexandria, VA 22304.)

Type, Teaching, and Learning

School is one place in which there are applications galore. It's worth noting again that school is where Typewatching began, as Katharine Briggs based her original classification of students on their learning differences—and teaching differences too.

A great deal has been written and published about education and personality types. We, too, have worked in and around educational systems throughout the country—primary, secondary, and college levels—and have seen Typewatching's tremendous relevancy for the teaching-learning dynamic. Here are some of our observations about how type plays out in the education process:

Sensors Do, iNtuitives Teach: The S-N Dichotomy

Grades K through six are heavily Sensing-oriented. It's hands-on learning with a great deal of student involvement. Kids are always "doing"—going to the chalkboard, making arts and crafts, filling out workbooks, having show-and-tell, and all the rest. Starting around seventh grade, theory increases, intensifies during college, and peaks in graduate school. Accordingly, our data show that grade school teachers are about two-thirds Sensing, high school teachers about evenly split between Sensing and iNtuitive, and college faculties about 70 percent iNtuitive (some graduate school faculties are as high as 77 percent iNtuitive).* This is significant when you recall that the U.S. population as a whole is 70 percent Sensing.

You can begin to imagine the problems this creates at the

* *MBTI Manual*, p. 133–36.

classroom level. Consider, for example, an iNtuitive college history professor lecturing to an auditorium full of Sensing students. "Today," he begins, "we'll examine the four causes of World War II. But before we begin, let me give you a theoretical frame of reference. . . ." At which point he launches into a fascinating but somewhat rambling dissertation explaining how World War II came about—but never specifically naming the "four causes." And at the end of the hour there sits a primarily Sensing student body wondering what it's all about and why they bothered to show up—to say nothing of the fact that they haven't scribbled a word in their notebooks. The iNtuitives, meanwhile, have had a fairly stimulating experience, or at least an informative one. And so the Sensing and the iNtuitive ships pass in the academic night.

NOT TOO LONG, NOT TOO SHORT

I'm an INTJ teacher and I tend to give very open-ended assignments. When students would ask questions like "How long should our reports be?" I'd say, "As long as it takes to make your point."

After learning type I realized I must be upsetting my Sensing students. But it remains impossible for me to assign a number of pages. The best I can do is give them a range.

"Five pages is probably too short and fifty pages is too long," I say.

The problems worsen when you realize that most intelligence tests are created in institutions of higher learning. That means that a group of overwhelmingly iNtuitive test makers are, in effect, determining the fates, educationally, of an overwhelmingly Sensing public. The inevitable result is that iNtuitives do better on the tests. Isabel Briggs Myers, in her book *Gifts Differing*, supports this notion when she points out that better than eight out of ten National Merit Scholarship finalists were iNtuitives.

And we wonder why our education often seems "irrelevant."

Explained in Typewatching terms, the irrelevance becomes clear. Sensors, as we've already seen, are hands-on "doers" in their approach to life. So a "relevant" education for them is one that is practical, tactile, and down-to-earth. It is more skill-oriented, preparing the Sensor to "go and do." For the iNtuitive college professor, on the other hand, you can never master enough theory.

Yet our culture rewards college degrees—the higher the better. Imagine the disappointment of the parent whose Sensing teenager announces, "I don't want to go to college," or, worse yet, "I want to be an automobile mechanic."

It hasn't always been this way. Today's car mechanic was yesterday's tool-and-die maker, watchmaker, or master craftsman. These were honored professions. But with our reward system today based on the theoretical, there's little motivation to seek such "lowly" skills now, let alone go to schools that are technical in orientation. Vocational education, you might recall, was designed for those who couldn't "make it" in the classroom. Our educational system was probably more Sensing-oriented back in the days of the three R's, when society recognized the skilled craftsman or apprentice as a worthy citizen.

So with low esteem and low reward, you get low motivation, which leads to poor training, which creates a society that technically can't take care of itself—cars that don't run, flying machines that won't stay up, and high-tech equipment that people can't service.

The S-N teaching-learning dichotomy results in Sensors becoming the *doers* of the various disciplines—the doctors, grade school teachers, engineers, and lawyers—and iNtuitives becoming the *teachers* of medicine, education, engineering, and law. That starts to explain why the bulk of the population views higher education as irrelevant, and why there is an increasing demand for internships across all discipline lines, from engineers to English teachers. In other words, after spending countless years learning about something, it takes a year of *doing* it before someone is fully competent; the apprenticeship system comes full circle. It was probably a Sensor who developed the adage that specialization is "learning more and more about less and less, until you get to know everything about nothing."

It was also likely a Sensor who promulgated the theory that "Those who can't do, teach." (And an iNtuitive who countered that "Those who can't teach, teach gym"—the ultimate Sensing experience.)

Type and Test-taking

Another S-N dichotomy can be seen in tests that require timed responses. Sensors prefer to read carefully each question, perhaps even more than once, to make sure they have understood it. They are less given to trusting the first thing that pops in their mind. Just the opposite is done by iNtuitives. On a test, they give the first answer that occurs to them, even if they don't fully understand the question.* It's not unreasonable to hypothesize, then, that timed tests favor iNtuitives, despite their constituting only about a third of the population.

Yet another difference in test performance has to do with Thinkers and Feelers. In 1973, two researchers, studying a group of students at Howard University, found that Introverted-Thinkers outperformed Extraverted-Feelers in memorizing a series of numbers, while the EFs outperformed the ITs in recalling faces.** This doesn't mean, however, that Feelers can't work with figures and Thinkers can't remember faces. It only means that they must apply different energies to do so successfully. A Thinker might recall numbers and a Feeler might recall faces, but if the test only deals with figures, the Feelers must appear to be slow learners. This dynamic plagues us all the way through education, but intensifies in college. A client of ours typifies this: he is an Introverted-Sensing student in a master's program and wrote a final exam mentored by three iNtuitive professors. They flunked him on the essay portion with the written critique, "You didn't flesh this out enough, it was too bare-bones." From the Sensor's point of view, he had

* Isabel Briggs Myers, *Gifts Differing* (Palo Alto, Calif.: Consulting Psychologists Press Inc., 1980), p. 59–60.
** Mary H. McCaulley, *Jung's Theory and the Myers-Briggs Type Indicator* (Gainesville, Fla.: Center for the Application of Psychological Type, 1981), p. 320.

written the facts; the rest was unnecessary elaboration. But the iNtuitives were the ones handing out the grades—and they handed him an F. As with truth, beauty, and contact lenses, intelligence is largely in the eye of the beholder.

Expression vs. Reflection: Extraverts and Introverts

There is an Extraverted learning model that says, "There is no impression without expression." In other words, "You don't know it if you can't say it." Introverts, on the other hand, live by the adage "There is no impression without *reflection*"—you must think something over, however briefly, before it is truly learned. You can imagine the situation: A teacher imparts some information to a classroom of students. To comprehend that information fully, Extraverts need to talk about it—to bounce it back to the teacher or other students—while Introverts need time to reflect—to integrate it, assimilate it, and internalize it—none of which can happen while others are busy Extraverting.

Which students will end up looking like the bright ones? The Extraverts, no doubt, who constantly "prove" their understanding out loud while the equally bright Introverts hardly have time to think it, let alone say it.

Structure vs. Spontaneity: Judgers and Perceivers

Judgers learn best when they know what the goals are and that an outline is being followed—all of which impedes the learning process for Perceivers. Completing an outline isn't as important for the Perceiver so much as hitching a ride on whatever train of thought comes along. Not following an outline frustrates the J, however. ("We said we were going to cover three points today, but we only covered one and then got into a class discussion.") The Ps would delight in a class in which the outline was abandoned in favor of an exciting digression. Of course, the ability to stick to an outline is directly related to the teacher's own type. Even though iNtuitive-Feeling-Perceivers are effec-

tive teachers at every level, there are very few of them in the
system as they are discouraged largely by Sensing-Thinking-
Judging administrators, who want week-by-week detailed
course outlines. That's simply debilitating to an NFP.

Learning Temperaments

If you recall from Chapter Four, a Typewatching shortcut is to
combine two letters which produce four types—NF, NT, SJ, and
SP—about which you can make some predictions. These four
types, called Temperaments, give us the most accurate predictions about our behavior. They tell us a lot about teaching and
learning too.

There is a great deal in the nature of education, for example,
that favors students who prefer iNtuition and Feeling—NF. As
Ns, they do well with theory, as Fs, they have a strong need to
please—teachers, parents, peers, whomever. As a result, NF
students often become high achievers academically and end up
in careers that are easy for them to pursue but which are typologically difficult for them to cope with. NF engineers, accountants, and scientists can be fish out of water because they followed a career course to be like a parent or personal hero. Such
analytical-oriented careers tend to be less rewarding for NFs,
however, whose career leanings are more people-oriented.

There are other Temperament differences.

For example, with three out of five public school teachers
being Sensing-Judging (SJ) types, the iNtuitive-Thinking (NT)
student is headed for trouble. NTs are driven by a need for
competence and expect their teachers to have it. So they test
them—along with parents, friends, and themselves—daily. As a
result, NT students are seen as counterdependent, obnoxious,
arrogant, and argumentative. In reality, they're merely testing
the teacher's competency and their own abilities to comprehend. A friend of ours, in her doctoral dissertation, correlated
by type the qualities of students well liked by teachers and
those not liked by teachers. She found that NT students generally, and ENTJs especially, rated poorly among teachers; ESFJs,

and Fs generally, had qualities the teachers liked most. ESFJs, as we describe in Chapter Ten, are the most gracious of the sixteen types. The study constitutes an argument for polished apples and other forms of teacher flattery.

Of course, teachers lure these nice students into the teaching profession (hence, 60 percent of public school teachers are SJs). The SJ student operates on the basis that "The teacher is there to teach and the student is there to learn." Consequently, they do well at memorizing things they must memorize and at having their homework in on time (and neatly done), all of which gets them a good grade and teaches them to be good teachers themselves. SJ students generally have a good definition of the roles and responsibilities of both teacher and student, and respond accordingly.

The losers in this educational system are the Sensing-Perceiver types. Living for the moment, it is hard for them to learn something that has no immediate application. (This is the type, you may recall, that says, "When all else fails, read the directions.") For them, learning is a hands-on experience that one must grapple with. "To learn" is to grapple successfully. An SP, for example, questions why it is necessary to study music theory in order to play guitar—or veterinary medicine in order to work with animals, something they do quite naturally.

Unlike the NFs, who, when motivated to please others, do well with theory, and the NTs, who are intrigued when intellectually stimulated by a theory, and the SJs, who learn theory because they "should do it," there is precious little theory the SP finds relevant. "If you can put it together without the directions," says the SP, "who needs theory?" Besides, the SP knows that "If I need the theory, I can always get it. And if I don't need it, I'm glad I didn't waste time studying something unnecessary."

This is portrayed dramatically in an ESTP we counseled, whose near-Mensa IQ score of 137 was the *lowest* of three tests he took—and yet he was diagnosed by a school counselor as "brain-damaged." Sadly, to this academically bright young man saddled with an SP's here-and-now restlessness, this diagnosis became a kind of self-fulfilling prophecy. Today, at twenty-six, he is divorced, the father of one child, unemployed, and, as a

Learning Temperaments

Everyone has the capacity to learn, but each type and Temperament has a unique style. Here are learning profiles of the four Temperaments, courtesy of Dr. Keith Golay, a therapeutic counselor in Fullerton, California, who applies Temperament theory in matching methods and approaches to clients' types.

NFs

Will be most responsive when learning *about:*

1. The value the various species have to cultures
2. How to communicate to people about endangered species and their protection
3. The issue of humane treatment of captured and protected animals
4. The effects that laws and enforcement have on people; do they in turn infringe on the rights of people

Will be most responsive when learning *by:*

1. Writing letters to various people
2. Reading books on the subject and doing a paper
3. Doing role playing to display problems with people
4. Giving the class a speech on the subject
5. Working in small groups and sharing information
6. Designing a means to communicate about endangered species to the public, or setting up a campaign to inform the public about the needs of endangered species

NTs

Will be most responsive when learning *about:*

1. Problem-solving—How to collect and analyze information related to endangered species
2. Ethology—How to collect and analyze information on the habits and needs of each species

3. Predicting—How to generate a prognosis for each species if various conditions do or don't exist
4. Explaining Why???

Will be most responsive when learning *by:*

1. Doing research in the library
2. Talking with an ethologist at a university
3. Reading books on the subject
4. Giving a lecture to the class
5. Having a debate on the pluses and minuses
6. Designing a test for students

SJs

Will be most responsive when learning *about:*

1. The laws, policies and governmental agencies related to endangered species
2. How to care for animals once they are caught
3. How to collect and categorize the data related to the habits and needs of each type of animal
4. Keeping account of the various animals—collecting and storing information
5. How to disseminate information to others
6. New laws needed to enforce protection

Will be most responsive when learning *by:*

1. Writing for information
2. Going to the library and getting information
3. Interviewing people for information—designing an interview format to use, i.e., the questions to ask
4. Giving the class a talk on the subject
5. Collecting information from the government and putting it in a document

SPs

Will be most responsive when learning *about:*

1. Locating and capturing the animals
2. How to set up game reserves and build facilities to care for the various animals
3. People who locate and capture hunters and poachers
4. The current methods of enforcing laws

Will be most responsive when learning *by:*

1. Interviewing people
2. Viewing films on the subject
3. Visiting a game reserve, taking pictures to show in class, acquiring films to show to class on the subject
4. Drawing pictures to portray information
5. Constructing a reserve to display information

high school dropout, lacks the academic credentials that would enable him to put his bright mind to work. Given the necessity to master at least some theory in order to advance himself academically, he is doomed to continue to fail.

The bottom line, educationally, is a system that rewards theory. And the more theory you have, the more you are rewarded with grades, degrees, and status. In dealing with the prospect of future rewards versus present gratification, the here-and-now SP swims against a strong current. The statistics bear this out: while constituting about 35 percent of the U.S. population, they are the least likely to receive college degrees.

Type and Career

We've already discussed how Typewatching operates in the workplace—how managers of one type gravitate to subordinates of the same type, for example, and how certain types are well suited for certain tasks. Similarly, Typewatching has considerable application in choosing—and changing—careers.

AS SIMPLE AS ABC

Sensing-Perceivers are notorious spellers. To these hands-on types, spelling is akin to theory: they would rather do it than learn about it. A supervisor we know, reporting to a group, once misspelled a word he wrote on an easel. The group called him on it. He replied, "I never could even spell 'cat' or 'dog.' I didn't need to. Why spell 'em when you can see 'em?"

On the other hand, an iNtuitive we worked with in a similar situation also misspelled a word in front of a group. When it was called to his attention, he commented with arrogance: "It's a small mind that can only spell a word one way."

Before we begin, however, a word of warning: If you like what you do for a living, even though your type isn't "ideal" for that occupation, don't let Typewatching theory lead you astray. It's an old Typewatching adage that any type can be successful

WHAT'S COOKING?

An NFP once reported, "I don't always have the ingredients for re-creating a particular recipe. But I'm not above substituting. If I don't have a spice, I'll put in another one—or none at all."

An ISTJ, hearing this, responded, "If it's not written down, I can't cook it."

It's not surprising that dieticians are overwhelmingly— about 70 percent—STJs. For them, "successful cooking" means "following directions."

in any career he or she chooses. Moreover, there are some types —particularly Perceiving types—who enjoy the challenge of being "miscast" in the "wrong" profession and, in the process, are often very successful in using those differences to creative ends. More often than not, however, miscast types aren't entirely successful at their chosen careers, and the type-career mismatch can lead to a host of other problems—at home as well as at work.

Miscast careers often result from the well-meaning but misguided reward systems found in many professions. The skills demanded at one level of a job are sometimes vastly different from those demanded at another level. Consider, for example, the police officer patrolling a beat. It's a job that requires flexibility, spontaneity, and concern for people's immediate needs, sometimes to the bending of rules and regulations. If the officer does the job well, a promotion to a "desk job" is often in order. But the new job demands a whole new set of skills: schedules, procedures, strict observance of departmental rules and regulations, and far less contact with people. Suddenly that exemplary employee is a fish out of water. The same phenomenon takes place in dozens of other professions.

There is a direct link between job-level skills and typology. Career counselors frequently divide careers into three types—those involving data (such as keypunch operator, desk clerk, accountant), those involving people (such as sales, teaching, management, lawyer), and those involving things (such as switchboard operator, crane operator, cabinetmaker). In each category, as you rise in skill you face different sets of typological demands.

As the chart on the next page shows, lower level tasks in the various types of careers can be done by an individual of almost any type. In the "data" category, for example, the ability to compare data—deciding whether two things are similar or different—demands no particular type. As you begin doing specific things to that data—compiling it, analyzing it, coordinating it, and synthesizing it—the typological needs become more specific. The lower levels of the "things" category require J-type activities—regularly emptying containers, operating a photocopy machine, maintaining equipment, and other tasks that require little or no judgment but demand punctuality and schedules, two characteristics in which Judgers excel. The top level of this category requires far more flexibility and perception, in modifying, altering, arranging, and installing various "things," characteristics best suited to iNtuitives and Perceiv-

Organizational Skills and Types

In the chart below, the functional skills within each area are presented as a hierarchy. At the top are the more complex tasks, at the bottom are the entry-level jobs. As you go up the chart, each level of skill includes all those below it.

Data	People	Things	
Synthesizing	Mentoring	Setting-up	Complex
Coordinating	Negotiating	Precision tasks	↑
Analyzing	Instructing	Operating/controlling	
Compiling	Supervising	Driving/operating	
Computing	Diverting	Manipulating	
Copying	Persuading	Tending	↓
Comparing	Speaking/serving	Feeding/handling	Simple

ers. The irony is that iNtuitives and Perceivers are likely to become frustrated working at the lower level activities, reducing the likelihood that they'll find their way to the top, and increasing the possibility that those who do rise aren't the best types for the job.

Occupational Choices by Type

The following are samples of representative occupations listed as attractive to each of the sixteen types, taken from the 1985 MBTI Manual. They are coded from a modification of the *Dictionary of Occupational Titles* (U.S. Department of Labor, 1977), and represent a fourteen-year data base from the Center for the Application of Psychological Type. The occupational listings in the manual are extensive; we have selected representative occupations from among those choices. In a few cases, we have included career choices based on our own observations; those careers are designated with an asterisk.

ISTJ
Administrative and managers (school, industry, medical)
Dentists
Police and detectives
Auditors and accountants
Military*

ISFJ
Nurses
Clerical supervisors
Teachers (preschool and speech pathology)
Librarians
Health technicians

INFJ
Education consultants
Clergy
Physicians
Media specialists
Teachers (English, art, drama)

INTJ
Lawyers
Scientists (life and physical)
Computer systems analysts
Chemical engineers
University teachers

ISTP
Farmers
Mechanics and repairers
Electric technicians
Engineers
Dental hygienists

ISFP
Storekeepers and stock clerks
Nurses
Dental assistants
Bookkeepers
Mechanics and repairers

INFP
Psychiatrists and psychologists
Writers, artists, and editors
Teachers
Social workers
Musicians and composers

INTP
Writers
Artists and entertainers
Computer programmers
Social scientists
Lawyers*

ESTP
Marketing personnel
Police and detectives
Managers and administrators
Retail salespeople
Auditors

ESFP
Child care workers
Receptionists
Salespeople
Religious workers
Teachers (preschool and coaching)

ENFP
Rehabilitation counselors
Teachers (art and drama)
Writers, artists, entertainers

Psychologists
Clergy

ENTP
Photographers
Marketing personnel
Salespeople
Journalists
Computer systems analysts

ESTJ
Teachers
School administrators
Surgeons
Factory and site supervisors
Lawyers

ESFJ
Medical secretaries
Clergy
Nurses*
Home economists
Hair dressers and cosmetologists

ENFJ
Clergy
Teachers
Actors and entertainers
Writers and artists
Consultants

ENTJ
Lawyers
Managers
Mortgage brokers
Administrators (computer systems and education)
Scientists

We don't happen to think it is appropriate to pick a career from a list simply because it's of the "right" type. It may be helpful, however, to recognize the particular strengths—and,

therefore, the potential weaknesses—of each of the eight preferences when mirrored against various career demands. Keep
in mind that every career requires some of each of the eight
preferences. Researching, for example, involves primarily Introversion in the striving for discovery. When a discovery is
made, however, "selling" that finding to various others is often
demanded, to gain financial support or professional credentials,
an activity better suited to Extraverts. Similarly, tough-minded
executive decisions require objective, directed action—Thinking-Judging traits—but, to be effective, require sensitivity to
the people upon whom the actions will have impact and the
flexibility to make adjustments as the situation demands—Feel-
ing-Perceiving traits.

It can be very helpful, whether you are a recent high school
graduate or someone making a midlife career change, to consider a potential job or career from a Typewatching perspective. The process involves asking a lot of questions. For example:

■ **Does the job involve working extensively with others, or working primarily on your own?** Jobs that involve working primarily
with others are better suited for Extraverts, particularly if they
involve selling, persuading, and motivating. Introverts can also
do these things very capably, but they may pay for it in their
expenditure of energy, leaving themselves drained. On the
other hand, if the job involves working primarily alone or being
accountable primarily to oneself, Introverts will find it far more
appealing. Such jobs tend to involve less "invasion" by others
and more self-directed tasks—ideally performed in an office
with a door that locks from the inside.

■ **Does the job require more hands-on activity or more imaginative speculation?** "Hands-on" means more than carpentry and
plumbing; it involves any profession where "doing" and "bottom lines" are the driving forces—as in accounting, trial law,
and civil engineering. These and other professions that have
short-term, tangible results are particularly satisfying to those
who prefer Sensing. On the other hand, imaginative- and spec-
ulative-type jobs—for example, those of financial planners, law
professors, and architectural engineers—that have longer-term

goals and more intellectually abstract rewards are more appealing to iNtuitives.

■ **Does the job call for objective, rational decisions or people-related concerns?** Clearly, Thinking types are drawn to jobs and professions that don't involve embroiling themselves in a lot of interpersonal relationships—journalism, for example, high-tech research, stockbrokers, and almost any job in the military. Their counterparts, Feeling types, are attracted to professions that involve more interpersonal dynamics—teaching, clergy, counseling, and nursing, among many others.

■ **Does the job have heavy structure and schedule demands, or is there room for flexibility and "flying by the seat of your pants"?** Judging types respond well to and are less stressed by jobs that require sticking to established procedures and schedules—everything from bus driving to brain surgery. There are, however, many jobs that require spontaneity, open-endedness, and flexibility—including those of entrepreneurs, journalists, strategic planners, and futurists—characteristics that have strong appeal to Perceiving types.

With this said, keep in mind that the specific careers that appeal to each of the eight preferences depend largely on an individual's other three letters. An Introverted Sensor, for example, will be attracted to jobs different from those appealing to an Extraverted-Sensor or an Introverted-iNtuitive.

When you look at your own four letters in terms of your values, education, age, and other personal characteristics, you can see that the key to type and career isn't a matter of choosing a job from a list of careers to which your type is "supposed" to gravitate. Rather, it is to ask yourself questions that can help you focus on you and your type, and on the career possibilities that fit both.

Let's assume for a moment that you are an ENTP—an Extraverted-iNtuitive-Thinking-Perceiver. A well-suited career would be one that involves:

■ working closely with other people, giving and receiving immediate verbal feedback, and allowing plenty of opportunity for interruption;
■ imagination, dreaming, and speculating;

- rewards for objective decision making and clarity of thought; and
- responding to constantly emerging situations and concerns.

Given this, it isn't surprising that many entrepreneurs are ENTPs. Other suitable careers include those that involve writing and journalism (which allow them to develop their own ideas, rather than follow others' prescribed plans), computer programming (which suits their need for development and creativity as well as their love for technology), and marketing and public relations (which use their Extraverted people skills and their iNtuitive creativity, as well as the flexibility to meet changing conditions).

There would be much more job satisfaction and fewer inappropriate professional choices if career counselors and executive-recruitment firms incorporated Typewatching into their operations. Obviously, career guidance for an ISTJ will look far different from that for an ENFP.

Indeed, we know of an unemployed ISTJ who was advised by a prestigious outplacement counseling firm to follow a largely ENP model for securing a new job: seeking contacts, promoting himself within his industry, being alert and open to possibilities, and remaining open to whatever comes along. After about three weeks, the counselor became frustrated with the ISTJ's reluctance to act on these suggestions, accusing him of being uninterested and unwilling to take control of his future.

We met with both counselor and counselee. It turned out that the ISTJ, despite his apparent lack of interest, actually had a rather clear vision about his professional future—his strengths and weaknesses, salary requirements, even to what cities or areas he would be willing to relocate. The problem, from his perspective, was that the counselor's instructions were simply too vague and general for him to implement. Moreover, they involved constantly selling himself in ways he felt weren't suited to his style—things like networking with strangers and attending cocktail parties and other social events. And there seemed to be no regular accountability on his part to the counselor, a factor the ISTJ felt was important.

It quickly became evident that it would have been better for the counselor to give the ISTJ one specific assignment per session—to make one new contact by a given date, for example, and to return with a report about it. That contact would best be made by letter, seeking a specific appointment during business hours, and being straightforward about the nature of the meeting. The results were dramatic. The ISTJ found a job to his liking within a few weeks.

The problem, it turned out, was the counselor. An ENTJ, he was imposing his EN style of networking on the ISTJ (who, as a J, further compounded the problem by his belief that there was only one right way to do things). The counselor's style, for the ISTJ, was ineffectual, unmotivating, and undirected.

The idea, in careers as in almost every other Typewatching application, is to find a job to fit an individual's preferences, rather than try to make that person fit a job for which he or she may be typologically unsuited. The better the fit, the less the stress, the greater the satisfaction, and the higher the productivity over the long haul.

WHAT COLOR IS YOUR PAIR OF SHOES?

The Extraverted-Sensing-Feeling-Judger is the most polished, gracious, and appropriate of the sixteen types. One ESFJ we know carries that appropriateness to the limit: she is color-coordinated in everything she wears. She claims that her underwear always goes with her outfit of the day.

Social Types: Who Does What at Parties

We're not going to belabor the obvious: that social situations make an Extravert's day, any day, and the more people there are, the merrier, or that Introverts would just as soon read a book, perhaps talk with one or two others, than attend a crowded affair. We've covered this situation amply here and in preceding chapters. What's interesting is how social situations bring out a variety of behaviors that are, for better or worse, unique to each type. From casual dinner parties to fancy affairs to nights on the town, you've seen them all:

- the one who never shows up on time
- the one who always arrives early
- the one who wants to be a part of everything
- the one who refuses to participate in anything
- the one who wants to make sure everyone is having fun
- the one who wants to make sure everyone knows the time
- the one who thinks "a good time" means "a good argument"
- the one who thinks "a good time" means "a planned activity"
- the one who thinks "a good time" means "whatever happens"

We've given quite a number of parties over the years and, because we know the four-letter type of virtually all of our friends and colleagues, we've had a lot of firsthand experience with types in social situations. It's fun after an event to go through the list to see who was the life of the party, who seemed out of place, who caused friction, and so on, and to try to see typological patterns. Almost inevitably, several patterns emerge.

We can say one thing with certainty: You'll never go wrong if you have a cross section of types at a social affair. Beyond that, there are some types who can guarantee success at an affair, and others who will make having a lively time more of a challenge.

Extraverts, of course, can help liven up any situation, although too many Es will drive the quiet types out the door early. We always seek a large number of Fs and Ps as well. Simply put, Extraverts, Feelers, and Perceivers love to make things happen. Even the relatively rigid Introverted-Judgers can be swept along by an infectious crowd of Es, Fs, and Ps. All of these observations, of course, are based on our own personal typological biases. Like most people, we tend to be true to our own types, gravitating to those whose types are similar to our own. Therefore, we find that we tend to have more Ns, Fs, and Ps in our own circle of friends.

Introverts can enjoy parties, too, of course, although their definition of "fun" may differ from Extraverts'. We gave a birthday party once in which the majority of guests were Introverts. We were convinced the evening was an absolute disaster because everyone seemed so quiet. (When you put twelve to twenty Introverts in a room, the noise level is roughly equivalent to four hearty Extraverts.) But the evening was by no means a disaster. The Introverts loved the freedom to be low-key, talking in depth with one or two other people.

Sensors, true to their names, tend to be more in tune with the sensual aspects of a party—what people wear, table decorations, the food (both how it looks and how it tastes), among other things. Meanwhile, iNtuitives tend to be far more tuned into the event as a whole—who is there (and who isn't), what's going on, with whom can they talk or dance, are there any good contacts they should make, how it's all going to end. They are more in tune with the overall ambience than with its specific components.

A Thinker assesses the party—"Should I be doing business or can I just 'have fun'?"—while their Feeling counterparts tune in to the people—"With whom should I connect, whom must I be sure not to slight, who's looking lonely and needs attention?" If all else fails, they can always be counted on to pass the hors d'oeuvres.

Judgers, for their part, arrive on time and expect the host to have things organized, judging the party a success if it goes according to plan. Perceivers, meanwhile, can't wait to get there to see what's going to happen, hoping, of course, for a few "surprises" during the course of the evening.

You get the idea.

Typewatching for Fun and Profit

We're constantly intrigued by the new and creative applications for Typewatching. Indeed, though some may accuse us of "overtyping," we've observed some very real type trends in almost every aspect of life. The excitement for us is in making some new connection between a seemingly unexplainable human dynamic and a possible Typewatching explanation for it.

Based on our firsthand observation of thousands of people in every walk of life with whom we have trained, counseled, or

PET THEORIES

As every animal lover knows, every dog, cat, fish, and bird has its own personality. Who could deny the Extraverted-Feeling of a golden retriever, or the Introverted-Sensing-Thinking-Judging nature of a German shepherd?

We once got two kittens from the same litter—a solid gray male and a solid black female. Although they never took the MBTI (we thought about giving them the indicator, but we knew they'd have trouble holding the pencil), it quickly became clear to us that each had a very clear and different four-letter type: the male is an ENTP, the female, an ISTJ.

The male prefers Extraversion (he is outgoing, loves people around, plays with other animals, walks through the house meowing); iNtuitive (he's often into new adventures and isn't bound by any known realities: he steps off of windowsills and other high places, as if to fly like the bug he's chasing); Thinking (he is not given to a great deal of warmth, and prefers to be nutured by being challenged with new games and activities); and Perceiving (he is very flexible and spontaneous—he can even be sidetracked by a new adventure en route to his food dish).

The female prefers Introversion (she is much more reserved, slow to make friends, and limits herself to only two or three people, and no other cats); Sensing (she is very precise about what she eats and her living conditions—she carefully and completely checks everything); Thinking (she is also very cool and aloof); and Judging (she is very neat, always tidying up after herself; she eats on schedule).

otherwise come into professional contact, here are a few of the many and diverse applications of Typewatching in which we're currently engaged:

Money: Who Saves, Who Spends?

Each of the eight preferences and sixteen types relates differently to money and finance. In a stockbrokerage firm we stud-
ied, for example, the ISTJs, year in and year out, had the most
conservative portfolios, delivering a small but reliable return on
investors' money. The company's ESTP and ENTP brokers
were by far the highest rollers, with the biggest portfolios yielding the biggest returns. They clearly outsold the others, although they also recorded the biggest losses. It would be a great
benefit to this and other brokerage firms and their investors if
the national financial climate could be assessed in terms of how
well ESTP and ENTP brokers would do in it, versus how well
the ISTJs would do: they could then deploy their brokers accordingly.

Another phenomenon we've seen is that Extraverts and iN-
tuitives tend to "round off" dollar amounts to suit their purposes. A $19.95 purchase, for example, becomes $20.00 if they
want to impress someone, but $19.00 (or "under $20.00") if they
want to downplay something's cost. Moreover, Extraverts and
iNtuitives tend to be more prone to brag about money, and are
more likely to disclose personal financial matters to veritable
strangers, often to Introverts' and Sensors' total embarrassment.

Sensors, in general, have a much more realistic view of what
money is, both its potential and its limitations, and often become frustrated with Perceivers', iNtuitives', and Extraverts'
attitude that, when it comes to money, "everything is relative."

Feelers, we've found, are not very money-conscious. They
tend to believe that money should be used to serve humanity;
not coincidentally, they are drawn to public service jobs and
other people-oriented jobs that are usually low-paying.

Judgers excel when it comes to financial planning and management, although Perceivers can be more responsive and find
creative ways to solve financial problems.

Perceivers, especially iNtuitive-Perceivers, tend to freak out as April 15 tax time nears. Sensing-Judgers, in contrast, are the ones who complete their tax forms just after Christmas and have their refunds in hand by Valentine's Day. Such behavior holds true for almost all bill-paying responsibilities.

Thinkers, Feelers, and Pets

We've made a couple of observations—unproven statistically—about how the decision-making function relates to pet preferences.

Thinkers: They love animals, but keep them in perspective. They want them for protection, company, and enjoyment, but not necessarily for nurturing.
Feelers: They are more likely to give the pet a personality —talking to it, speaking for it—and create a whole life scenario on its behalf. They identify with the pet, and it can become an extension of the Feeler's personality.

Weight: Who Gains, Who Loses?

What started out for us as a fascination with type and dieting has expanded to include eating disorders and smoking cessation, and can probably shed light on other types of dependencies and addictions too. We have heard from people all over the country who believe we're on to something with our ideas about type and weight. We plan to continue to refine our observations.

One of the most fascinating things we've found came from a workshop we conducted at the University of Maryland in 1983 for a group of dieticians, counselors, and weight-control specialists. The group reported that, based on their work with type and eating disorders, the bulk of those suffering from anorexia and bulimia were INFPs and ENFPs. That tracks closely with our finding that Extraverts, iNtuitives, Feelers, and Perceivers have much more difficulty with weight-related issues than Introverts, Sensors, Thinkers, and Judgers. The reason? There are several:

- Extraverts, in general, are more gregarious and orally oriented, which results in a lot of social eating and drinking. Introverts, in contrast, tend to focus more of their attention inside themselves and are more withholding of themselves. Whereas Es tend to eat for the sake of eating, Is are more likely to think about eating before actually doing it.
- Sensors, more grounded in here-and-now reality, are more aware of sensation: "Am I full?" On the other hand, iNtuitives, often theorize on how to lose weight—while continuing to eat.
- Thinkers are more objective and tend to eat when it is rationally necessary to do so. Feelers, who tend to be more nurturing, may feed others (or themselves) to solve a problem ("Have a cookie. You'll feel better") and eat so as not to offend others. Whereas Ts may politely refuse food offered them when they aren't hungry, Fs are more likely to partake "just to be nice."
- Judgers, more planned and goal-oriented, stick to schedules, including diets, with less difficulty. Perceivers are very responsive to the moment and like to take in new information—even if that "information" is something to eat. Their classic motto: "I can always start my diet tomorrow."

A similar finding came from another study, this one conducted in a smoking-cessation class at the National Defense University. The study found that iNtuitives, Perceivers, and Extraverts had the most difficulty stopping smoking (only 62 percent, 55 percent, and 54 percent, respectively, of these preferences succeeded.) The highest success rates were found among Introverts (80 percent), Judgers (76 percent), and Sensors (73 percent). The results were inconclusive as to Thinkers and Feelers.

We've also made observations about the kind of diet that works best for each type. Extraverts, for example, need to contract with others when dieting, making it a kind of social event. For example: "I'm thinking of going on a diet. I need to lose about five pounds. I'll keep you posted as to what happens." The simple fact of making it known to the world that they're dieting makes them more accountable for the results.

Dieting is generally difficult for Feelers, for whom food covers a multitude of sins. Eating together is a way of expressing intimacy and harmony with others. Food is a gift that Fs give to others and must accept appreciatively from others. Food is often a comfort for Fs and they use it as a personal reward. For them, dieting (and stopping smoking) works best when motivated by some interpersonal relationship.

Judgers tend to have the edge in dieting because it involves setting and reaching a goal, often involving a highly structured meal plan and a rigid time schedule. Keeping lists of what is eaten, weighing and measuring food, and other exacting diet techniques play to the J's strengths—and often sets Ps up for frustrations, sending them directly to the refrigerator for instant gratification.

There are strong links between diet and other addiction control efforts and the Temperaments we discussed in Chapter Four. The NF dieter, for example, is motivated interpersonally and probably demands more regular affirmation from "significant others." They may therefore get into more eating difficulties when interpersonal relationships go awry. There's a tendency for NTs, who are natural competitors, to compete with themselves when dieting. Always having "a better idea," they like to take an already existing diet, improve it, and rise to the challenge of their innovation. In general, iNtuitives are driven more by the intrigue and mystery of dieting than by the actual mechanics of the diet itself. SJs, for their part, are the most responsible about good eating habits; when they run into problems, it's usually because their Extraversion or Thinking-Feeling preference has led them astray. All Ps, and especially SPs, stay away from setting goals and making lists. They diet best "one day at a time."

Humor: How Types Tell Jokes

Jokes, humor, and the overall ability to be funny have a fascinating relationship to type. Indeed, the eight Typewatching preferences give us a frame of reference: Extraversion legitimizes laughing at others; Introversion legitimizes laughing at ourselves. Sensing helps us laugh at the absurdity of reality; iNtuition permits us to find humor in the seemingly unrelated aspects of life, facilitating puns, among other things; Thinking helps us laugh at life's less than funny moments, while Feeling facilitates laughing at the intimacies that sometimes scare us. The structured, organized nature of Judgers facilitates effective joke-telling, while Perceivers' flexibility and spontaneity make them skilled at one-liners and repartee.

There's more. Extraverts, you can probably imagine, would rather tell a joke than listen to one. Puns and limericks are the domain of iNtuitives, while literal humor (Q: "What's the book about?" A: "About 250 pages.") belongs to Sensors. Thinkers tend toward harsher humor—such as sexist and racist jokes—while Feelers, who laugh at (but are filled with guilt by) such humor, much prefer jokes that are warm, happy, and reflect life's good times. Morbid humor is primarily the bailiwick of Thinkers and Judgers.

The skilled joke-tellers, by and large, are Extraverted-Judgers, followed by Introverted-Judgers. One-liners and spontaneous humor in a situation belong to Extraverted-Perceivers, followed by Introverted-Perceivers. We find iNtuitive-Feelers to be far and away the most schmaltzy and idealistic humorists; they tune out if the prevailing humor is inconsistent with their ideals. Meanwhile, iNtuitive-Thinkers are the ultimate punsters and riddlemeisters; they do them well and love to be challenged by them. They are also the purveyors of bad jokes—the ones that make us groan. Sensing-Perceivers are the practical jokers—they don't mind being the victim because they enjoy the challenge of getting you the next time. Sensing-Judgers, especially Sensing-Thinking-Judgers, are perhaps the harshest joke-tellers and, because their stories are most apt to have beginnings and endings, among the most skilled humorists.

Sex: Who Does What, Where, and When?

At the risk of dealing with this sensitive subject too lightly, let us share some observations. First and foremost, we've found that Judgers consciously or unconsciously schedule sex. They often have their rituals and timing techniques that include the sex act as part of a week's activities. We know a J husband who walked in his front door on schedule at 5:05 P.M., in anticipation of a 7:30 dinner party he and his wife were giving that night. To his surprise, he found his perceptive, spontaneous P wife scantily clad and in a seductive, playful mood. The husband's immediate reaction was something less than romantic: he was abrasive and quick to remind her of the dinner party on the schedule. She felt rejected and hurt. The episode not only didn't result in intimacy but ended up ruining the entire evening: they held the dinner promptly at 7:30, but did so under a dark cloud of anger (on her part) and guilt (on his).

This is one of the obvious potential problems. Far more subtle are those resulting from the rich imagination of the iNtuitive— an imagination never quite fulfilled by reality. There is the Sensor, who likes to fantasize about sex—*after* the fact. And problems stem from the Extravert's need to talk before, during, and after sex, particularly problematic for the Introvert, who may need to go inside and quietly savor the experience—before, during, and after. Strong, objective Thinkers, for their part, enjoy analyzing—Feelers would say overanalyzing—their sexual performance with the aim of improving competency; Feelers, meanwhile, shrink from such analysis for fear that the subjective power of the experience will fade beneath the scrutiny. To speak of these matters without an understanding of typological differences is to run the risk of hurt, rejection, denial, frustration—and all the way down the line to separation and divorce.

Sports: Who Wants to Play, Who Wants to Win?

We're not exactly suggesting that potential gold-medal winners can be picked typologically, but we've found some intriguing links between athletic competence and type. Clearly, the more severe contact sports have a great deal of appeal to Sensors and Thinkers, who desire immediate gratification. The need for athletes to be well-rounded typologically has been demonstrated in the recent attempts to put football players through the rigors of ballet, a discipline considerably more iNtuitive and Feeling than life on the gridiron.

If you analyze almost any sport, you begin to find that each has a typological configuration. Golf, for example, could be said to be an INTP sport: you're always competing against yourself (Introversion); you contemplate every move against your environment—the fixed lay of the land and the changing weather and other factors (iNtuition and Perception); based on that information, you make objective decisions (Thinking), which can only be foiled by such things as superstition ("If my towel isn't draped over the nine iron, I'll flub the shot"), interpersonal factors ("I wish Ben wouldn't talk when I'm putting"), and other subjective dynamics. An offensive lineman on a football team—the one who blocks the defensive rushers while runners and passers gain yardage—is likely ISTJ: he is responsible for his own turf and accountable first and foremost to himself (Introversion); he must memorize cold various plays, including precisely where he must be at a given moment in each play (Sensing and Judging); he is objectively out to destroy the opponent, without regard to how the opponent feels about it (Thinking)—indeed, opposing members can be the best of friends off the field. As an ISTJ, his commitment to the greater good makes him a powerful team player. In contrast to golf and football are hockey and skiing, both action-oriented SP sports; the hockey player easily could be an ESTP and the skier an ISTP. The first is a team sport and reactive to the crowd (Extraversion), while the second is highly self competitive (Introversion). Both sports provide instant gratification (Sensing) and demand the participants' total concentration upon constant yet insistently changing events (Perceiving, and especially Sensing-Perceiving). Cool objectivity (Thinking) provides the edge in successfully winning over the opponent, the environment, or one's self. And both demand precise concentration and split-second accuracy. "If you stop and think, you're too late," is the motto of the SP athlete.

Participation in sports at the youngest level might better be approached typologically instead of through parental and social pressures. Feeling children, for example, often can't relate to intense competitive sports, but bow to pressure from parents and friends and end up participating in body but not necessarily in spirit. It is possible that physical coordination comes more slowly to iNtuitive-Perceptive children; they are less interested in specifics, which makes it difficult for them to concentrate on the details needed to be a good athlete. A parent could well use Typewatching skills when considering whether to encourage a reluctant child to pursue a given athletic activity. On the other hand, it would not be wise to discourage a child who has natural athletic inclinations, simply because the chosen activities seem typologically inappropriate.

Religion: Who Are the True Believers?

Churches, and the religious experience, often reflect typological bias. It can be said that the no-frills, down-to-earth religious experience typical of Methodists and Baptists is more attractive to Sensors, for example, while the symbolic and liturgical styles of the Lutheran and Episcopalian churches have more attraction for iNtuitives. The conceptual and liberal thinking behind Unitarianism and Christian Science often appeal to Thinkers, especially iNtuitive-Thinkers. The charismatics (a.k.a. Holy Rollers and speakers in tongues) have particular appeal to Sensing-Perceiving types, while the conservatives and fundamentalists appeal more to the Sensing-Judging types. Ultimately, of course, one's religion has mostly to do with one's heritage and upbringing, although we believe that one's type may influence the fervor with which one practices a religion.

There are typological differences even within some religions, such as Catholicism and Judaism. The different orders of the Catholic Church—Franciscans, Jesuits, and Oblates, for example—each has its own typology that attracts certain people and repels others. (Franciscans, for example, tend to be SFPs; Jesuits NTs and NFs; and Oblates NFs.) There are also typological attractions within Judaism: reform Jews reflect far more iNtuitive leanings; conservatives and orthodox Jews are far more Sensing and Judging.

I'm an NF and my wife is an SP, and one of the places we notice the difference is in the way we pray. I give thanks for all sorts of abstract things, like the Bible, the church, the good feeling in our home and marriage. She gives thanks for the house, the car, our food and clothes.

Interestingly, many clergy are Introverts who feel drawn to the inner richness of theology, only to discover that the job involves a lot of "sales" and demands a great deal of Extraversion. The parochial-school nun is predominantly ISTJ. In general, the predominant clergy profile is Extraverted, iNtuitive, Feeling, and Judging. This fact notwithstanding, the "ideal" clergy—whether priest, rabbi, or minister—would more appropriately be Introverted (reflective and introspective), iNtuitive (imaginative and symbolic), Feeling (subjective and interpersonal), and Perceiving (responsive and spontaneous). Ironically, most congregational boards reflect Extraversion (go beat the bushes to get members), Sensing (get the money, pay the bills), Thinking (run a good ship for everybody's benefit), and Judging (everything in good order). It isn't an accident that church groups' guidelines are often known as "disciplines"—a strong ESTJ model for living.

Politics: Who Make the Best Leaders?

Typewatching as applied to politics is still largely speculative—politicians as a rule aren't generally inclined toward psychological tests, so there isn't much of a data base on them. But there is a great temptation here for any student of human behavior. The politician able to grab the limelight is far more likely to be an Extravert, while those with sharper distinctions between public and private life probably prefer Introversion. It's no surprise in a country predominantly Extraverted, that our most Extraverted contemporary presidents—Truman, Eisenhower, Kennedy, Johnson, Reagan—are also the best liked, while the

Introverted leaders (Nixon, Ford, Carter) had a harder time capturing the public's affection. (Nixon, of course, had other problems in addition to Introversion, but that analysis lies outside the scope of this book.) In general, it takes longer for history to judge the more Introverted presidents because they are simply not as visible to us. One reason it is easier to judge the Extraverts is because they are quick to tell us how they're doing.

With key advisors and public relations gurus having so much influence on both the style and the substance of politicians, it is often difficult to determine a politician's type. But about some politicians there can be little doubt. Clearly, "give 'em hell" Harry Truman's take-names-kick-ass, blunt, earthy style was Extraverted, Sensing, Thinking, and Judging. His style was quite different from the smooth-talking, shoot-from-the-lip, conciliatory style of Ronald Reagan, the Great Communicator, who reflects Extraversion, iNtuition, Feeling, and Judging. It is probably not coincidental that this is the same profile of the predominent clergy style, and probably of the ideal used-car salesman.

We could go on. Typewatching, as we hope by now we've made perfectly clear, can explain an almost endless range of human activities. As you become proficient in your Typewatching skills, you may well develop your own theories based on your observations and experiences. We'd love to hear about them. You may contact us at Otto Kroeger Associates, (3605-C Chain Bridge Road, Department B, Fairfax, VA 22030; 703-591-MBTI.)

10

The Sixteen Profiles

"How could we lose when we were so sincere?"

We are not the first to compose portraits of each of the sixteen types. David Keirsey and Marilyn Bates, for example, created very readable descriptions in their book *Please Understand Me;* Isabel Briggs Myers's portraits in her book *Gifts Differing* are considered to be classic in their faithfulness to Jung's theory. Having tested, counseled, taught, or otherwise come in contact with thousands of people over the decade and a half we have been Typewatching, we think the profiles that follow effectively combine the theoretical with a large data base of real-life individuals. We do not intend these profiles to be the final statements; rather, they are intended as points of reference for insight into yourself and others.

The potential danger in creating type profiles is that they are usually viewed as rigid boxes encompassing an unvarying and static set of characteristics. That can make them more confining than liberating, ironically defeating the whole point of Typewatching, which is to allow room for others to "be themselves."

As you read your own portrait, you will find that some parts "fit" better than others. But don't let a few statements that aren't right for you lead you to discard an entire portrait as invalid. Chances are that others may see in you parts of the portrait that you might not recognize in yourself. If you seriously doubt the accuracy of your typological portrait, you might want to read that of your four-letter opposite—the ENFP portrait if you are an ISTJ, for example, or the ISFP portrait if you are an ENTJ. That might help put your own portrait into perspective. It is even possible that after you read your portrait, you may need to rethink your type and adjust one or more of its four letters.

Typological portraits have been accused from time to time of being like astrological horoscopes: general statements broad enough to encompass everyone. That's simply not true. We believe our portraits reflect a combination of sound Jungian theory and years of clinical research. Admittedly they are more positive than negative. But in the world of behavior, psychology, and the Western model of "sickness," we think that's a refreshing change.

ISTJ
Doing What Should Be Done

Perhaps no type is more driven by a sense of responsibility and "bottom-line" behavior than Introverted-Sensing-Thinking-Judging types. In the name of responsibility, these Introverts have acquired social grace, ease with words, and all of the appropriate interpersonal skills demanded at any given moment. They can be so outgoing under clearly defined circumstances that they are sometimes mistaken for Extraverts. But make no mistake: as the most private of the sixteen types, these Introverts can don Extraverted clothing when the occasion warrants it without changing their essentially Introverted inner nature.

The ISTJ's highly responsible nature is shaped by the Sensing preference of the information-gathering function. In other words, ISTJs focus inwardly, concentrating on data that are objective, immediate, concrete, and pragmatic. Their affinity for the here and now leaves them to assume nothing, to take nothing for granted. What they see they translate objectively and tangibly (T), which they immediately organize and schedule (J). Since this comes easily and naturally to them, they expect similar behavior of virtually everyone else. They are extremely demanding at home and work, even at play, engaging at times in very compulsive behavior. To some observers, these seem to be your classic Type A personalities—driven, impatient, and obsessive.

Like INTJs, with whom they share three preferences (I, T, and J), they often excel at school and work, rising to senior positions of responsibility as class presidents, school heroes, project managers, and community leaders—all of which may seem out of character for an Introvert. But for the ISTJs, this is not out of character at all; they are simply doing their duty— "doing what should be done" (though *not* what comes naturally. Indeed, *should* is a key part of the ISTJ's mantra, as it is for all Sensing-Judgers, and in this context the result is that the preferred and more "natural" Introverted behavior is dutifully abandoned for the more difficult Extraverted style.)

While all Thinking females swim upstream in our society, this is particularly true for female ISTJs. The responsible, driven nature of this type, while admirable, flies in the face of traditionally "feminine" traits. Moreover, as traditionalists at heart, ISTJ females are inwardly conflicted about trying to balance the conventional feminine roles—mothering and nurturing—with their objective, organized (TJ) nature. Male ISTJs, in contrast, are "naturals" in conforming with this type's attributes, so much so that ISTJ is often dubbed "the macho type"—a label with which few women would feel comfortable (but which doesn't necessarily bother those ISTJ women.)

ISTJs have homes that are neat and they carry out their domestic activities with efficiency and dispatch. They like to eat breakfast at eight, lunch at noon, and dinner at six, no matter what. Holidays and other family affairs are extremely important, and become the focus of family life, no expense or inconvenience spared. Family members of other types who fail to fall in step may be subject to considerable grief and guilt. ISTJs' homes and personal appearances tend to reflect their life preferences in general: traditional and probably somewhat austere. You can often spot an ISTJ's home from the outside: the yard is sparse— the few bushes and plants are neat and orderly—the house color is rather subdued, bikes and toys are put away, and the entire presentation can only be described as tasteful but reserved. A place for everything and everything in its place.

For ISTJs, parenting is a lifelong responsibility that is undertaken seriously. They impose rules and regulations upon their children—and sometimes on their spouses—and expect them to be followed and not questioned. After all, when the ISTJ was a child, things were done in this way; now that they themselves are in authority, they expect things "should" continue to be done as they were before. Roles, for the ISTJ parent, are clearly defined: parents are parents, children are children, and each has appropriate responsibilities. It is not uncommon for an ISTJ to assign family duties for a whole weekend so that no time is wasted. To the ISTJ, an idle mind is the devil's playground and "honest work" is good for all. Even relaxation is scheduled and dutifully executed.

These same driving forces define ISTJ children. Homework is done neatly and on time, and in general they are good students. Bedrooms are kept orderly. They show up on time for meals, expecting them to be served on schedule. Like their ISTJ elders, they live by a series of "shoulds," which they often impose on their parents. For them, too, the parent-child lines are clearly defined. They can become stressed when they encounter a family member of a different type who resists their rules and regulations, or when a parent or other authority figure is working on a schedule different from theirs. Ultimately, they'll give in to the adult, but not without considerable unpleasantness. Such unpleasantness may be a test to make sure the authority figure is being responsible to his or her role.

In an intimate relationship, an ISTJ's word is as good as gold, and having once declared "I love you," they can be trusted to be true to that sentiment for years to come—though they may not give voice to it often. The reason is simple: For the ISTJ, actions truly speak louder than words; the continued expression of love comes not in the saying but in the doing—being there day in and day out, providing unfailingly, being a veritable Rock of Gibraltar. This nonverbal style of affection often gets ISTJs in hot water because it can be perceived as uncaring; they are often described as having "ice for blood."

But ISTJs do care—and show it through their strong sense of responsibility. (Indeed, they would rather die than be seen as irresponsible.) They are fiercely loyal, both to individuals and institutions, sometimes responding fanatically to the "shoulds" and "oughts" of their commitments. They make good soldiers, literally and figuratively. In fact, based on a sample of more than ten thousand of the U.S. military—from enlisted personnel through four-star generals and admirals—their predominant configuration is ISTJ.

Other professions to which ISTJs gravitate are similarly oriented toward achieving practical and tangible results, and include such careers as general surgery, law, and accounting. These careers have appeal because they frequently involve working alone (I), are very results-oriented (S), require objectivity (T), and generally have prescribed ways of doing things (J). While they may be successful at any career, ISTJs are less drawn to those that require abstract thinking and interpersonal spontaneity. Whether as supervisors or subordinates, with their work as with everything else they like to play by the rules. They expect those who follow the rules to win, those who don't, to lose.

In their later years certain ISTJs may behave in somewhat bizarre ways. It is that period of their life when they wish to give in to the more subjective and spontaneous parts of their personalities. Suddenly the rather rigid parent may become the playful, doting grandparent. The hard-charging executive tries on new hats—from the painter's beret to the camper's cap. Overall, the older ISTJ becomes aware that things that used to seem all-important aren't quite as crucial in the bigger scheme of life.

Some famous possible ISTJs include auto-maker Henry Ford (described as a man of few words who gave customers a "choice" of "any color, as long as it's black"); George Washington (whose blueprint for the country comprised immediate practical procedures to be implemented); Johnny Carson (who calls himself an Introvert, sets a style for American male dress, and has maintained a constant program schedule for a quarter century); and Calvin Coolidge (who was austere, simplistic, and noted for his cryptic and terse remarks).

ISFJ
A High Sense of Duty

ISFJs like to work behind the scenes. Quick, easygoing, neat, orderly, and given to a higher sense of duty and obedience, they find their source of energy within (Introversion) and their reality in those things they can see, hear, feel, taste, and smell

(Sensing). That energy is then focused outwardly in the service of others (Feeling), always in an orderly and timely fashion (Judging). As a result, ISFJs find meaning in life by serving human needs and making others happy.

One appropriate image of the ISFJ is that of the dependable bulwark who will always be there when needed, waiting silently. As Judgers, they might complain about being intruded upon, but ultimately their high sense of duty compels them to do what needs to be done, without complaint.

Mates and friends of ISFJs often criticize them for letting others continually take advantage of their goodness, even though these same mates and friends may be guilty of doing so themselves. Indeed, ISFJs take commitments and obligations very seriously and often do allow others to take advantage of them. Possibly more than other types, they allow themselves to become the doormats of a marriage, family, job, or whatever situation in which they find themselves. More often than not, this is a result of their high sense of obligation and allegiance, coupled with their strong values and commitment to serve humanity.

Gender issues for ISFJs are complex for the male and almost too simple for the female. ISFJ characteristics are almost stereotypically female—quiet, reserved, gentle, steady, dependable, caring, dutiful, obedient, neat, and tidy. In fact, ISFJ females may be quietly critical when females of other types don't behave "like the other girls." For the ISFJ female, her feminine "script" may be so tightly written that if, later in life, she exerts her individuality, the action may both surprise those around her and result in negative reactions from others.

If the ISFJ profile is a female stereotype, it's to be expected that the male ISFJ will face special problems. The gentle, caring, quiet, and dutiful attributes are the opposite of typical "male" behavior. As a result, male ISFJs may be pressured to suppress their natural behavior in order to act more typically male. In such cases, ISFJs may go overboard, becoming supermacho, drinking or smoking to excess, or becoming highly competitive to "prove" themselves.

In relationships, as with most everything else, the ISFJ's strong sense of duty and commitment dominates. They are typically careful and exact in the words they use, words that represent bonds and contracts to be taken very seriously. Relationships may develop slowly but surely for an ISFJ and when a declaration comes, it may—at least by the ISFJ—be considered permanent. ISFJs, more than other types, may remain in relationships that long ago went bad, simply because of their sense of duty and obligation.

Their sense of loyalty may make them appear quite serious. It may take another type individual to mitigate the seriousness of life's demands on an ISFJ. Some ISFJs are quietly tantalized by the bizarre and extreme. However, they give in to such longings only on special occasions or vicariously—by way of a movie, perhaps, or a friend's tale of intrigue. Beyond those exceptions, it is generally "work first, play later"—and then only if the work is completed. For the ISFJ, there is almost always some work somewhere yet to be completed.

Parenting for an ISFJ is another serious responsibility, one that ISFJs more than other types may recognize as a lifetime commitment. As a consequence, they often assume a quiet, guardian-like role. Generally, as parents, they are diligent, protective, and extremely patient with the many facets of the job. While each of these characteristics is admirable, when maximized in ISFJ parents it often means subjugation of the parents' needs in favor of the childrens'. Though ISFJs never really feel like saints, that is probably the way most children of ISFJs would describe their parents.

Because duty, obedience, and responsibility permeate all that the ISFJ does, the entire living style is marked by caring and concern for others, expressed in an orderly, well-regulated way. Relaxation can come only when all work is completed and, as stated earlier, it rarely is. ISFJs generally schedule their leisure activities; indeed, such leisure may become part of the ISFJ's repertoire of duties.

It is ISFJs, more than other types, who will complain about all the work, responsibilities, or demands placed upon them, and yet be dismayed and disappointed if someone tries to spare them such agonies. Cooking a big, festive family meal, for example, or taking care of an aged parent or arranging a class reunion, may all engender a variety of protests or complaints from the ISFJ. In fact, there is nothing that ISFJs would rather be doing. Should someone try to rescue them, they would be hurt and consumed with guilt.

As children, ISFJs are a treat that every parent should be allowed to experience. Content to play by themselves, they are relatively undemanding, neat, and obedient—in general, model children and hardworking students. As both child and adult, ISFJs may be given to streaks of stubbornness that seem entirely out of character. But even that stubbornness will give way if authority, role definition ("I'm the teacher and I want it done this way"), or some other sense of responsibility can be appealed to. ISFJs respect authority and respond accordingly.

As students, ISFJs prefer teachers and courses that are organized and practical. They like following outlines and doing homework and assignments that are highly defined. For them, learning, like most other aspects of life, is best when nobody makes waves and everything happens as it should—according to schedule.

Family events for ISFJs are very meaningful occasions, a chance to gather and observe tradition and ritual, to express in action and deeds the family's importance. For the ISFJ, the meaningfulness of the event is directly related to the extent he or she contributes to it—by cooking, cleaning, whatever; such efforts are a direct expression of love. No matter how reserved the behavior, the ISFJ has depths of loyalty that should not be underestimated; to do so is to seriously miss the inner quality and strength unique to this type.

Work, for the ISFJ, is fun, rewarding, satisfying, and ultimately fulfilling. If it is not, the ISFJ will likely work harder in the hopes that things will improve. It must have been an ISFJ who said of heaven, "Whatever else is there, it must involve work or it wouldn't be heaven." In general, a happy ISFJ is one who has most of the hours of the day filled in some sort of service to family, friends, or employer. For ISFJs, work builds character; it brings growth, maturity, satisfaction, and fulfillment. In fact, parenting, relating, mating, teaching, and managing are all forms of work through which ISFJs express their sense of duty and service.

As an older person, the ISFJ employs tried and true methods

in every activity. Later years may allow some relaxing of the schedule and more extraverted expressions of the self's needs. Though such expressions are still tempered by a larger sense of social responsibility, this is still a refreshingly liberating opportunity for the ISFJ to pursue his or her own needs with a bit more zeal. ISFJs may enjoy some risk-taking as they grow older; by some other types' standards, however, they may still appear to be overly cautious. Retirement, if there is such a thing in ISFJ terms, is yet another thing to be filled with meaningful activity.

Famous likely ISFJs include Bess Truman and Nancy Reagan (whose loyalty to and defense of their respective husbands made them seem the real powers behind the presidential thrones); and "Radar" on *M*A*S*H* (who would spend endless hours dutifully waiting at the ham radio for an important message, despite whatever chaos might be going on around him).

INFJ
An Inspiration to Others

INFJs are gentle, compassionate, and accepting, yet given to streaks of extreme stubbornness. The INFJs' driving force is their iNtuition (N), which is directed inward (I), generating a never-ending stream of possibilities and ideas. In fact, the more the INFJ introverts, the more malleable and open-ended life can seem. But the external world has a way of interfering with this flow of inspirations and creativity because INFJs feel called upon to render service to humanity (F) in a very orderly and demanding way (J).

Consequently, when INFJs are committed to an ideal or cause, the stubbornness surfaces. These otherwise compliant, reserved individuals become extremely rigid and demanding of themselves and others, when pursuing a goal in the external world.

INFJs are dreamers whose genius, caring, and concern can be an inspiration to many other people. Their quietness gives them a low profile and their concern has a way of being intense in most situations in which they find themselves. In almost any interpersonal activity, from a board meeting to an intimate family gathering, the INFJ's quiet strength is felt by others. Their hope, aspiration, and caring have limits, however, and those limits can be invoked by the INFJ at any given moment. Such limits may have no apparent relationship to external events, and may leave others feeling frustrated, confused, possibly even deprived.

INFJs often need an Extraverted type to tap the reservoir of their inner richness. Otherwise it can be lost, either in the INFJ's introversion or as a consequence of pressure from the typically scheduled life of those who prefer the Judging function in their outer worlds. When in the presence of more Extraverted types, they are likely to share jokes, ideas, whimsical thought, and many inventive models or theories. Those close to the INFJ may feel frustrated that so much of what is inside the INFJ is so rarely fully tapped. The frustration continues as those close to INFJs recognize that while they must respect INFJs' space, doing so diminishes INFJs' contributions to the world.

INFJs often have, without formal training, skills in group dynamics. Almost psychically, they are aware of various levels of interaction between and among people. However, such awareness remains largely their own, and efforts to make these observations known to others can be frustrating to INFJs.

Though they may maneuver themselves to receive affection, INFJs may be quite sparing in dispensing it to others because of their naturally Introverted manner. For the INFJ, talk is cheap, and the resulting sparsity of their communications can have a negative effect on relationships at work and home.

Gender differences can be seen with the INFJ. The female INFJ clearly has the advantage. As a Feeling type, she has the nurturing qualities traditionally associated with femininity. Often, however, because of her Introversion, the INFJ female does not project those qualities, even though they are very much a part of her nature. At home as well as at work, she tends to be aloof, so that the sense of her caring and concern is ultimately lost, particularly to those types more demanding of overt affirmations. A common complaint about the INFJ female is that she is "nice but seems removed." People feel this about her even though they would admit that in fact she's always there when needed, quietly dependable, steady. Female INFJs must work hard to be understood and may find themselves being taken for granted because of their own failure to make their needs known. Consequently, when they do express their needs, it seems out of character and can lead to general disbelief, which, of course, is frustrating to the female INFJ.

Male INFJs have a more problematic situation because the qualities naturally preferred by INFJs are not those traditionally considered to be "male." To counter the image of being weak, male INFJs can become stubborn, often to a degree disproportionate to the situation at hand. They are capable of taking a seemingly small issue and making it seem as if the entire world—or at least their masculinity—were riding on the outcome. This behavior unfortunately belies the fact that both male and female INFJs are reservoirs of quiet, intellectual introspective imagination who can inspire insight and growth in men and women alike. INFJs are often great thinkers whose pondering of the immense can bring great ideas to the forefront. Typically, they seek to spread their ideas in a quiet, deliberate way—more typically by the pen than by the sword.

At home, INFJs are given the ultimate arena in which to act on both their idealism and their humanitarian concerns. Their longing for harmony is such a driving force that they sometimes create tension in their relationships by working so determinedly to eliminate it. They would do better to work out tensions within themselves than to focus on external conflicts, because they often carry very heavy inner burdens. In some ways, this fosters a sense of martyrdom typically of Feelers generally. Over the long term, the inner tension that plagues them as a consequence of imperfectly realized aspiration toward total harmony can do little except induce guilt in INFJs and others. The INFJ goal of harmony is particularly difficult to achieve because the model for it is rarely articulated, though the drive toward it is nonetheless unrelenting.

Parenting to an INFJ means accepting intense responsibility to help young minds and spirits develop on their own. By example and by direct involvement, the INFJ exerts great energy to see that all children are afforded every intellectual opportunity available. There is considerable allowance for differences—as long as each individual exerts himself or herself. The INFJ parent strives to be stimulating, resourceful, and helpful in everything. A young spirit is considered a terrible thing to waste.

Toward that end, if a child shows interest in any kind of self-development, no matter how different from the preferred activities of the INFJ parent, that interest would still be encouraged. To the best of their abilities, the INFJ parent will provide whatever is necessary to foster growth.

The home and living style of the INFJ seem relatively neat to outsiders, but just below the surface lie a million books, articles, and projects to be addressed at a later date. It is more important for the home atmosphere to be congenial, stimulating, and accepting than for it to be precisely neat and tidy. The home is a reference library for a wide variety of interests and pursuits. Most everything has some symbolism or meaning and rarely is anything discarded. The fantasy is that some day, the INFJ will wander through the Pandora's box of goodies and attend to each of the many projects contained therein. Usually that remains only a fantasy for the INFJ.

As children, INFJs are frequently very complacent. Except for the stubbornness exhibited around values they prize, their love of harmony, coupled with a general curiosity and hunger for knowledge, makes them compliant children and excellent students. If anything, parents, especially Extraverted ones, may be amazed at how content the INFJ seems, though somewhat concerned about their daydreaming. But the dreaming typically gives way to good scholarship and the INFJ child finds school, at most levels, quite rewarding. Clearly, their Introverted-iNtuition prefers theoretical and abstract course work, but their desire to please teachers and parents makes them successful and productive in most subjects. Learning enriches the mind and the INFJ learns very early on that his or her mind is the gateway to the world.

Family events are opportunities for INFJs to explore and learn, so they are attended with eagerness and satisfaction. INFJs are especially sensitive to family tension and have a tendency to personalize those tensions, even blaming themselves for problems they did not create. If family events are sources of tension, INFJs will tend to shun them, even be terrified by them. If, on the other hand, they are filled with warmth and joy, INFJ can become quite involved, though often in a more passive than active way.

Wherever the INFJ is, there is work, particularly if the work offers some opportunity to grow and learn. As managers, INFJs are fairly open and very interested in both the people and the product. Though usually slow to give positive strokes, they are nonetheless inwardly proud of their subordinates' accomplishments and open to their desire for self-improvement. The biggest bane of the INFJ's work is conflict and tense interpersonal relationships. In general, INFJs are adept at helping others actualize their goals and eager—as both workers and managers—to actualize their own. They are at their best in situations that encourage personal enhancement.

INFJs can benefit from their mature years if more leisure time and less compulsiveness give them the freedom they need for dreams and inspirations. To daydream, fantasize, theorize, read, build something, or simply "follow a star" allow the INFJ to bring forth all sorts of inner creations. Later years can also be pleasant for INFJs who allow themselves to drop the world's many troubles, problems, and issues from their shoulders. Though this is very hard for them to do, and few succeed completely, it can be sweet relief for a type that, by virtue of their unique combination of preferences, tends to allow many of the world's cares to be heaped upon them.

Famous likely INFJs include: Thomas Jefferson (whose creativity, genius, and idealism helped to forge the Republic, even though his own aristocratic value system was different from that of the Constitution he helped to author); Jimmy Carter (whose Introversion kept him from being understood, and whose iNtuitive-Feeling preference enabled him to be a powerful mediator in bringing Menachem Begin and Anwar Sadat to an accord); and Sigmund Freud (whose iNtuitive psychological theories revolutionized the world, and whose strong Feeling preference kept him working to help people his entire life, although others' criticism of his work made him ever more rigidly entrenched in his own beliefs).

INTJ
Everything Has Room for Improvement

INTJs have an inner world rich with endless possibilities that, when combined with their Thinking-Judging preferences, gives them a drive toward constant improvement of everything. Indeed, these are the "better idea" people of the typological world. Everything—words, plans, designs, ideas, even people—has room for improvement. In the INTJ's eyes, even the best can be made better.

INTJs have a natural propensity for organization, and as such they often rise to the top of any system in which they find themselves. They tend to be "big picture" people (iNtuitive) who can see the forest as well as the intricacies of its component parts. (To an INTJ, there's more to a forest than merely trees.) With their capacity for follow-through (Judging), they have a high completion rate in their many undertakings. People naturally look to them for a job well done, a word aptly spoken, an opportunity seized. And they usually rise to such occasions with aplomb.

INTJs are among the most independent of the sixteen types. Their theme song may be "My Way." As with other NTs, this independence often gives them an aura of arrogance that makes in-depth relationships develop slowly. At both work and play they can often seem aloof and sometimes argumentative. For INTJs, such behavior is simply the result of their attempt to stimulate the world around them. They can be stunned, even appear hurt, when others accuse them of being distant and seemingly uncaring, but it is, ironically, the INTJs' caring that has been the source of the provocation. They may even seem surprised at others' taking offense when their motivation was fostering improvement. Again, as with other NTs, INTJs learn by arguing, part of their continuing quest to understand the universe. The problem is that an INTJ's "friendly discussion" may be seen by others as hostile, even obnoxious behavior.

Statistically, there are more male INTJs than female. Not surprisingly, the INTJ female's independence, intellectual aloofness, and argumentative style may result in her feeling somewhat out of step with those attributes more traditionally associated with femininity. For an INTJ female to be true to herself may put her out of step with the mainstream.

As parents, INTJs' relentless pursuit for self-improvement becomes a model for their children as well. They encourage a child's independence and self-sufficiency, the sooner the better.

What may be seen by others as uncaring or unaffectionate is, to INTJs, the ultimate in caring: teaching their children to stand on their own. The situation may best be illustrated by the way in which an INTJ parent likely teaches a child to swim. An INTJ parent may allow the child to dive into deep water that other parents might consider risky—all the while supervising intently —in the name of learning how to swim. Other types may stick to shallower waters, wanting the child to feel more comfortable in the learning process. To the INTJ, the issue of comfort or fear is irrelevant. What's important is learning how to swim. An old Chinese proverb was probably INTJ-inspired: "Give a man a fish and he eats for a day; *teach* him to fish, and he eats for a lifetime."

The same model drives all INTJ relationships: any relationship that's good today can be better tomorrow and both parties must be directed to constant self-improvement: learning, growing, confronting, and anything else that leads to mutual self-competency. As lovers, mates, and companions, INTJs must be ever improving. When thwarted in this quest, they can become critical and often depressed over the seeming stagnation.

An INTJ's home reflects his or her current conceptual pursuits. Theoretical and practical books abound. To a casual visitor, the home may seem neat, but its more private corners reflect a series of half-started projects, collections of mementos, and an assortment of potential challenges: a guitar to be mastered, a file to be organized, a household repair to be made. Dreams and visions are the INTJ's form of relaxation. Unfortunately, seemingly ambitious plans may go unfulfilled if the INTJ falls into the trap of being seduced by the intellectual excitement of the plan without ever getting to the actual hands-on accomplishment. Such a dilemma sets them up for self-criticism, which leads, in turn, to frustration and depression.

INTJ children crave much of the same independence as their parents. Unless their parents are of the same type, this quest may be the root of an ongoing parent-child dispute. While sufficiently neat to pass parental muster, their rooms may be laboratories of endless explorations and experiments. For a parent to invade this territory may be seen as an invasion of privacy and result in a struggle for power. Often, in high school, INTJs can be "underachievers" who score well on formal tests but are unstimulated by the details of day-to-day classroom learning. Similarly, family events may be exciting if they are stimulating and challenging, but the final decision on whether to participate must lie with the INTJ child, not with his or her parent. A lack of understanding this by both parties can cause considerable tension. Clearly, in this context, such otherwise simple decisions as when to go to bed or whether to attend a family function can become major battlegrounds.

For the INTJ, work is the laboratory in which blueprints become reality—and give way for new blueprints. Consequently, INTJ managers strive to stimulate and stretch themselves and subordinates. INTJ subordinates, in turn, strive to stimulate and stretch themselves and their supervisors. They also want to be given a free hand to experiment, and if too tightly controlled, may become frustrated and resentful. They frequently master the language of whatever it is in which they find themselves: whether managers or counselors, they know all the correct words and phrases for the situation at hand.

In short, the workplace is one more "system" that can be organized and improved. As such, all assignments are undertaken with that underlying expectation. When improvements are not forthcoming, the INTJ may be subject to self-criticism. Careers particularly appealing to INTJs include those that provide mental challenge (teaching, especially college and research) and inventiveness in both business and science (program analysts and architects). They can become restless and frustrated in career choices that demand too much detail or a high demand for personal services.

Midlife, as with most other types, finds a moderating of some preferences. Their iNtuitive searching for the abstract begins to lean toward a desire for immediate Sensing fulfillment. Similarly, they may also "discover" the emotional and subjective sides of their Feeling nonpreference, which may be at once exciting and frightening. Later years could easily find INTJs inspiring themselves with more sociability.

Best guesses of famous INTJs include Thomas Edison (who was given to almost daily inventions, upon which he was always improving); Richard Nixon (whose political genius made him a man ahead of his time, but whose grasp for control ultimately undid him); and Katharine Hepburn (whose private nature belies her take-charge, I'll-do-it-my-way style).

ISTP
Ready to Try Anything Once

ISTPs may best be described as reserved, aloof, and interpersonally cautious, yet ready to try almost anything once. They focus inward (Introversion) and when that tendency is coupled with their objective decision-making preference (Thinking), it is natural that they should be more inclined to wait and see where conversations may go or what others might do before tipping their own hands. Their view of the world is very concrete (Sensing) and that in combination with the open-ended way in which they relate to the outside world (Perceiving), can result in their taking a more active, spontaneous role than their apparently detached nature would seem to warrant. They may, for example, be prone to unexpected bursts of humor, a take-charge attitude, or a sudden drive to fix whatever's broken. Such displays of involvement often confuse others, keeping them off guard—which is exactly the way the ISTP feels most comfortable.

The motto, "Don't tread on me," could easily be of ISTP origin. It reflects that type in many ways. It could mean "Don't tread on me because I don't know how I'll react," or "Don't do it because I wouldn't think of doing it to you," or "Don't do it because it is a waste of time and energy."

ISTPs are especially skilled with their hands and often get satisfaction from accomplishments that are both tactile and immediate. When some*thing*—as opposed to some*one*—needs attention, the ISTP's powers of observation (related to both their Sensing and Perceiving preferences) make it possible for them to plunge into the task at hand without feeling it necessary to follow procedures or read directions. This is how the ISTP prefers to work, and when the result is success, the ISTP feels a wonderful sense of accomplishment. If, midway into a project, the need for directions becomes apparent, the ISTP will refer only to sections that are directly relevant, so that no time or energy is wasted—a matter of great consequence to ISTPs.

The ISTPs' area of interest will take precedence over assigned tasks that are perceived as dull, boring, or not practical. They can become so engrossed with their own projects that other obligations, if not abandoned outright or forgotten, take second place. In situations that excite them, they work with great accuracy and precision, often to the amazement and envy of others. They thrive on and prefer "working on the edge," even putting themselves at risk, if that's what it takes to get the job done.

There are dramatic gender differences between male and female ISTPs. So much of the ISTP's drive and gratification is related to activities traditionally associated with the male. Contact sports, heavy equipment, auto racing, carpentry, and other adrenaline-driving occupations are exciting and rewarding for the ISTP. Obviously, ISTP women who have the same tactile skills and satisfactions will be seen as tomboyish if they act on them.

The ISTP female who seeks more traditional channels for her preferences, such as homemaking, business, and accounting, may adhere to a more conventional female model while satisfying her need for immediate, tangible rewards. Life presents many demands for hands-on professional skills, which are sexually neutral as far as society is concerned. The ISTP female has many opportunities to fulfill her aspirations in the workplace and feels no less than 100 percent female in doing so. Problems are far more likely to arise in the social sphere. Cool, aloof, and socially cautious behavior combined with an interest in manual skills and activities may make people ill at ease with the ISTP girl or woman. Moreover, if she excels in any such activities, she can be downright threatening to her friends, partners, or colleagues.

Relating to ISTPs can be both fun and confusing—fun because of their spontaneous, easygoing view of life, confusing because of their mixed communication messages. Because ISTPs alternate between enthusiasm over things of immediate interest to them and quiet reserve about other things, one can never predict which reaction to expect from them.

ISTPs can often be enigmas, especially to Extraverts and Judgers, who find their unpredictability and apparent social indifference so disturbing that they may try to change them. Not only will the ISTP resent such impositions, he or she may get an inner thrill or satisfaction in not behaving according to expectations, always remaining somewhat mysterious.

ISTPs' nature is to be quietly observing, collecting data on all things at all times. They do not think of themselves as watching in order to do something with the information; they are merely scanning the universe because it is part of their nature to want to take in all that is occurring. The often dramatic outcome, however, is that when an emergency occurs, they can move swiftly to the core of the problem and correct it. What seems like instinctive action is actually the result of long periods of observation that enabled the ISTP to be aware of all the details of the picture.

ISTP parents do not believe in planning. They tend to wait and see what each day brings, and then do what is needed at the time. ISTPs, in their general living and certainly in parenting, know that the best-laid plans go awry. Given that, the plan is not to have a plan, just to be ready for anything, do what needs to be done, and expect that things will work out for the best as a result. Above all, they strive not to get excited, become emotional, or lose their cool, for good reason: It takes extra energy which, if expended, could make them less than ready for whatever will happen next.

ISTP parents are true to type with their low need to impose themselves on their children. Individualism, space, different levels of interest and development for each person in the family —these are the ISTP's values and much effort goes into living up to them in both word and action. When a conflict erupts, however, ISTPs may react with loud, explosive demands, which give way to calmer presentation of several alternatives once the ISTP has cooled off.

So strongly does this seemingly hands-off, laissez-faire style characterize the ISTP that the price can be isolation. ISTPs think each person should be afforded his or her own space (whatever it may be) and should enjoy or use that space according to individual tastes and desires. This emphasis on individual rights is much more important than neatness, orderliness, or routine—and that makes living with an ISTP quite challenging and varied, to say the least. But it does mean that those around the ISTP enjoy a high level of personal freedom. Whatever they need to establish their individuality and define their space, be it tons of papers from a project, piles of material from a hobby, an automobile engine or two, or tubes of paint and stacks of canvas —the ISTP is more than willing to allow them, in return for reciprocal treatment.

When not involved in an enterprise or adventure of the kind that compels all their attention, ISTPs relax. They do not unwind by engaging in the kind of routine chores that other types may find both relaxing and worthwhile. As a result, life is one long relaxation to the ISTP, frequently interrupted by various exciting hands-on challenges to repair, understand, improve, or experience whatever comes along.

Judging parents have great difficultly understanding ISTP children. Their yearning for new adventure and their fascination with the mechanical and sensual often separate them from other members of a family. By other types' standards, the ISTP child always seems to be heading for trouble—taking things apart to understand and learn about them, plunging in and trying things without first getting approval. They are often drawn to motorcycles (both to ride and to repair), which can cause concern within the family.

Learning is most enjoyable for the ISTP child when it is relevant and experiential. The ISTP believes that the only way to learn is by doing. The more abstract and removed from the immediate concerns of everyday life the learning becomes, the more restless and uninterested the ISTP student becomes. Hands-on projects, experiments, and other practically oriented experiences keep the ISTP involved and the course work palatable.

Family events are a mixed bag for the ISTP. The ISTP child and adult both may eagerly anticipate a special family event—Christmas, birthday, a reunion—although the activity of preparing for the event (baking a special cake or making and wrapping gifts) often holds more interest than the social demands and pressures of the event itself. Other types may see that behavior as uncaring or unsupportive or actively antisocial. This simply isn't true; it's just that the ISTP has little need for the social activities. When the event is over, the ISTP may encourage a few close friends to linger, and it is there that he or she experiences the "real" party: a good time with a few carefully chosen people.

Work that is routine (such as administration) or too open-ended (such as research) is of little interest to the ISTP. This kind of work is an energy drain. The new, the unexplored, and the unexpected, however, are energizing and really not considered by the ISTP to be "work" at all.

The later years of an ISTP's life may involve a new Extraverted focus and more time devoted to the family side of life. ISTPs may find appealing the chance to turn back to work on some of the activities that have unsuccessfully competed for their attention during the earlier part of life. Their senior citizenship may involve an acting-out of some idea or dream they have long had in mind but never had the time and energy to realize. *Now* is the time, and the ISTP will not only be ready but will greet the opportunity with the same sort of aloofness that has accompanied his or her earlier years.

Some famous likely ISTPs could include Burt Reynolds (who classifies himself as an Introvert and who is most comfortable playing high-risk daredevil, and athletic parts); and Red Adair (the guy who is constantly being whisked off to some risky assignment, such as hanging from a helicopter or capping a burning oil well, yet who shuns publicity and remains very private).

ISFP
Sees Much But Shares Little

Though they struggle constantly to maintain visibility, there is in the ISFP a love and sensitivity for others, as well as serenity and appreciation for life. The combination of Introversion, Sensing, Feeling, and Perceiving puts ISFPs more in touch with both themselves and the world around them than any other type.

ISFPs have a very low need to lead and control others, and yet are driven by a desire to see everything—plants, animals, and people—living harmoniously. ISFPs are not invaders of any living creature's space but instead want to relate to and encourage all life to fulfill its potential. As a result of being so much in tune with and respectful of the natural boundaries of life around them, it can become difficult for ISFPs to understand the need of some people to impose limits or structure on others. Unfortunately, in their desire not to influence, they often forgo expressing themselves and their wishes in favor of blending in with others. This nonimposing nature and seeming lack of direction is so much a part of ISFPs that they can easily be either overlooked or overpowered by others. In a sense, they are the most invisible of the sixteen types.

This type, often creative, artsy, and skilled in a variety of practical disciplines where people and nature are served, tends to be shy about offering his or her services—depriving the world of their contributions as a result. All too often, more aggressive, demanding and less capable types fill the void.

ISFPs may be unconventional in their approach to problem-solving, but not because they value contrariness as such or because they relish developing new ways of doing things. It happens because they see the clearest way to do something and then simply do it—often to the consternation of others who prefer to follow the prescribed methods. ISFPs are often oblivious to the "standard" way, indeed even puzzled by why anyone would consider doing something in a way that is obviously cumbersome and impractical.

Feeling (warm and nurturing) and Perceiving (open and flexible) are more traditionally feminine characteristics; Introversion (reflective and reserved) and Sensing (practical and grounded) are more traditionally masculine traits. Put the four together and you have a type who has little need to lead or influence, who relates to the world with little desire to change or control it, or even to understand it, but simply to take it all in. Thus, ISFPs of either gender do not project a strong image, nor are they competitive in nature.

Male ISFPs are successful and highly regarded in various roles, and if someone is looking for a nurturing male, this type is a natural. Both female and male ISFPs often sell themselves short. As a result, most any compliment an ISFP receives can be dismissed as "not really meant" or "just an accident."

Parenting is an opportunity for an ISFP to relate to children, not to control them. As a result, children who also have strong Perceiving tendencies are probably allowed to wander too much; they may not be given the basic sense of structure that may be helpful later on. Judging children, by contrast, are often frustrated by the ISFP's lack of direction and guidelines, which may set up the parents to feel like failures. They are not failures —they simply fail to offer much direction. Different types find it difficult to understand the ISFP's low need for control or influence. Clearly, it is intended to allow others to grow more freely, although the ISFP's quiet, subtle style may never receive full credit.

Children learn that the ISFP parent is always near, very much in touch with the child's needs, and very supportive and loving of the child's development, but in a quiet and unassuming way. "Love" is not so much spoken of as displayed—quietly, and in myriad ways. "Nothin' says lovin' like something from the oven" could be an ISFP motto. The cookies or dollhouse furniture or handmade sweaters are symbols that say, "I love you." An ISFP's child knows he or she is loved because in these kindly acts and gentle deeds, love is conveyed.

The ISFPs' living style is generally relaxed but active. Hands-on activities keep these Sensors busy. Interestingly, this does not always involve "what needs to be done" so much as what they want to be doing. As Sensing-Perceivers, they usually prefer doing something to doing nothing, but the activity is often spontaneous and scattered rather than goal-oriented. While this can be a source of fun, the result may be a long list of unfinished activities that can be frustrating, not only to others but to ISFPs themselves.

To relax ISFP-style is to do something "for the fun of it." Such "fun" things might include gardening, painting, needlework, or whittling. Some ISFP hobbies, such as creating "miniatures," for example, often demand high dexterity.

ISFP children are often curious explorers who seem unhurried about getting anywhere in particular. Content with their own company, they see the entire world as a place for discovery. Often unaware of rules, time, and other family demands, they explore the world around them. Plants, animals, brothers, sisters, and parents are all part of that world.

As Perceivers, ISFP children march to a somewhat different drummer. They are likely to be playing when they are expected to be at meals, watching TV when everyone else is in the car ready to leave, or rearranging toys when company is about to walk in the door. They want very much to please but often go about it in such a way that the person to be pleased—parent, teacher, sibling, and so on—becomes impatient, even exasperated. The message the sensitive ISFP gets from these individuals is: "You never seem to do anything right!"

As Sensors, ISFPs are a very "now" type and so learning needs to be tactile and immediately relevant. They have little interest in the conceptual and abstract and are most responsive to what is pragmatic: "What does it look like?" "How does it feel?" "What can I do with it?" "How does it work?" Questions like these spark interest in a project; the theoretical side of things is more difficult, less interesting, and often produces very negative responses from ISFPs. Such responses often lead to negative labels—"slow learners" and "daydreamers," to cite a few. The labels are inaccurate, but they contribute to the ISFPs' tendency to avoid formal education, especially higher education.

Family events for ISFPs are best when they just "happen." Too much planning, work, and structure can block things from unfolding freely. Family rituals indeed merit attention, but only once they are in process. It is not uncommon for an ISFP to be doing something totally unrelated to an event minutes before it is supposed to begin. Somehow, ISFPs *know* that all will take care of itself if only they are sensitive to others' needs, in touch with their own feelings, and open to whatever happens. The occasion will be great—or at least long-remembered.

Bedtime for ISFPs is "when you're tired." If there are projects, people, pets, or other forms of life that need attention, then bedtime may take second place. Once these other things are tended to, and *if* one is tired, it is time for sleep—whenever and wherever one happens to be. Again, others may find such behavior difficult, even "flaky."

For ISFPs, work must be rewarding, and to be rewarding it must be personally gratifying and of use to others. Money is secondary; the primary concern is that service be rendered, to whomever or whatever requires it. If a great deal of formal education or abstract theory is necessary for a certain career choice, then ISFPs will likely seek fulfillment elsewhere. Vocational education, however, is often appealing for ISFPs who desire to work in the area of hands-on, practical trades and skills, including everything from car mechanics and repair to cosmetology, carpentry, and clerical tasks.

When they are enthusiastic about themselves and confident in their abilities, ISFPs find that their four preferences give them a natural edge to excel in a variety of vocations, including psychology, veterinary medicine, botany, and theology. When they make it to managerial levels, their styles tend to be nondirective. They create an open and diverse environment, which can be fertile ground for those subordinates capable of developing themselves.

ISFPs seem to carry this easygoing nature into maturity. Adapting to each day as it comes, with little need to plan, they tend to "wait, see, and hope for a surprise." Retirement allows some special time for the kinds of hobbies that are open-ended and can result in high levels of personal satisfaction related to the process, not necessarily the product.

Two famous likely ISFPs include *Peanuts's* Charlie Brown (whose Introversion demands that he constantly rehearse what he will say to the little redheaded girl, but prevents him from actually delivering the goods, whose Feeling often raises the question, after he's been beaten badly in baseball, "How could we lose when we were so sincere?" and whose need for action *demands* that he try to kick a football, fully knowing Lucy will always foil him); and Saint Francis of Assisi (whose quiet, reflective way of relating to animals around him brought scorn and misunderstanding from his colleagues, but whose need to serve inspired an entire new order).

INFP
Performing Noble Service to Aid Society

If there is a single word that defines this type, it is *idealist*. As Introverted Feelers, they discover their ideals through a subjective interpretation of the world, and put those ideals to use to help others in a variety of ways. They are often the "Joans (or

Johns) of Arc" who seek fulfillment through performing noble service to aid society.

INFPs have their own self-imposed "codes" for life, and while they have little need to share or impose them on others, they can be very strict with themselves about following these regimens. But in general, INFPs tend to be easygoing and congenial. They would prefer to "fit in" harmoniously rather than to create waves—as long as they can do so without violating their ideals. Yet when others do trample on INFPs' codes, INFPs can become very demanding and extremely aggressive, often to the surprise of both themselves and others. This tendency may be best illustrated by the mother who feels her child has been treated unjustly by his or her school. The normally quiet INFP mother leaves no stone unturned in full pursuit of rectifying the injustice and creating a better environment—not only for her child but for others, who will also benefit from the change.

Male INFPs can be seen by others, particularly macho traditionalists, as too gentle, even wimpy. The INFPs' generally passive, live-and-let-live exterior, however admirable, may lack the take-charge quality often associated with maleness—until they feel that their value system is threatened, that is. Then, the easygoing ways (of male and female INFPs alike) can give way to harsh rigidity. For staff, friends, and mates who don't understand this characteristic, the INFP can seem, at best, a source of mixed signals—pliant one moment, rigid the next—and, at worst, a deep, complex, even somewhat melancholy person who is hard to understand. When a male INFP marries an Extravert, society may view his mate as domineering and demanding. In actuality, for the marriage to succeed, the mate must quickly learn the limits of her mandate to take charge.

These very same qualities in an INFP female are more socially acceptable, even admired. While the INFP male's quiet stubbornness can make him seem simultaneously unforceful yet rigid, the INFP female may be respected for her inner strength. Her determination conveys power and makes others feel secure.

INFPs resist being labeled and are often driven to do things that shake the way others view them. This can on occasion lead INFPs to be unpredictable, even outrageous. A docile INFP we

know was invited to a staff costume party where guests were
instructed to dress as "who you really are." She came as Ma-
donna, the eccentric eighties rock singer, bedecked in jewelry
and silky clothing. Her colleagues were shocked by her display
—but she wasn't.

Like all iNtuitive-Feelers, the INFP strives for self-identity,
self-knowledge, and self-definition. "Who am I?" is an all-important question. More so than all other NFs, however, the INFPs
find in their preferences further material and inspiration for
this never-ending quest. Their Introversion fosters inward reflection, their iNtuition ensures an endlessly ramifying sense of
the possibilities inherent in the self, their Feeling guides them
to reflect on how such potential could benefit both themselves
and their relations with others, and their Perceiving keeps
them open to a constant flow of new data. It's not unusual for an
INFP to get out of bed reflecting (Introversion), "Who am I and
where's my life going today?" There may be a number of possible answers (iNtuition)—"I'm a father," "I'm a mate," "I'm a
teacher," and the like—as well as a consideration of how those
attributes might be deployed in the service of self and others
(Feeling). Deciding these are all interesting issues to contemplate, the INFP may then, in the search for more information
(Perceiving), set off for school or work, there to start the process
again. Even if these questions are not consciously raised, the
identity issues are always percolating. The INFP's reflective,
open-ended approach to life produces far more questions than
answers.

The INFP's home and work area may be rife with little piles
of "to-do's"—reading, ironing, artwork, writing. These things
will always be there. In fact, they will increase as the INFP's
interests and concerns grow throughout life. It's helpful for
INFPs to learn to live with this rather than punish themselves
for seeming "failures." In general, home and family relationships are more relaxed than rigid; schedules are always subject
to change because of others' immediate needs. Neatness often
takes a backseat to interpersonal warmth and affirmation, except when company is expected, in which case perfection is the
name of the game in the desire to serve others. INFPs prefer to
give in to others rather than to argue points that may lead to

disharmony. Still, all of this may fly out the window if an INFP's "codes" are "violated," and then a relaxed home gives way to strict rules and schedules.

The same dynamic applies to parenting. An INFP parent may focus on a few carefully cultivated values. If these are respected, the INFP parent is typically easygoing and quick to meet a child's needs. In general, the INFP parent is positive and affirming and a child will find in that parent a friend in whom they can confide. If there are parenting weaknesses, they are probably related to INFPs' first preference, Introversion: INFPs may be slow to give overt, positive strokes, not because they don't feel approval, but because they find it difficult to express; and to their last preference, Perceiving, which may cause them to avoid providing the structure and organization that a child may need.

Introversion may also plague INFPs' relationships: they may feel far more love and warmth than they are able to express. In any relationship involving INFPs, there will be growth, affirmation, and self-fulfillment for both of the parties involved, but sometimes the combination of the Introversion and Feeling preferences causes them to avoid discussing issues that they fear may cause disagreement. For example, an INFP may, after much inner debate, conclude that some kind of change is necessary, and may then spring this conclusion on an unprepared partner. Thus, the INFP's decision to quit a job and go to graduate school (or convince the mate to do so) may be presented as a fait accompli, not a subject open for discussion, and the unsuspecting mate may be shocked into a new view of their relationship when a formerly pliant INFP shows new drive, determination, and rigidity, far out of proportion to the issue involved.

This INFP complexity—an easygoing exterior masking a compulsive interior—may make for inner stress. The result can be a variety of serious health problems: ileitis, colitis, and other stomach or intestinal problems. They may be particularly prone to such ailments when the needs of others prevent them from being able to relax and enjoy themselves. INFPs can easily make martyrs of themselves.

As children, INFPs' deceptively easygoing natures may cause others to take them for granted. INFP children have a high need to please parents—and be stroked for it. Generally, they are tender and sensitive to the world around them and, like their INFP elders, often give in to others at the expense of their own needs. If such self-sacrifice is not appreciated or, even worse, is criticized, the INFP child can become sullen, self-critical, often overpersonalizing each remark. The potential for martyrdom begins early. INFP children can spend a disproportionate amount of time daydreaming and being preoccupied with inner thoughts. They are often good students and expend a lot of energy pleasing their teachers. They tend to do well in high school, and often excel in college. To please others, they may take courses they do not like—and even succeed in them. The potential for self-doubt and self-criticism, however, is always close to the surface. Even when told they have done a "good job," INFPs know the only true judge is themselves, and may punish themselves for work they consider less than perfect.

In general, while INFPs love to learn, grow, excel, and please others, they are always their own worst critics; they often remind themselves that they could have done better. It is a lifelong struggle between self-approbation and self-depreciation. In the end, INFPs almost always tend to sell themselves short.

Family events for an INFP are expressions of the essentials of life, and a lot of energy can be directed to celebrating such family rituals as birthdays, anniversaries, or graduations. Loyalty and service to the family can keep an INFP a "child" at any age and always close—psychologically, if not physically—to parents and family.

The values that shape INFPs' family life and personal growth patterns highlight their career choices: integrity, hard work, idealism, sensitivity, and concern for other people. INFPs also bring their self-criticism and perfectionism to the workplace, which can sometimes hamper their natural skills. An INFP may be an excellent musician or a superb teacher, but even if showered with accolades, INFPs may never quite be satisfied. Their high learning abilities may lead them to careers in which they excel academically but for which they are typologically somewhat miscast. The daughter of an engineer may pursue that career to please her father—and find it academically very attainable and challenging—although as an NFP, she may find the world of engineering foreign, even hostile, turf.

Those careers that involve human service are the ultimate home of the INFP: psychology, teaching, family medicine, and church work, for example. In the long haul, what INFPs choose as a career must serve their own idealism. If it doesn't, they can become restless and stressed and their work can become sloppy and counterproductive.

Retirement tends to be relished by INFPs because the little piles of to-do's they have been amassing for years can be rearranged, pondered, and finally tackled. They tend not to "slow down" in later life, approaching their postcareer hobbies with the same intensity they once reserved for children and careers. They may approach retirement with a particular joy if it allows them to leave a traditional career or job that imposed the kind of structure and rigidity that INFPs resist. Still appearing externally relaxed, they tend to continue to be internally driven by a call to serve humanity—in the form of children, grandchildren, organizations, causes, or any other local or world issues.

Abraham Lincoln quite possibly personifies the INFP. As a young man, seeing slaves loaded into a boat, he took the cause of freedom into his heart, ultimately imposing his crusade on the entire nation. Isabel Briggs Myers, another INFP, carried on her mission—that people learn how to use their personality differences more constructively and creatively—throughout her entire life. From age twenty to eighty, she endlessly created, researched, and refined the Myers-Briggs Type Indicator. Carl Rogers, one of the pillars of American modern psychology, saw the need for a therapeutic model that enhanced individual self-development—itself, an INFP cause—and spent his life developing nondirective counseling.

INTP
A Love of Problem-solving

If any type personifies the absentminded professor, it would likely be the INTP. Their inner reflectiveness—Introversion—enables them to explore all the imaginative possibilities their iNtuition preference provides. Their objectivity (Thinking) demands the analysis of all that information, and their open-ended and flexible attitude (Perceiving) prompts them to be responsive to whatever new data present themselves.

Such a combination of preferences keeps the INTP caught up in the paradoxical goal of always trying to make a coherent whole out of an endlessly proliferating amount of data. Whether it's an article, drawing, a plan, scheme, thought, or theory, the INTP struggles to fit all its pieces together into a complete picture that keeps expanding with the continual discovery of new pieces. As a result, all thoughts, ideas, and plans, however final they seem, are subject to last-minute changes when "new data," from either internal or external influences, become available. This is very exciting to INTPs and very frustrating to others, especially those with a preference for Judging.

To arrive at what seems like perfection, only to have it challenged by a new insight, is at once exciting and challenging to INTPs. As a result, they are their own greatest critics and pride themselves on being the first to knock down their own theories or correct themselves with a better word or improved idea. The quest for flawlessness, cleverness, competency, conceptual perfection, and self-mastery is a driving force for INTPs. When maximized, however, these goals can become tiresome, self-punishing liabilities.

Any project, from fixing a leaky faucet to writing a business plan to taking a vacation, presents itself as a mental challenge to the INTP, who thinks through every stage of the task at hand, from beginning to end. Such thinking may well involve computers, drawing boards, resource books, and anything else that will help the INTP focus the project and create a plan open-ended enough to allow for improvements. Once such a plan has been developed, either on paper or in the INTP's mind, a considerable amount of energy must then go into critiquing and improving the "rough draft." This process, which may go on for hours, days, even weeks, is always more exciting, challenging, and stimulating to the INTP than actually doing whatever needs to be done. Sometimes, once an INTP thinks a project through, he or she may lose interest in it, for in the mind of the INTP that project has been completed—even if that's the only place it exists. Indeed, when INTPs are conceptualizing—and they usually are—it can be difficult to interrupt their high power of concentration.

Gender issues are especially pointed for the INTP female. While all of the internal conceptualizing, however misunderstood, may be tolerated in a male, society is less likely to tolerate the same characteristic in a female. The absentminded professor is another image more conventionally male than female. This creates at least three special problems for the INTP female: First, women historically have not been looked upon as the architects of much beyond their own homes and families. The constant desire to make life conform to a theoretical model, while true to the INTP preference, flies in the face of traditional female roles. Second, conceptual originality is similarly not a traditional female trait. Some INTPs, asked the time of day, would be tempted to expound on the philosophical meaning of time; this eccentricity in a man may be looked upon as the result of overintelligence, in a woman it may result in her being labeled "dizzy" or even "dumb." Finally, the Thinking preference of INTPs directly counters most females' scripting to be subjective, soft, and caring. Even worse, when an INTP female's feeling side does surface, it often does so with intensity, an outpouring that can be frightening to both herself and others.

In relating to an INTP, male or female, expect an intellectual challenge. Words spoken and thoughts shared with an INTP will be construed as an invitation to expand, clarify, argue, and rethink. Though less immediately reactive than their ENTP relatives, they are sure to be thinking about and rehearsing a response that will cause all involved to reevaluate the issue at hand. Such discipline and rigor brings growth and new direction to a relationship. But social deftness and poise are generally secondary to an INTP's intellectual pursuits. As a result, when INTPs are absorbed in thinking or questioning, they can often appear hard to reach, at best, or even downright rude, to those of a different type.

Parenting for the INTP is seen as an opportunity to help young minds develop and grow. Very patient and accepting of differences in children, INTP parents want their children to grow up enjoying, expressing, living through independent thought. Clearly preferring a child to develop "mind over body," INTP parents have an amazing tolerance of and support for each child's pursuit of his or her own course. If anything, they may be too nondirective of their children's development. It is an INTP model to open new possibilities for the child by *suggesting*—not demanding and rarely imposing—alternatives to whatever thought or action the child may be pursuing; if the alternative is not adopted, the typical INTP response is simply —"At least I tried." But sometimes children, even when they seem rebellious or uninterested, welcome a parent's pushing and imposing new ideas. Those who do are out of luck if they have INTP parents, for "pushing" and "imposing" are two words foreign to INTPs.

It is a live-and-let-live life-style for most INTPs. Study, follow one's inspirations, master the situation, then move on to some new "problem." At times, their love of problem-solving may overshadow their other inclinations. So, for example, while not particularly mechanically inclined, they may find the challenge of repairing a broken appliance totally consuming, and be willing to expend great bursts of energy to master the situation. Having mastered it, they will instantly move on to something else. They are the quintessential Jacks (or Janes) of all trades and masters of none.

As children, INTPs can be viewed variously as socially shy or terribly argumentative, with little in between. In school they may be seen as unfocused, pursuing too many things unrelated to the curriculum. Worse yet, they are seen as raising the wrong questions at the wrong times, although this may be more a reflection of a teacher's rigidness than a student's disorganization. Still, the INTP's behavior can be seen as disruptive, particularly in females. The result, inevitably, is that INTPs must work harder than most to tolerate and survive grade school. When they are successful, they will likely thrive in college. The inquisitiveness encouraged in higher education is the INTP's dream come true. For INTPs, whatever the subject, the joy is in learning.

Family events for INTPs are generally fun because they are opportunities to explore what makes such events and people tick. While an INTP may be remiss in remembering anniversaries and belated in honoring them, such events are considered important and the forgetfulness is inadvertent. At the very least, family occasions offer material for thought about the meaning of family and its place in the sequence of life. As an INTP grows and matures, even bedtime may seem a stepping-off place for exploration, because it opens the door to dreams, which provide more opportunities for understanding and growth.

Work that does not involve intellect and the opportunity for mastery soon becomes drudgery for INTPs. In fact, if a job doesn't afford the INTP such challenges, he or she will be better off seeking new employment. Otherwise, on-the-job listlessness will result, over the long term, in stress, accident proneness, and overall poor performance.

Senior years for INTPs ought to afford time to theorize and dream with much less accountability. During some of that time INTPs may experience more Extraversion and subjectivity (Feeling), which may be simultaneously scary and quite exciting. As that phase passes, the INTP will settle into a senior citizenship of developing new thoughts and ideas to present to younger generations.

Famous likely INTPs include Linus of *Peanuts* comics fame (who brings rationality to the contemplation of the theological implications of absolutely everything in the world and intimidates everyone with the universal questions he ceaselessly raises); C. G. Jung (whose revolutionary and complex theories of personality were comprehended by few, although his intent was simply to raise questions for all to explore); and Albert Einstein (an intellectual Goliath who devoted his entire life to exploration and questioning, and yet was known to show up at a dinner party having forgotten to wear pants).

ESTP
The Ultimate Realist

The classic ESTP slogan may be "When all else fails, read the directions." This heavily action-oriented type, more than any other type, lives for the moment. If reading the directions delays "the moment," it may therefore be a waste of time.

The ESTP is the ultimate realist with the lowest tolerance for unrelated theory. The ESTP's focus is directed toward people and things (Extraversion), and information gathering is grounded in what's real according to the five senses (Sensing). The information then is assessed objectively and analytically (Thinking) at the same time that the ESTP remains spontaneous, flexible, and open to any new alternative (Perceiving). These four preferences combine for quick, exact, tactile, objective, externally expressed responses to any situation.

The ESTP believes that time spent making plans and getting ready may mean missing what is going on right now. So, for example, going to school makes sense only as long as what's taught is relevant and immediately usable. But the ESTP would rather plunge into the "real world" and deal with real (as opposed to textbook) problems using one's innate talents instead of what one learns in books.

The ESTP would always rather be doing something than nothing. And the consequences of action can always be postponed to another day. Act now, pay later. Such tendencies in their personalities earn them very negative reputations from other types: they are "fidgets" and "hyperactive," for example. Certainly the ESTP can seem exceedingly restless.

As outgoing realists with objectivity and flexibility, ESTPs demand a return on every investment of energy they make. If something doesn't seem worth their while, they move on to the next thing. Rarely, if ever, does one find the ESTP finishing a book that doesn't appeal; while some other types may wade through a dull book just to finish what they've started, or because they think it will be intellectually "good for them," the ESTP views this as a silly waste of time. Similarly, it may be a waste of time to clean a room simply because it *should* be done. Better to wait until one needs to find some specific lost item. Then, cleaning the room has a purpose and the task makes sense.

Entertaining and gregarious, with a short attention span, the ESTP can often be found on center stage. The ESTPs' quick repartee, with a special knack for practical jokes, makes them fun to be with. People are easily drawn and engaged by an ESTP. Their capacity to tackle and complete tough jobs, their fearlessness in trying anything at least once, and their keen sense of competition, make ESTPs doers, problem-solvers, and people upon whom one can count when an exciting challenge lies ahead. Not that the job will be done according to the rules. That's part of the pride and cleverness of the ESTP. If the job becomes routine, the ESTP will lose interest and become bored, causing him or her to want to move on or change setting.

One ongoing dilemma for this type is that they are often oblivious to established norms and procedures. As a result, they can be in continual trouble with those in authority. Some other types are specifically anti-authority and enjoy testing its legitimacy—not the ESTP. This type is simply oblivious to authority. Looking at a job or problem, he or she begins to see a way to complete or solve the dilemma and leaps right in, not having checked first as to whether there are established procedures for doing something. As a result, what may have been intended as a good deed by the ESTP may be seen as something completely different by others, who may end up dubbing the ESTP a "troublemaker" or similar term. The well-meaning ESTP ends up not a hero but a failure. Fortunately for them, ESTPs are not given to much self-punishment and simply move on to other endeavors.

ESTP females tend to be out of step with the mainstream. As a type, they are often given to athletics, especially competitive, hands-on, contact sports. If an ESTP female, true to her preferences, is a natural at these, she may be deemed a tomboy. Moreover, the hard-charging fix-it-or-forget-it model of the ESTP is not one readily associated with women in our society.

In a relationship as in most other things, the ESTP demands center stage. While deeply committed in a serious relationship, the expression of commitment may vary from day to day according to changing situations.

ESTP parents often have very realistic expectations of their children and mates. It isn't necessary for the ESTP's children to excel, or even go to college, but they simply must do something constructive and practical with their lives. More specifically, ESTP parents want their children to find something that will make them happy.

The ESTP life-style has a certain restlessness to it. There is always too much going on, with still more to do, never enough time. That, in itself, brings much excitement to the ESTP. Almost any event can be the excuse for a party: an athletic event, the end of summer, a baptism, a new job, a good grade, whatever. An ESTP can become quite involved in preparing and participating in such events. Sometimes all this flurry is only flurry, especially when ESTPs are disorganized, doing things in spurts and accomplishing very little. Then their lack of orderliness can be extremely frustrating to those around them. Their need for center stage can, at times, make them appear very abrasive to other types, as can their impatience with theory or even with long explanations.

As children, ESTPs are woefully misunderstood. These are the children we call "hyperactive" or "slow learners." There is often a war between high-strung ESTP children and parents of a different type who think it necessary to "quiet" these apparent troublemakers. Actually, ESTP children are very creative and resourceful, often in the face of repeated attempts to get them to conform to more standard ways of behaving. With guidance instead of control, ESTPs do very well. They love family events but often do unexpected things. It's common for an ESTP—child or adult—to plan some special event and then forget to show up at the appointed hour. They find this perfectly natural behavior, but it can be very frustrating to others.

Work that is flexible, varied, and open to creativity can be challenging to an ESTP. Routine and predictability are considered a drag and lead to stress and low productivity. ESTPs want to learn as they go; they'll read the instruction manual only when absolutely necessary (and then only the parts of the manual that are relevant to the moment). They prefer to trust themselves and to rely on common sense to accomplish whatever is at hand. They are adept at entrepreneurial activities, and there are many ESTP small-business owners. Sports, auto racing and repair, maintenance or operation of special equipment, and anything else that changes from day to day or moment to moment and is unpredictable has special career appeal.

As ESTPs age, they still require new mountains to climb. Though the mountains needn't be quite as high, they are still needed. A bit more reflective time is needed, too, although the preference continues to be for challenges that test common-sense skills and abilities. Without these challenges, retirement would be nothing but drudgery for an ESTP.

Famous likely ESTPs include General George Patton (who clamored for the limelight and always did the opposite of what was expected, usually at high risk); Lee Iacocca (who loved the thrill and challenge of taking on Congress, solved Chrysler's many problems one day at a time, and by his own words would never have taken the job if he had examined it first); Chicago Bears quarterback Jim McMahon (who loves the spotlight and does whatever is necessary on the field, no matter how unexpected or how risky); and *Peanuts*'s Peppermint Patty (she often sleeps through class, finding the daily lessons boring, yet is always ready to play ball with Charlie Brown).

ESFP
You Only Go Around Once in Life

Of all the sixteen types, ESFPs are most in touch with the here and now and live primarily for the moment. As with ESTPs, their slogan could easily be "Act now, pay later." As Extraverted-Sensors, their only certainty is the here and now. They personify the bird-in-the-hand-is-worth-two-in-the-bush philosophy. When the bird is in hand, they have all they need; when there is no bird, their energies are focused on getting one. While their Introverted counterparts might reflect a bit before acting, ESFPs' are driven by their Extraversion to act first to achieve the immediately tangible.

ESFPs may be the inspiration for Madison Avenue pitchmen: they exemplify such slogans as "You only go around once in life . . ." and "If I only have one life to live, let me live it as a blonde."

Their focus on the immediate leaves them with a low tolerance for procedures, routines, and anything else that stands in the way of immediate gratification. The combination of Extraversion, Sensing, and Feeling drives ESFPs to make each moment a successful interpersonal experience. They are very accepting of others and believe people should "Live and let live." So strong is their need for harmony that they constantly tend to accentuate the positive, denying and repressing anything that is less than positive, often employing diversionary tactics to circumvent a conflict. If an argument erupts, ESFPs may quickly start a conversation about something pleasant, hoping that the combatants will join in and forget their differences.

Although Extraverted-Sensors are the ultimate realists, with a firm grasp of the outer world, they tend to lose their way very quickly in the nether regions of their inner world of abstraction. They tend to experience it as an ominous place in whose coil they become quickly enmeshed. Like their ESTP first cousins, given half a second to speculate, they can proceed to the worst possible conclusion. A mate or guest who is late for dinner is presumed, after a moment's reflection, to be killed en route; when the guest then shows up and offers a perfectly plausible excuse, it will be viewed with distrust and suspicion. The imagination of the ESFP tends to run wild if given half a chance.

All of this gives ESFPs an uncanny skill for making life a three-ring circus, juggling many activities and people, and, for the most part, enjoying the hustle and bustle, and the spotlight that is on them. Unfortunately, they have low tolerance for those times when the circus lights are down or the curtain is closed. Their need for action can earn them negative labels like "flighty," "hyperactive," or even "egotistical," which may appear to be accurate even when they are not. In the presence of an ESFP, one often feels positive, enthused, and excited, albeit somewhat tired and out of breath from trying to keep pace and follow each new dynamic as it surfaces.

Gender has a lot to do with how ESFPs are viewed by others. Female ESFPs, unfortunately, are often cast as "dizzy blondes" (whatever their hair color), while male ESFPs are viewed, at best, as "spacy" and, at worst, as wimps. Both males and females constantly bemoan the fact that "no one takes me seriously."

The characteristics usually linked to ESFPs are considered more traditionally female than male, such as "works well with children" and "enjoys serving others" as well as "conflict-avoidant" and "fuzzy-headed." As a result, when a male ESFP demonstrates some or all of these traits, his masculinity may be suspect. Because of their tendency to be somewhat abrupt and quick-spoken, ESFPs can be seen at first blush as harsh—although in the long run, they are caring and sensitive—so an

ESFP male sometimes must work harder at giving in to his natural "soft" side without feeling his masculinity is threatened.

In general, both male and female ESFPs are often misperceived. The spontaneity and immediacy of their nature (Perceiving) and their firm grounding in "what is" (Sensing) as opposed to "what can be" may make the ESFP appear lacking in depth, direction, and purpose. But this is not the case. It's just that their depth, direction, and purpose are always interpreted in light of the demands of the existing moment. "I don't need a long-range plan if I make the most of what I'm doing right now," they are likely to say. It is precisely such sentiments that cause them to be perceived as shallow.

Like all Extraverted-Perceivers, ESFPs make more starts than finishes, and it is therefore vital that they somehow develop a system of benchmarks against which their accomplishments and progress can be measured. This will act as a check on the ESFP's tendency to live only for the excitement of the moment, with no real long-term satisfaction, or sense of self-worth.

ESFP parents bring their three-ring circus into their homes as well as their jobs. Multidirected, they can pack into a single evening for their children everything from Little League to dance class, a church meeting, and a home-cooked dinner. While this can be very exciting for all involved, it also results in a feeling of overextension and scatteredness that can ultimately cause guilt and self-flagellation over all the things left undone. (One of those things left "undone" can, unfortunately, be paying attention to a mate.) Even when they themselves are not overextended, ESFP parents can make their children feel that way, especially children of a different type. In fact, ESFPs can seem like competition to their children. After all, as believers in "living for the moment," they'd much prefer to be one of "the kids" and get involved in an activity than to sit on the sidelines as spectators with all the other parents. All of this makes ESFP parents very popular with the neighborhood kids (and their parents) but may lead an ESFP's child to conclude that "Dad doesn't care about me personally, he's always off with my friends. There's never time for just me." For the child, there are times when the circus needs to stop. But even children who find life with ESFP parents tiring will enjoy their warm, supportive, easygoing ways.

One possible drawback to being so easygoing is that it can frustrate the family with not enough restraints, direction, and general discipline, to say nothing of "thinking about the future" —any or all of which may be important to family members of different types. Judging children, for example, while appreciating their parents' fun-loving nature, may go to bed frustrated, hungering for a plan, a schedule, an overall pattern for their lives.

The thrill-a-minute intensity ESFPs bring to parenting also characterizes their intimate relationships. They are good at translating the excitement of falling in love, or the intensity of commitments, into each day's experiences. Today's passion, for example, may be tomorrow's home-cooked meal, and the next day's "special surprise." All of which, while exciting, may be misunderstood by a mate of a different type. An Introverted mate may wonder why the relationship needs constant external affirmation; the Judging mate may long for less upheaval and more stability.

As with everything else, relaxation for an ESFP involves "doing." Remember: to spend too much time alone or reflecting can lead an Extraverted-Sensing-Perceiver to leap to all sorts of bad conclusions. So, "doing anything" beats "doing nothing." "Relaxation" can include a great many demanding activities that other types might not find so relaxing. But for the ESFP, such activities provide not only fun and relaxation but the chance to do more of the many things they've "always wanted to do." Going to the beach for a relaxing weekend may result in a variety of activities that may include exploring all the interesting shops on the boardwalk or gathering a multitude of shells and making them into gifts for friends.

An ESFP child must often struggle to be understood. The ESFP child sees himself as entertainer, dancer, garbage collecter, car washer, train engineer, the identities changing daily. As a result, these children can often be seen as hyperactive, constantly needing strokes and affirmation. The plus side is that they are very capable of self-entertainment—though their activities may not necessarily meet with parental approval.

The need to be "doing" also applies to learning. When learning is fun and social and a chance to entertain or be entertained, the ESFP excels. When it begins to become more abstract and theoretical, the ESFP starts to withdraw and ultimately loses interest. While Sensing-Perceiving types tend not to do well in college (which requires considerably more facility for the abstract and the conceptual than earlier education) and often drop out before graduation, ESFPs do well once they learn that college can be a four-year party at parents' expense. They may not excel academically, but they manage to perform well enough to stay in school, making the most of campus social life.

At bedtime, ESFPs, like other Extraverted children, would rather fall asleep at the top of the stairs than miss any excitement that may be going on downstairs. And if any of the activities can serve as an opportunity to be in the spotlight for one more moment, the ESFP child is ready, willing, and able. Therefore, family rules, bedtime rituals, study hours, and all other regimens will be stretched to the limit—as will be the patience of the parents.

ESFPs generally make family events exciting and entertaining, though they generally are "happenings" rather than carefully planned rituals. The lack of planning can cause family members of different types (particularly Judgers) to become highly stressed as the event approaches, although they may greatly enjoy the outcome. ESFPs can work wonders at the last minute, pulling together a successful party in mere minutes, often to the consternation of those watching on the sidelines.

Career choices for ESFPs often include service to humanity such as teaching, especially elementary school, or working in the arts or theater. They love athletics and anything else that provides relatively instant gratification and allows for self-expression, concern for others, and a challenge to accomplish, improve, and grow. Conversely, careers requiring adherence to rigid routine or other kinds of constraints will not only have low appeal for ESFPs but, in the long haul, will be very frustrating. They are challenged by things that are different, fun, and require some special effort to accomplish.

In later life, the hunger for the unknown and the unexpected does not end. This may best be illustrated through a woman we know who when her husband died, met with a minister the night before his funeral. When asked by the clergyman whether there was anything special she wanted included in the service, she thought briefly, looked up, and replied, "Surprise me."

Famous likely ESFPs include people who are viewed as flighty by all but those who know them well. The character played by Gracie Allen—flighty to everyone but George Burns, who viewed her as the backbone of their team—could easily be an ESFP. So could Edith Bunker, seen by the audience as flaky, called "Dingbat" by husband Archie, who nonetheless recognized that she was his Rock of Gibraltar. Both of these women viewed the world in very concrete, literal-minded terms, which made for much of the comedy of their roles. They were usually to be found in the midst of a variety of activities, juggling several people's problems and doing so in caring ways, accepting of others' perceived eccentricities.

ENFP
Giving Life an Extra Squeeze

ENFPs are generally described as dynamic, enthusiastic, highly skilled with people, affirming, and gregarious. The combined preferences of Extraversion, iNtuition, Feeling, and Perceiving give them an exceptional capacity for dealing with a variety of people, events, or challenges—often simultaneously.

ENFPs prefer to perceive the world through its possibilities (N) and translate these possibilities inter- and intrapersonally (F). All this takes place in lively interaction with the outside world (E), and their Perceiving attitude (P) keeps them open to a never-ending flow of alternatives in any situation.

The ENFP has a high need to be affirming of others—and to be affirmed. This drives them in such a way that they may appear overly positive, even insincere, in praise of other people's simplest deeds. Craving such affirmations, ENFPs will overexert themselves—physically and psychologically—to please. They may also expend extra energy giving strokes to everyone and trying, at times desperately, to get strokes in return. It is not uncommon for ENFPs to work themselves into exhaustion while following an inspiration or seeking an approving response from someone important to them.

This ability to see the potential in people and be positive about them gives ENFPs a decided edge in interpersonal dynamics, especially when combined with their almost psychic awareness of what's going on with people around them. Sometimes in their Extraverted enthusiasm, however, they may share some of these iNtuitive insights and be so accurate as to be intimidating rather than helpful to the people involved. These unsolicited but freely offered insights can often win them disapproval rather than approval, although that may only make the ENFP try harder the next time around.

Because of their enthusiasm for life, it is easy for ENFPs to rally support around any number of exciting ideas or causes. Unfortunately, somewhat like their first cousin, the ENTP, ENFPs make more starts than finishes. So while a crowd may be attracted by an ENFP's charisma, it may soon grow frustrated by the lack of organization and follow-through.

Gender differences can be significant for males because the qualities most associated with ENFPs are more traditionally attributed to females: sociability, desire/need to please, intuition, spontaneity, and concern for other people. As a result, when an ENFP male "plays" into those natural preferences of his personality, he can find himself outside the male "establishment." Ironically, this may set him up to overcompensate and behave in ways atypical for ENFPs—to be, for example, competitive or overly argumentative. Seeking group approval, he may get involved with contact sports or other "tough" activities, though he would really prefer to be elsewhere. ENFP males, somewhat more than other F males, may also fall into the trap of physical seduction as a way of establishing their masculinity. Indeed, both male and female ENFPs can be intellectually and physically seductive.

By virtue of their enthusiasm and generally accepting nature, ENFPs are highly resistant to categorizing and "putting people in boxes," and they are equally resistant to being put in boxes themselves, since they enjoy their own multifaceted personalities. With a little bit of effort they can "get into another person's moccasins" and identify with that individual's thoughts and feelings so readily that they run the risk of virtually losing their own identity. This beautiful quality of effortlessly taking on both the characteristics and the problems of another type is seen by others as very supportive and accepting. However, it can become a problem to the degree that it leaves ENFPs adrift, wondering who they are and what they should be doing. Obviously, this tendency has a restlessness to it, as well as an unfinished quality that haunts ENFPs lifelong.

In a relationship, ENFPs are rarely complacent. While highly committed, they can never give up thinking that either "This relationship could be better if I worked harder" or "There's a better relationship, still out there waiting for me." Such ambiguity and tension can be disconcerting for mates who are of a different type, particularly Judgers and most especially Sensing-Thinking-Judgers.

Parenting is fun for the ENFP and with the ENFP. The home, while often not the world's neatest, is a playground for fun, creative explorations. "The more the merrier" is the theme and each person and his or her differences must be affirmed. Expression, affirmation, and growth happen all the time. All life is a party and so even family chores must be converted to play in order to be worth accomplishing. If there is a family or individual job to do, it must either put it off (if it is boring) or involve others (so it becomes fun). The ENFP home is a gathering place for the neighborhood and friends. If the children are not ENFPs, they may not only misunderstand such a social whirl, they may also be confused or affronted by their parents' "immature," childlike behavior.

The basic theme of the ENFP's life is self-expression. The 1960s emphasis on self-awareness and group dynamics, the conversation pits where talk of peace and love and "flower power" took place, epitomize the values of the ENFP. The more that people can be themselves—and be affirmed for being themselves—the more growing they will do and the more they will contribute to the good of society. ENFPs believe that and will give their energies to help others achieve their goals. It's possible, however, for their enthusiasm to lead them in so many directions simultaneously that they can squander their best intentions, leading to frustration and self-punishment.

Obviously, relaxation—even in play—does not come easily to ENFPs. In fact, they almost have to "work at it." ENFPs go in fits and starts, and so when they become excited, they lose all sense of time, physical needs, and anything else. They follow their enthusiasm until totally fatigued, then collapse. As a result, relaxation, unless as part of a creative adventure, may take a backseat, sometimes even at the expense of the ENFP's physical well-being.

As children, ENFPs are a delight and yet often thoroughly exhausting and exasperating to parents. Everything around is material for daydreaming about who they are and might be. So, an upright vacuum cleaner becomes a radio microphone and the ENFP is a disc jockey. Tomorrow, a tree house will be built, and the ENFP is an architect, artist, painter, or interior decorator. Still another day, he or she may be program director for a large playground, responsible for many activities. All of this, while exciting for the ENFP, may be something of a merry-go-round for the parent, as the ENFP solicits parental approval and help in implementing each of these activities. While desperately wanting such approval, ENFP children, in their enthusiasm, can sometimes do things in direct conflict with the affirmation they're seeking: talking incessantly instead of listening, for example, or losing something they were entrusted not to lose, messing up their rooms in the name of straightening, or coming home later than promised.

In their quest to be liked, ENFP children are hypersensitive to the criticism of others, especially playmates. With a tendency to personalize everything, they are easily crushed by a harsh remark, so that their trademark phrase could be: "Everyone is so mean to me!"

ENFPs approach learning as they do everything else: it is a creative adventure that, if done well, will bring affirmation. They may be the ultimate apple-polishers. They want to be liked and they want to like the teacher, their classmates, the school, the administration, and everything else. As Extraverted-iNtuitive-Feelers, they generally do well academically and are people-pleasers. Interestingly, more than other types, they may suffer test phobias, because even those who do very well in class and know the material feel boxed in by fact-oriented exams that have only one "right" answer. On the other hand, they do well on essay tests, which give them the opportunity to integrate their knowledge into a bigger picture.

Family events for ENFPs are parties. If they are not, the ENFP will make them so. The Irish wake was probably designed by an ENFP who preferred to celebrate a life rather than mourn a death. One of the beauties of ENFPs is their ability to take an ordinary family event and, with almost no planning, using only the people and materials at hand, convert the occasion into a virtual work of art, an expression of affection or family affirmation that will be long remembered.

In this and many other ways, ENFPs are great improvisers. In the pursuit of pleasing others, their capabilities can be boundless. They may, for example, reach into the refrigerator and pull out whatever is at hand, and transform it into an impressive, spontaneous dinner, served with artistic flair. While this is clearly admirable, they still have a tendency to be hypercritical of their own performance. So after the dishes are done, they may decide that the dinner would have been better had they only, say, planned a day earlier, or remembered to defrost the brownies. Such "what-if" speculation can haunt ENFPs, turning otherwise successful occasions into opportunities for needless self-criticism.

For the ENFP, work, too, must be play or it is probably not worth doing. Worthwhile tasks are those that affirm and enlarge the self and involve more fun than drudgery. Like other EPs, ENFPs have a great deal of difficulty settling on just one career, for three reasons: They truly believe they can do most anything they want; the search for ever new fields to master is always more fun than remaining in a career already conquered; and they usually *can* do almost anything they set their minds to. Unfortunately, their career choices, like so many other things, may result from trying to please others. To please parents, for example, ENFPs may find themselves in careers involving the kinds of skills that, over the long haul, may become frustrating or stressful for them. They generally find more satisfaction and greater rewards in careers that involve human services, such as family medicine, psychology, teaching, and theology, than in such fields as engineering or accounting. As managers, they are far more advocates and mentors than "bosses," believing that their role is to help everyone achieve their individual goals.

In later years, the ENFP may cultivate the more objective, grounded (Sensing) side of life. In combination with the opportunity to take more time for quiet reflection (Introversion), these preferences may give greater stability to the ENFP's life of enthusiastic work and play. Good growth will allow this settling process to take place in a way that the ENFP will find welcoming.

Famous likely ENFPs include Will Rogers (who "never met a man I didn't like" and whose entire performance each night consisted of appearing onstage and responding to the audience), Tevye, the main character in *Fiddler on the Roof* (whose life was one of hope and possibilities in the face of austere oppression and unsettling change), and Charlie Brown's dog, Snoopy (whose imaginative imitations range from vultures through snakes to little kids; whose leadership style among his bird friends consists of setting a good example; and whose great ENFP lines include "I think I'm allergic to mornings" and "I'm going to get organized—tomorrow").

ENTP
One Exciting Challenge After Another

ENTPs are highly inventive types whose enthusiasms lead them into a variety of activities, vocational and avocational. Their inventiveness is attributable to their rich iNtuition (N), which gives them a world of endless possibilities, which, when combined with their objective decision-making facility (T) and directed outwardly (E), converts everything to ideas and schemes.

Like most Extraverted-Perceivers, they are more excited about pursuing a new idea than about following through on an existing one, which can be a cause for frustration and anxiety—both for themselves and for those around them. To the ENTP, all the world is a chessboard whose pieces must be moved in such a way—by the ENTP—that all the players will get the best and the most out of life. Constantly bombarding themselves and others with ideas, ENTPs burst with an excitement that, at best, leads to tackling one exciting challenge after another and, at worst, to an endless series of delayed or unfulfilled dreams.

The ENTP is a "big picture" person who finds it challenging to see how many ways there are for fitting the various pieces of the whole together. In fact, it is their ability to see the big picture that enables them to generate so many creative alternatives for just about any system—whether that "system" is a family, a vacation, a record collection, or a major corporation. They know that any system, no matter how successful, can always be made better or more effective. Such perceptions can at times make them seem almost psychic about future developments in a variety of disciplines. Clearly, these qualities make them well suited for a variety of entrepreneurial adventures.

ENTPs are high rollers and risk-takers with their own resources and others'. Like other Extraverted-Perceivers, when they win, they win big, and when they lose, they lose their shirts. As a result, life for an ENTP (and for those around them) can be a roller-coaster event with great highs, thrills, scares, occasional stops—and lots of unexpected jerks and turns.

All Thinking-type women swim upstream in society, and this can be especially problematic for ENTP women. When the ENTP's objectivity presents itself in an enthusiastic, witty, competitive, argumentative woman, she is not likely to endear herself to most men. The ENTP female frequently has a struggle with traditional female "scripts" that call for a given behavior at a given time. It is the nature of all ENTPs to test the limits of any system or person, especially traditional ones.

Most iNtuitive-Thinkers learn by discussing and challenging, and this is especially true for ENTPs. They get pleasure and intellectual stimulation from arguing both sides of a subject, or from doing something unusual or unexpected just to get a reaction. ENTP women can be fun to be around, but their competitive, testing nature can be intimidating and tiring. Interestingly enough, all these same qualities can be seen as positive in ENTP males, although they, too, can become tiring, particularly to those of a different type.

In relationships with an ENTP, one can expect to be challenged—usually by whatever comes along that is new, different, or on the cutting edge. Just coping with an ENTP can be stimulating, a fact attested to by ENTPs themselves ("I find myself very interesting—but tiring").

The ENTP sees the parenting relationship as one more opportunity for the growth and development of everyone involved. The ENTP's house may be crowded with the latest books, gadgets, fads, or all of the above. Children will be introduced to all of these things, which are used to challenge them—something far more important than neatness, schedule, and order. The ENTP's parenting model is "Stretch thyself," and successful parenting involves whatever helps the child to achieve this goal. Most ENTP parents generate more ideas and possibilities per day than their children will ever be able to complete. This in itself can be tiring and, to a child of a different type, very frustrating. It was probably an NT parent, most particularly an ENTP parent, who first said, "A mind is a terrible thing to waste." Helping the child to realize and expand the self is the ENTP's most basic principle of child-rearing. This quest may be made at the expense of hugs, kisses, and expressions of affection, although for the ENTP the process itself is the ultimate expression of love.

This focus on challenge, extremes, pursuit of ideas, and independent thinking characterizes all aspects of the ENTP's living style. The result can be a variety of kinds of instability. There may be big financial swings, as well as a lot of physical disarray and disorganization. When intellectual sparring and "doing your own thing" take precedence over completing yesterday's tasks—cleaning the house, the office, the yard, or whatever—the result can sometimes be chaos. Generally, the ENTP's home is an open haven to all, especially to those who are interested in whatever current scheme is unfolding and those who, like the ENTP, thrive on the intellectual stimulation of one-upmanship —whether they are one-upping or being one-upped.

Being allowed to dream up and pursue possibilities without any follow-through or accountability is the ultimate form of relaxation for the ENTP. It is also probably the greatest source of ENTP creativity. To give free rein to the imagination, instead of getting bogged down in the sticky details or dull routines that may be part and parcel of the idea, allows ENTPs' creativity to flourish. They find not only stimulation and growth in the process, but relaxation too. Stress comes from being tied down by too many details.

Like their adult counterparts, ENTP children are often whirlwinds. Lots of friends, laughter, projects, and ideas fill their waking hours. Each new day is a new opportunity to design systems, challenge friends, and scheme. A single request by a parent—"to take out the garbage," for example—can lead an ENTP child to spend hours if not days designing some sort of invention that will get the garbage from the kitchen to the backyard without human intervention. The design might demand calling friends, experimenting, or any number of other possibilities—all of which will be more exciting than actually completing the chore.

This is exactly the way an ENTP approaches learning. It is a group exchange of ideas, arguments, challenges, and projects. ENTPs would much rather learn by "getting involved" than by being lectured to. In true entrepreneurial spirit, if their involvement results in something that can be used, shared, and marketed (a new garbage-removal system), so much the better. Teaching that encourages such exchanges and opportunities is exciting to an ENTP. That which is routine, redundant, rigid, or overly detailed is boring. Assignments may be completed late (or early) and may be done sloppily. If dull or unchallenging in their original form, the ENTP student may even change or reconstruct assignments in the name of "learning." This typically ENTP behavior may be frustrating to students and teachers of different types and may result in a no-win situation—for the teacher, because he or she loses the ENTP's respect and attention, and for the ENTP student, who may do poorly in school.

Like most other things, family rituals and events are seen as opportunities to exchange ideas. ENTPs never like to miss such opportunities. Though not always given to appropriate behaviors, the ENTP is always an active participant in all such family moments. Sometimes late, sometimes underprepared, they will still be there and will more than likely engage whoever is present so that the time spent together will be fun, maybe competitive, and certainly memorable.

Work that allows the ENTP to be challenged and stimulated

will be highly attractive. Work that binds an ENTP to standard operating procedures will be ultimately frustrating and, quite possibly, stress-inducing. Computer science, financial investment counseling, college teaching, and other theoretical pursuits are highly attractive to ENTPs.

Later life might bring to ENTPs the opportunity to slow down some and not only "smell the daisies," but bring to fruition some long-shelved projects and hobbies. Pausing for introspection, appreciating what their senses are telling them, and respecting some of the more tender and emotional moments of life, will all have special appeal at this time.

Famous likely ENTPs include Ralph Kramden of *The Honeymooners* (who regularly came home with some new scheme to make them rich or their lives easier), *The Odd Couple*'s Oscar Madison (whose chaotic life-style undermined his obvious talent), and W. C. Durant, founder of General Motors (whose restless inventiveness and entrepreneurial skills turned a single car-company into a conglomerate).

ESTJ
Life's Administrators

ESTJs perceive the world "as it is" (Sensing) and translate those perceptions objectively (Thinking); as Extraverted-Judgers, they have a driving need to impose their judgments on the world around them with structure, schedule, and order. They are life's administrators.

It is as natural and inborn for ESTJs to manage (although not necessarily to lead) as it is for fish to swim. Grounded, organized, exacting, socially deft, gregarious, academically capable, and always appropriate, ESTJs are seen by others as dependable, practical, and able to get the job done—whatever the job may be. It is easy for ESTJs to end up in the top positions of any organization. Their inherent administrative skills make the family, the work force, the neighborhood, the church, or any other group appropriate arenas for them to administer and manage. ESTJs' need for control prompts them always to say yes when asked to assume positions of responsibility.

Often given to a raucous sense of humor, the ESTJ is a partygoer and party-doer who is always ready with a quick joke, a ready exchange, or an unsolicited opinion on almost anything. Whether or not one likes an ESTJ, one usually knows where the ESTJ stands on virtually any subject. Among ESTJs there are some sharp differences between genders, because of all the sixteen types this is the most conventionally masculine. Each of its four components—Extraversion, Sensing, Thinking, and Judging—falls on the tougher, more objective side of the line between the preference alternatives.

As a result, ESTJ males tend to be very "macho," and their humor often the most sexist and racist of all sixteen types. ESTJ outgoingness, assertiveness, practicality, firm-mindedness, and decisiveness tend to make them good protectors and providers —roles more generally associated with the male of the species.

The ESTJ female, though satisfied with her own femininity, may be torn between inner promptings that say, "Be tough, assertive, firm-minded, and decisive," and the traditional feminine model, which says, "Be soft, passive, gentle-hearted, and adaptive." The ensuing struggle is more dramatic for the ESTJ female than for any other type. While all Thinking-type females swim upstream in our society, in no type is that more apparent and prevalent than in the ESTJ.

In relating, as in all else, ESTJs are comfortable taking charge. Decisive and opinionated, they are easy to get along with as long as they are listened to and allowed to control. Generally, ESTJs and ISTJs would prefer to surround themselves, both at home and at work, with yes-people, though they would deny it.

ESTJ parents have sharply defined roles, and each family member (mate and children) is expected to respond according to the ESTJ's definitions. A "father" is the provider and final judge, for example, a "mother" keeps home and does wifely duties, and "children" obey and respond to the authority of their parents. (ESTJs may allow a "father" or "mother" to be a "friend" as well, but only at scheduled, defined intervals.) When family members respond to ESTJ expectations, things tend to go smoothly for all concerned. The problems come when a mate or child of another type has more resistance to the ESTJ's control (ENTJs or ISTPs, for example), or is more driven to self-determination (particularly NPs).

Home, family, parenting, and children are among the central

and motivating commitments of the ESTJ's life. When all else fails, appeals to an ESTJ's parental duty and responsibility will bring the parent around to considering, if not going along with, whatever program is being offered. Our hunch: More encyclopedias, home-learning kits, how-to-raise-better-kids books, and other "family programs" have been sold to ESTJs by appealing to "parental responsibility" than to any other type.

The ESTJ's living style, like most other things, is controlled and organized. Family is one more thing to manage. Hard work, tight schedules, and solid merit-based rewards are hallmarks of the ESTJ life. Fun, relaxation, and free time are scheduled and doled out (to self and others) according to how well one has adhered to standard operating procedures and other regulations. Good work brings good rewards; hard work is its own relaxation. Certain male activities—such as golf, beer-drinking, and poker—are scheduled for relaxation, as are certain female activities—gardening, tennis, or shopping, for example.

As children, ESTJs are usually socially active, take-charge types. Such behavior is much more welcomed in boys than girls, but ESTJ girls display it just as readily as the boys. As a result, ESTJ girls grow accustomed to hearing "Little girls don't behave that way." (Ironically, this is most likely heard from an ESTJ male parent.) Such statements may have considerable impact on their future feminine development. In general, ESTJ children play hard, give orders to all (parents included), and want two main things: that their parents be parents and act accordingly; and that structure, schedule, and definition be imposed upon them by someone. They may protest such imposition, but in the long run an ESTJ appreciates—indeed, relies on —the security that such authority brings. ESTJ children are both responsible and testing—responsible to parents and friends who take command, but sure to keep testing that authority in order to reassure themselves that it can be relied upon. This may best be illustrated at bedtime, as the ESTJ child resists and protests going to bed, yet appreciates immensely a parent who enforces bedtime rituals.

Things are no different in the classroom. A teacher's job is to teach, be organized, be a good role model, dress appropriately, be decisive, and follow a lesson plan. ESTJ students will respond and prove to be rather scholarly students, albeit somewhat mouthy and argumentative. Courses that are the most structured, with practical, tangible results, will appeal most to ESTJ students. Their academic prowess continues up the academic ladder, although they tend to have less patience with the more abstract theories at the college level. They are frustrated by iNtuitive-Perceiving professors (who dominate at the college level), whose lectures don't follow stated outlines and whose material isn't limited to the factual and concrete.

Family events and rituals are the symbols of an ESTJ's cultural heritage, whatever that culture may be, and therefore must be honored with the strictest adherence and most loyal obedience. ESTJ children and adults alike look forward to the birthdays, holy days, and annual family reunions. Though, again, ESTJs may protest, sometimes vehemently, about attending such events, it would never occur to them not to be present. They might even be surprised to hear that another type was "hurt" by their protesting.

Two slogans that describe ESTJs' philosophy in the workplace are "Don't fix what ain't broken" and "Anything worth doing is worth doing well." Both statements drive ESTJs. Fiercely loyal and extremely compulsive, they move up the administrative ladder in any organization. They spend money well and are naturals at marketing and at selling their own effectiveness. They are superb at developing sound management policies and committed to their own models as the best ways of doing something. They are quick to venture into many areas, take charge of those areas, more often than not prove successful, and develop a following of subordinates who come to trust the ESTJ's take-charge nature.

ESTJs are very conscious of the chain of command. For them, work is a series of goals, to be reached by following rules and regulations issued by the upper ranks of an organization's hierarchy. The system, and its regulations, are good, self-protecting, and self-perpetuating. By following them and working hard, ESTJs believe the system will, in turn, serve them. ESTJs give loyalty to the office and to the organization as a whole, though not necessarily to specific individuals therein.

Hard work carries ESTJs to the end of life. Rewards, degrees, gold watches, and certificates are given in due season. Retirement is one more thing to be scheduled and planned. Except for an occasional respite, ESTJs' later years are still scheduled and regimented, though sometimes less so than before.

Famous likely ESTJs include Harry S Truman ("Give 'em hell" Harry knew where the buck stopped and never shirked responsibility); *Peanuts*'s Lucy van Pelt (who has an answer to most any problem brought to her psychiatric booth—and never fails to collect her fee immediately); Archie Bunker (who abrasively protests all his wife Edith's sensible suggestions, but ultimately gives in and plays his responsible parental role); and Joan Rivers (whose quick, macho wit and steamroller style are often caustic and abrasive).

ESFJ
Hosts and Hostesses of the World

The Extraverted-Sensing-Feeling-Judgers' four preferences equip them to be gracious and effective in dealing with others. They use their subjective Feeling decisions to bring harmony and goodwill to almost any situation in which they find themselves, at the same time imposing order and structure on any situation—gently, yet firmly. They are exceptionally in tune with specific individual needs and especially sensitive to the nuances that make for happy and wholesome lives.

As a type, ESFJs probably personify "motherhood." Their gentle, caring nature, in its Extraverted way, takes them beyond their own needs to serve the world around them. As a result, they are the hosts and hostesses of the world. ESFJ males, who have less need to be "in charge" than to be concerned with others' needs, may as a result be torn between expressing the more conventionally masculine parts of their personalities and giving in to opposing tendencies. The male's Sensing-Judging temperament, sometimes described as "stabilizer-traditionalist," demands macho, objectively cool, yet aggressive behavior, while the Extraverted-Feeling preferences demands a warm or more caring and gentler role.

If the ESFJ male is something of a fish out of water, the ESFJ female, in contrast, often represents the epitome of femininity. She always wears the right clothes, says the right words, and behaves the right way. ESFJ girls are the perfect children who never get dirty, and even as adults, never seem to get mussed. There's something about an ESFJ—especially the female—that just reeks of appropriateness in all aspects of life.

Don't think that ESFJs have found perfection, however. As EJs, for example, they are given to quick, abrasive comments whenever their routines are interrupted. As SFs, however, they are critical of their own EJ behavior and compensate for their abrasiveness with extra sweetness. To paraphrase Isabel Briggs Myers, they have many "shoulds" and "should nots," and they express them freely. They may especially overlook facts when they find a situation disagreeable or a criticism hurtful. As a result, they may sweep problems under the rug rather than seek solutions.

The ESFJ's home is the center of his or her universe: it is the focus of family life, the place for entertainment, the bastion against the harshness of the outside world, the ultimate womb for all family members. The ESFJ's home is generally neat and orderly, however much activity takes place there. It isn't advisable to tell an ESFJ to relax as long as there are unmade beds or messy kitchens. Relaxation for the ESFJ comes both from doing such chores and from knowing that they are done. (As an EJ, they may complain about the mess and about how much work must be done, but they nevertheless are happiest in serving others in this way.) Like all Js, ESFJs schedule their relaxation, whether it be reading a book or being with friends.

As a rule, home can be a place of fun, happiness, and affirmation for the ESFJ. These things must take place on schedule, however, and in an "appropriate" manner. Parties, for example, are great, but only when sufficiently planned; "spontaneous fun" is a contradiction in terms. "Appropriateness" extends to dress, decor, and behavior. ESFJs mete out assignments to family members and expect them to be done correctly and in timely fashion. They readily impose behaviorial "shoulds" on other family members, and when disappointed in their expectations of others they become either hurt or upset.

This need for appropriateness also drives ESFJs' parenting style. The child of an ESFJ parent probably feels loved and generally satisfied, albeit somewhat restricted by the "shoulds" and "oughts," coupled with the constant need to put work (homework, housework, etc.) before play. ESFJs are generally very patient with children, although even patience can be subject to other demands and responsibilities. An ESFJ parent is likely to be looked upon as being somewhat strict, but still very loving and caring.

The same, in fact, may be said of ESFJs in relationships. They are very loyal, almost to a fault, often sacrificing their own needs in favor of the mates'. This, combined with their drive for harmony, often puts their personal welfare low on the list of priorities and can result in their feeling more like hired help than lovers or mates. The paradox is that while it is difficult for them to acknowledge their own needs, they may resent those who take them for granted.

ESFJ children bring the same graciousness, caring, and punctuality to their young lives. They tend to be neat and easy to be around. At school, ESFJs like teachers who stick to a lesson plan and generally "follow the rules." They respond well in such situations with good work habits and punctually completed assignments. In one study, ESFJs were rated by teachers and school psychologists as the ideal type to have in the classroom. Many of the qualities desired by teachers come naturally to ESFJs: they are helpful, cooperative, and eager to please.

They are like that at home too. But difficulties may arise with ESFJs, as with all Js, if some of the demands placed on them conflict with strong inner needs. Bedtime, for example, can be difficult for the gregarious Extraverted child, whose social needs may conflict with the night's hour and parents' demands. Still, ESFJ children think "parents should be parents" and appreciate rules and regulations imposed by those in authority. Like their SJ adult counterparts, they may protest such authority, at the same time respecting and expecting it. Role clarity is important.

ESFJs' careers often lean toward those that serve humanity: nursing, public school teaching, clergy, and psychology. Sales and other public service–oriented jobs also have particular appeal. More impersonal tasks (related to computers, for example, or bookkeeping) and jobs that demand theory and speculation (such as college teaching, consulting, and especially investment brokering) can be particularly stressful to an ESFJ.

In their later years, ESFJs may mellow somewhat, but they still are guided by the same values that shaped their earlier years. After a life devoted to meeting the needs of those around them, they may turn their attention to more abstract, universal concerns. Even in retirement, however, they tend to be driven by "shoulds" (and, perhaps, a few "shouldn'ts"), though the "shoulds" may be of a more leisurely kind, with perhaps less emphasis on service ideals—for example, learning a language, tending to neglected hobbies, or meeting some self-directed needs. In general, home, children, and grandchildren play central roles; they prefer to have family nearby and accessible, and may also enjoy the occasional unexpected visitor. For them, the ultimate symbol of security may be the continually replenished woodpile for the fireplace around which the family gathers.

Some famous ESFJs could include Dwight Eisenhower (although he was never seen as a brilliant military strategist, he could do no wrong. *Life* magazine called him "the most popular man in the world" in the 1950s; indeed, his highly successful campaign theme was "I Like Ike"); and Felix Unger of *The Odd Couple* (who rages at his sloppy roommate but is constantly there to take care of him).

ENFJ
Smooth-talking Persuader

The ENFJ may best be described as a smooth-talking persuader. The ENFJ's combination of preferences makes this type a natural when it comes to motivating people—even motivating them to do something they may not initially have wanted to do.

Their focus and direction is toward other people (Extraversion), and they are highly skilled in understanding others' needs and motivations (Feeling). These tendencies, along with their gift for imagination and inspiration (iNtuition), are expressed in an organized, effective way that allows them to make their imaginative ventures become reality. Hence, the ENFJ is a highly credible leader who attracts many followers.

The ENFJ has the capacity to size up a situation iNtuitively and, in a very caring and concerned way, say just the right thing. This is part of why people are drawn to ENFJs, and why ENFJs are such natural leaders. They are seldom at a loss to iNtuit just what the group needs or how to help it reach its goal.

Because of these group-leadership abilities, ENFJs, more than other Feeling types, often rise to the top of a cross section of organizations. They are, indeed, natural and often well-liked leaders. The ENFJ sees the entire world as filled with people whose endless needs and concerns are waiting to be funneled into organizations and institutions that can serve those human needs. ENFJs have a zeal for imposing "what's good for humanity" upon humanity—and, fortunately, more often than not, humanity is better off as a result.

Paradoxically, one of their biggest difficulties derives from one of their greatest strengths. While very accomplished at working with other people and groups, ENFJs can become depressed, wounded, even bitter, if their ideas meet with resistance. They take conflict or rejection very personally, and often carry a grudge against the individuals or groups involved. Disagreements tend to escalate into win-lose issues and become personalized, with loyalties sharply marked, even when the other side had only intended to raise some valid questions. Such behavior by ENFJs in influential positions has divided families, organizations, and systems.

The female ENFJ has an advantage because many of the nurturing, caring qualities associated with this type are considered feminine. However, when an ENFJ female assumes leadership beyond the family and moves, quite naturally, to larger systems, she may have trouble. The system, and especially its male members, may resent her. Suddenly all those qualities for which she was rewarded at home, in college, or in other organizational ranks, now become the basis for scorn because she has "overstepped her bounds" as a woman. She is not doing anything differently from what she has done successfully in the past; the end result, however, can be conflict.

ENFJs are such effective leaders that the male is often seen as a "man among men" and seductively appealing to women. Both men and women look to the male ENFJ for leadership and decisiveness in a supportive climate—and rarely are they disappointed. This notwithstanding, all ENFJs, including males, are often criticized as insincere or superficial because of their smooth and glib way with words. ENFJs may respond to such criticism with incredulity, often followed by depression and self-doubt, because their sincerity and concern are their driving force and motivation.

Relating to an ENFJ is usually fairly easy. As a rule, an ENFJ wants a happy and affirming relationship because that is how everyone works best. Highly articulate, with excellent social skills and a quick sense of humor, ENFJs are often the life of the party. If it is a party of two, the ENFJ will still work just as hard at making the occasion a lively and memorable one. Unfortunately, as with most Extraverts, if an ENFJ works too hard at it, all the other person is likely to remember is how much talking the ENFJ did and how little listening.

Parenting, for the ENFJ, is a responsibility and a pleasure. There are young lives just waiting to be molded by the ENFJ's value system. Unlike most other types, especially Perceivers, ENFJs don't wait for a child to develop. Instead, right and wrong, good and bad, and other models are imposed in a very warm, supportive, and clearly defined environment. A child will know where an ENFJ parent stands on most things, and how he or she is expected to behave. When behavior is appropriate, affirmation abounds. Negative behavior, however, often makes an ENFJ parent feel like a failure, which in turn can give the child who picks up on these feelings a sense of guilt about failing to please mother or father.

When harmony prevails, the living style of the ENFJ is lively and fun. But there must be order before relaxation, and fun must be balanced by a good measure of work. Peaceful and joyful living are certainly a goal—and an expectation. However, achieving that goal generally requires either following the ENFJ's good intentions or letting the ENFJ show you "the error of your ways" and redirect you toward "real joy"—whatever the ENFJ deems that to be.

As a general rule, people are central and important to ENFJs. This means that if people's needs end up in conflict with rules and schedules, the ENFJ will generally put people first—though not without a sense of martyrdom or possibly guilt.

ENFJ children's verbal skills develop early and stay with

them. They are often advised to become public speakers, preachers, or announcers "when you grow up." ENFJ children are pleasers, wanting strokes from adults. They are also hero-worshipers, often imitating those they idolize, whether it be a parent, sibling, teacher, or anyone else who has had a dramatic influence on them. Since imitation is the sincerest form of flattery, it is not surprising that ENFJ children are often teachers' pets and parents' favorites.

Learning, for ENFJs, is also imitation. They seek to learn by emulating their heroes, and how *they* learn. In fact, somewhat like ENFPs, so strong is their desire to please and be stroked that ENFJs can end up in careers far removed from their natural abilities if they can think that will endear them to the heroes they are emulating.

Family events are fun for an ENFJ. Almost without being asked, the ENFJ child or adult will assume a responsibility for making events entertaining, harmonious, and enriching for all. The ENFJ is usually tuned in to the family event, ready to provide games, entertainment, wit, wisdom, or whatever else may be needed. Generally, family members appreciate this dimension of the ENFJ, and, of course, the ENFJ then feels affirmed and fulfilled.

Clearly, any opportunity to be with others, to entertain, serve, involve others and be involved, is far more rewarding than sleep or any other solitary activity. In fact, too much time alone can make an ENFJ pensive, moody, self-punitive, and depressed. More than other types the ENFJ needs to move among and be engaged by people. Even a negative stroke from another person is better than being ignored.

ENFJs are drawn to careers that serve others with minimal potential for interpersonal conflict. Work that involves too many specific details, an abundance of paperwork, or too much time alone will be boring if not stressful to ENFJs. They are especially drawn to religious organizations, academia, and psychological services and approach these careers with enthusiasm and commitment. They are natural teachers and preachers, although they can become frustrated with the accompanying administrative demands, ending up somewhat disillusioned.

Senior citizenship may bring some Introversion and objectivity to the ENFJ, and with reflection may come the insight that the world is not going to be saved by anything the ENFJ can do, that life is going to continue—and probably quite well—without the ENFJ. Unless there is some respite from service to others, the ENFJ can suffer burnout. If that is avoided, the natural growth cycle can afford the ENFJ the chance to stop, "smell the daisies"—and quit trying to save the entire world. As a result, retirement, though perhaps still characterized by the service ethos, can also allow more focus on personal needs and a more relaxed, less compulsive way of life.

Famous likely ENFJs include Ronald Reagan (who is socially gregarious—ENFJs are naturally "great communicators"—and whose emotional stance on issues translates into rigid, not very negotiable positions); Jerry Falwell (who believes all would be well if people followed his moral preachings, and whose visions have indeed garnered a great following); and Martin Luther King, Jr. (whose highly idealistic dreams and charismatic leadership created a fiercely loyal following).

ENTJ
Life's Natural Leaders

Hearty, argumentative, and *robust* are three words that accurately describe ENTJs. Their unique preferences combine to give them very high need for control and unusual leadership abilities.

Their focus and energy are directed outwardly (Extraversion) toward a world of endless possibilities and meanings (iNtuition), which are translated objectively into systems and products (Thinking) in a very timely and orderly fashion (Judging).

Like their cousins, the ENTPs, the entire world seems a chessboard to ENTJs, with pieces in need of being moved—by them—for the greater good. Life is a system of forces to be understood, mastered, harnessed, altered, or defeated, as appropriate, from day to day.

For the ENTJ, all life unfolds through confrontation, arguing, and engaging with one another in the name of learning. The ENTJ starts with the basic assumption that he or she is right and must be proven wrong. This proving process will be beneficial only to the extent that there are others who have the gumption or audacity required to mount an effective challenge. When the engagement is over, if the ENTJ was right, everyone will be better for having gone through the process. If the ENTJ is wrong, then there will be profound admiration and respect for whoever was strong enough to prevail, as well as gratitude and respect for the new lesson learned.

In some ways, life for the ENTJ is a variation of the children's game King (or Queen) of the Mountain. The goal for others is to try to push the ENTJ down from the mountaintop. So long as they are unable to do so, they must remain "beneath" the ENTJ. The process of being challenged is as important to the ENTJ as the outcome.

As a type, ENTJs have low regard for people who refuse to engage them or are intimidated by them, and high regard for those who stand up to them and challenge them intellectually, emotionally, or any other way. The problem of intimidation is intensified by the ENTJs' arrogance, which is often so much a part of them that they are unaware of its existence. Those around them are usually keenly aware of it.

ENTJs are often impatient, more so than most other types. Their impatience may show itself in the form of a quick temper, inappropriate complaints over relatively small matters, and an urgency to move on to bigger and better things. Their strong egos can trick them into thinking they can do or handle anything, including details and intense interpersonal matters, but details and interpersonal skills are simply not the ENTJ's strong suits.

When an ENTJ "fails" at such matters, the resulting stress, frustration, and feelings of incompetence can result in self-flagellation and criticism, often totally out of proportion to the issue at hand. Indeed, when it comes to criticism of self or others, ENTJs are usually in a class by themselves. Sharp-tongued, harsh, seemingly unforgiving, ENTJs can be devastating to those they criticize—including themselves.

ENTJs are especially gifted with language. Clarity of thought and speech make them excellent communicators. It also sharpens the precision of their critical abilities.

Clearly, gender issues are especially significant for ENTJ females. As a type, their arrogant, confrontational manner and need for control can appear to be quite "unwomanly" to others. Efforts by parents and others to mold them into more traditional female images are usually met with rebellion. Other women usually resent the arrogance of ENTJ females and can feel "talked down to." As a result, an ENTJ female may unwittingly find herself to be a loner, something particularly difficult for Extraverts.

Of course, the problem intensifies for the ENTJ female when dealing with men, even male ENTJs. Their demanding, objective, competent, and independent nature is not particularly endearing to most men. These qualities may obscure the fact that ENTJ females can be quite nurturing and caring. For them, femininity is not defined by traditional roles. It is reflected in the total involvement and commitment they bring to each moment of life.

Though the qualities of ENTJs may be more acceptable in males, they, too, may find people shunning them, often avoiding confrontations in order to escape their arrogance. As with their female counterparts, ENTJ males may be plagued by staff, family, and personal relationships in turmoil, leaving them with more time alone than their Extraversion can deal with.

To their frequent surprise, ENTJs are often told they appear angry, even when it is just their enthusiasm for a point that has gotten them so worked up. Such encounters can be frustrating for ENTJs—as well as for those around them—and they may find themselves in the rather ironic position of having angrily to defend their nonanger. The sense of futility that results may make the ENTJ try even harder or, as is often the case with female ENTJs, may make them give up and move on to some other project. In either case, the result can be debilitating to all involved.

The ENTJ's home is the arena for all sorts of pursuits. Relationships there tend to be open, honest, and stimulating. While to others ENTJs may seem somewhat abrasive, those who know them well understand that, as with other EJs, their bark is usually worse than their bite. To an ENTJ, relationships grow and develop over time.

As parents, ENTJs see children as fun because they are young minds to be encouraged, enlightened, and stimulated. As they grow, the children, too, become eligible to be drawn into hearty discourse about a variety of subjects. And they become candidates for the molding and shaping that ENTJs like to do for those they care about or have responsibilities for.

The ENTJ style of living is fairly compulsive and family members must know their responsibilities within the system. When rebellion is encountered, the ENTJ may enjoy the exchange, even admire at some level the boldness of whoever is rebelling, but still use maximal powers of persuasion to quell the revolt and ensure that all family members continue to march to the beat of the ENTJ drummer. If the rebel manages to win, that person also wins the ENTJ's respect. Each day, at work or at home, the ENTJ may win some and lose some, but there are few, if any, draws.

Relaxation does not come easily to most ENTJs and when it does, it is only because it has been scheduled. Even then it is viewed as one more assignment to master, and ENTJs attack such challenges with zeal and compulsiveness.

ENTJ children are rather direct with both their peers and adults. Though they are often bossy and argumentative, they make friends easily, are quick-witted and gregarious, and have strong needs, like other Extraverts, to include others and be included by others in everything they do, from working to studying to partying. In the eyes of peers, ENTJ children can be simultaneously respected for their capabilities and resented for the obnoxious, overpowering conviction that accompanies their ideas. Competitive in most anything they do, ENTJ children start early to criticize their own shortcomings. They rarely rest on their laurels. Even the best, they believe, can be better. That, indeed, is how the ENTJ approaches everything.

Teachers, of course, may not always understand these attributes, and the result is often some very hostile moments, power struggles that the student is likely to lose. If there is no face-saving way out, the ENTJ can be resistant to subsequent learning experiences. While a good, challenging, competitive engagement that involves an exchange of ideas is enjoyable for ENTJs, the one-sided teacher-student power struggle can be damaging and alienating.

Family events are fun for the ENTJ. They are yet another

chance to plan, organize, lead, and show off. It is a time for intellectual exchange and robust encounter. ENTJs look forward to such events with great enthusiasm.

With their natural leadership and systems-planning abilities, ENTJs often rise to upper levels of management fairly quickly. They may alienate some people along the way, but that's all part of the price one pays to express ability and prove competency. Moreover, if one achieves one's goals and has caused learning and growth for self and others, then the alienation was not in vain. Approaching these interpersonal dilemmas objectively, they find it surprising that anyone would be hurt, disappointed, or intimidated by their aggressiveness. In their objectivity, they don't understand why anyone would personalize an argument or competition that was, to their mind, well intentioned, meant only to result in the growth and betterment of all concerned.

Older age for the ENTJ is still a time for conceptual and intellectual expansion. Good development will bring more respect for reflection, with less need to control everything, less compulsive behavior. However, the later years must still include some form of mental challenge, the more competitive, the better. For the ENTJ, the rewards of maturity are the opportunities to read, argue, organize, or theorize—in other words, to continue on his or her lifelong path, but with less accountability. Retirement, if it ever comes, will see a continuation of these activities in some form or another.

Famous likely ENTJs include Douglas MacArthur (whose Extraversion kept him clamoring for the limelight, who viewed himself as a strategist of a high military system with no patience for detail, and whose objectivity always kept a sharp distinction between his mission and the people involved); Eleanor Roosevelt (whose social gregariousness kept her in headlines, whose intuition made her a futurist always looking at the big picture, and who loved managing complex systems); and Frank Lloyd Wright (who implemented his iNtuitive-Thinking architectural visions with buildings and systems, whose Judging nature produced guidelines for other architects to follow, and whose Extraversions brought those systems to the public's view).

A Brief History of Typewatching

The idea of classifying people is as old as humanity itself. The particular means of classifying personality types that is employed by Typewatching is based on the written works of Swiss psychologist C. G. Jung (1875–1961), which first appeared in English in 1923. Jung's orientation was both medical and psychological and was based more on wellness than on illness—that is to say, normal rather than abnormal psychology. He had what we would today call the most holistic view of life among the theorists of his time, believing that many physical and emotional illnesses were the result of imbalances of the mind, body, and spirit. Jung believed that we are born with a predisposition to certain personality preferences. He also believed that healthy development was based on lifelong nurturing of those preferences, not on working to change them. The maturing process for Jung meant being able to deal more effectively with and being less threatened by the preferences you do *not* choose.

Independently of Jung, Katharine Briggs, who had no formal psychological training, had developed classifications of her own, based on her observations of personality differences. Her goal was to quantify her theory that people's behavior was not as random as some believed. Her observations told her that the issue had to do with subtle differences in how they approached life. She had formally classified these differences when she encountered the newly translated book, *Psychological Types,* by

Jung. She recognized that her theory of personality types was consistent with Jung's, and became an exhaustive student of his.

Briggs's only offspring, Isabel, was an extraordinarily brilliant child who was taught primarily at home by her mother and who attended Swarthmore College, graduating at the head of her class (having married Clarence Myers in the interim) with a major in political science. After graduation, she spent the next twenty years as wife, mother, and author of two published novels, all the while observing differences in people and trying to fit them into the classifications created by her mother and Jung.

In 1942, prompted by World War II—and the two women's conviction that the war was caused, in part, by people not understanding differences—Isabel, with her mother's guidance, began to develop a series of questions to measure personality differences. The result was the Myers-Briggs Type Indicator. With painstaking care, and thousands of three- by five-inch cards containing sample questions, Isabel spent years sorting, analyzing, and validating people's responses to the MBTI. She validated her early observations against groups of people whose preferences she knew to be well defined. Later, she tested individuals in a cross section of society and further validated the MBTI against other psychological instruments. By the early 1960s the data indicated that the MBTI was not only a valid measure of personality differences, but seemed to be reliable in reporting those differences over time.

Not everyone in the vast field of psychology agreed with the MBTI's validity. For one thing, the instrument had been developed by two women, which did not endear it to the primarily male psychological community. Even worse, neither woman was a psychologist. Further, not many psychologists subscribed to Jung's esoteric theories; even Jung felt that his own theories couldn't be quantified. The MBTI seemed to be an instrument whose time had not yet come.

It was in 1956 that Educational Testing Service (ETS) in Princeton, New Jersey, agreed to publish the MBTI, albeit with some reluctance. Some on the board of ETS felt that a personality test was beyond the organization's mission, which was to publish more educationally oriented material, such as the Scholastic Aptitude Test. William Chauncy, the president of ETS, prevailed, and the MBTI began to gain credibility. ETS placed stringent requirements on those working with the MBTI. It could be used only for research, for example, and the data were not to be made available to the general public. Few professional psychologists even knew of the Indicator, let alone put it to use.

During the 1960s a number of dramatic things happened that helped launch the MBTI. In 1962, Isabel published a manual on her research, the first formal document on it. That same year she was invited to speak to the American Psychological Association, a major breakthrough in the process of her gaining recognition in the field of psychology. Over the next few years there emerged several pockets of research using the MBTI, studying everything from dormitory living configurations to learning styles.

In 1969, Isabel met Mary McCaulley, a clinical psychologist who was in charge of the Health Center at the University of Florida in Gainesville. Together, the two women started a typology laboratory at the university that would become a research and resource center for all MBTI-related work. As the laboratory grew in size and scope, it was established in 1972 as the Center for the Application of Psychological Type (CAPT). It remains the principal research facility for Typewatching. The accumulation of Typewatching data warranted the establishment of such a center to facilitate the growing amount of interest in the field of typology. In 1975, while the MBTI was still considered only an instrument with limited research potential, CAPT sponsored the first of what would become a biennial conference on Typewatching. Fewer than one hundred people attended that first conference; a decade later, more than eight hundred people attended the Sixth International Conference, in Evanston, Illinois, mirroring the growth of interest in Typewatching.

In 1975, Consulting Psychologists Press became publisher of the Myers-Briggs Type Indicator, and the MBTI became available to a wider professional circle. At the 1979 CAPT-sponsored conference, the Association of Psychological Type (APT) was born. It is a membership organization for anyone interested in Typewatching. Among APT's interests is to foster professional standards in use of the MBTI and to encourage diversity among schools of Typewatching. Among the most popular of the varying approaches is the Temperament Theory espoused by the California-based David Keirsey and Marilyn Bates, authors of *Please Understand Me.* Keirsey, a behaviorist and clinical psychologist, while very different in his approach from Myers-Briggs and Jung, introduced some variations on the theme that we find to be very helpful. But by itself, Keirsey's theory, with only four type classifications, is considered more limited than the MBTI. Together, however, Keirsey and the MBTI provide a more thorough perspective on Typewatching differences than either can provide by itself.

By the mid-1980s, the growing interest in Typewatching theory—and Jung—coupled with people's natural tendencies to classify behavior, helped to create the fertile environment we now have for Typewatching. Today, several million Americans have taken the Myers-Briggs Type Indicator; exact figures are unavailable, due to a lack of centralization of data. The MBTI has also been translated into Japanese, Spanish, and French, and, as of this writing, a German version is expected. APT itself has gained an international membership.

Dominant, Auxiliary, and the Complexity of the Introvert

In Typewatching, we have looked primarily at the four letters that constitute one's preferred way of dealing with life and people. When we combine those four letters, we get a "profile" that gives us a bigger picture of what that person is like.

There is another concept in Typewatching that goes beyond the four-letter profile, one that was originally developed by C. G. Jung and more fully developed by Isabel Briggs Myers. It focuses on only two functions of our personality: the information-gathering function (Sensing or iNtuition) and the decision-making function (Thinking or Feeling). These show up as the second and third letters of our four-letter profile, for example, E*NF*P.

In Jung's theory, as one grows and develops, one of these two functions becomes the favorite. It is the most reliable, dependable, measurable, manageable, and predictable function of one's personality. It is the function that, given the chance, determines behavior. It is referred to as the Dominant Function. Isabel Briggs Myers called it "the commanding general" of one's personality. Simply put, it's the boss.

The remaining function is called the Auxiliary Function. We like to think of it as the Avis of your personality—the number two function that may from time to time "try harder" to take charge. The Auxiliary Function provides support for the Dominant Function. Isabel Myers called this one "the loyal lieutenant."

Extraverts focus their lives and energies through their Dominant Function. With the Extravert, "what you see is what you get." Extraverted-Feelers impose their "commanding general" —Feeling—on the whole world, and do so for the world's good. (Most clergy are Extraverted-Feelers, and impose their value systems very freely on congregations, individuals, and communities.) Extraverted-Thinkers, in contrast, impose their Thinking—they love to organize anyone or anything within their reach and are the administrators of the world.

Introverts' energy and attention, in contrast, is directed inwardly, because that is where the Dominant Function of their personalities remains. Hence, one does not meet the commanding general of the Introvert's personality without an appointment—and the "appointment" is "trust." Even then, it's a matter of the Introvert's "letting you in" rather than the Introvert's personality "coming out." As a result, Introverts deal with the outer world through their Auxiliary Functions, and consequently all external matters are subject to final approval of the information-gathering or decision-making of the Dominant Function.

Not only are Introverts outnumbered three to one in our society—making them sociologically disadvantaged—they are more psychologically complex in that the focus of their energy and attention is directed inward.

In Typewatching, it is important to keep in mind that Extraverts are more vocal in sharing their personality preferences while Introverts are considerably harder to read. Moreover, when an Introvert "Extraverts," the action is always subject to subsequent Introverted scrutiny. That means, for example, that an Introvert's "final" spoken decision may not be final following a bit of reflection and reconsideration. Similarly, an Introvert's apparent "flexibility" may be far from truly flexible once the Introvert has had the opportunity "go inside" and think it over.

For Extraverts, the external world is positive, affirming, and energizing, and they typically feel free to use the best-developed parts of their personalities in the external world, keeping that which is second-best inside.

Introverts reverse that process. It is the inner world which Introverts prefer to trust and find positive, affirming, and energizing—so it is inwardly that Introverts direct the best-developed parts of their personalities, the Dominant Function. The outer world is energy draining but inescapable—everyone must get up and face the world each day—and is clearly a necessary evil for the Introvert. Therefore, for that which is less preferred and second class, the Introvert prefers to use only the second-best—the Auxiliary Function. A twist of an advertising slogan may accurately express the Introvert's view of the process: "We do not care enough to send the very best."

The bottom line is that Extraverts Extravert their favorite and best function, the Dominant. Introverts, on the other hand, Extravert their second-best function, the Auxiliary.

Dominant and Auxiliary of the Sixteen Types

Here are the Dominant and Auxiliary Functions for each of the sixteen types:

ISTJ
—Dominant is Introverted *Sensing*—factual and practical
—Auxiliary is Extraverted *Thinking*—objective decisions and structure

ISFJ
—Dominant is Introverted *Sensing*—factual and practical
—Auxiliary is Extraverted *Feeling*—interpersonally based decisions and structure

INFJ
—Dominant is Introverted *iNtuition*—inspirations and possibilities
—Auxiliary is Extraverted *Feeling*—interpersonally based decisions and structure

INTJ
—Dominant is Introverted *iNtuition*—inspirations and possibilities
—Auxiliary is Extraverted *Thinking*—objective decisions and structure

ISTP
—Dominant is Introverted *Thinking*—objective decisions
—Auxiliary is Extraverted *Sensing*—factual and practical observations

ISFP
—Dominant is Introverted *Feeling*—interpersonally based decisions and structure
—Auxiliary is Extraverted *Sensing*—factual and practical observations

INFP
—Dominant is Introverted *Feeling*—interpersonally based decisions and structure
—Auxiliary is Extraverted *iNtuition*—possibilities and abstract observations

INTP
—Dominant is Introverted *Thinking*—objective decisions
—Auxiliary is Extraverted *iNtuition*—possibilities and abstract observations

ESTP
—Dominant is Extraverted *Sensing*—factual and detailed perceptions
—Auxiliary is Introverted *Thinking*—objective decisions

ESFP
—Dominant is Extraverted *Sensing*—factual and detailed perceptions
—Auxiliary is Introverted *Feeling*—interpersonally based decisions

ENFP
—Dominant is Extraverted *iNtuition*—possibilities and abstract observations
—Auxiliary is Introverted *Feeling*—interpersonally based decisions

ENTP
—Dominant is Extraverted *iNtuition*—possibilities and abstract observations
—Auxiliary is Introverted *Thinking*—objective decisions

ESTJ
—Dominant is Extraverted *Thinking*—objective decisions and structure
—Auxiliary is Introverted *Sensing*—factual and practical

ESFJ
—Dominant is Extraverted *Feeling*—interpersonally based decisions
—Auxiliary is Introverted *Sensing*—factual and practical

ENFJ
—Dominant is Extraverted *Feeling*—interpersonally based decisions
—Auxiliary is Introverted *iNtuition*—inspirations and possibilities

ENTJ
—Dominant is Extraverted *Thinking*—objective decisions and structure
—Auxiliary is Introverted *iNtuition*—inspirations and possibilities

About the Authors

Otto Kroeger, ENFJ, is founder of Otto Kroeger Associates, Inc., a consulting firm based in Fairfax, Virginia, working exclusively with the Myers-Briggs Type Indicator. A former Lutheran clergyman, he has been working in organizational development and the behaviorial sciences for more than two decades. He has lectured on Typewatching extensively throughout the United States, and in Europe and Asia, and has worked with hundreds of corporations, including AT&T, Xerox, IBM, Marine Midland Bank, Ford, Exxon, and the World Bank. He has worked extensively with the Defense Department, presenting Typewatching for all four major branches of the military; his seminars are now required course work at many military schools and training facilities.

Janet M. Thuesen, ENFP, president of Otto Kroeger Associates, Inc., has had an extensive career in education, business, and counseling. She has taught at grade levels from preschool through college and has worked with emotionally disturbed adolescents and chemically dependent women. She also served as White House assistant director of organizational development and at the Department of Education in executive and management development. She has trained hundreds of professionals in administering and interpreting Typewatching skills, and has spoken extensively on the subject.

About Otto Kroeger Associates

Otto Kroeger Associates, Inc., formed in 1977, is a psychological and management consulting firm located in Fairfax, Virginia. It provides consultation and training in organizational development, conflict resolution, goal-setting, and communication to a wide range of organizations, using the Myers-Briggs Type Indicator as a basis for understanding differences. It is one of only two organizations certified to provide qualifying training for professionals in administering and interpreting the MBTI. In addition, it has developed a variety of Typewatching-related materials, including videotapes, audiotapes, and a series of sixteen T-shirts.

Suggested Readings

These books and other related MBTI materials can be found in some bookstores, or may be obtained directly from Otto Kroeger Associates.

Bates, Marilyn, and Keirsey, David W., *Please Understand Me.* Del Mar, Calif.: Prometheus Nemesis Book Company, 1978.

Bennet, E.A., *What Jung Really Said.* New York: Schocken Books, 1983.

Bolen, Jean Shinoda, M.D., *Goddesses in Everywoman.* San Francisco: Harper & Row, 1984.

Calaway, Bernie L., *Forty-Four Fun Fables.* Wilton, Conn.: Moorehouse-Barlow Co., Inc., 1982.

Campbell, Joseph (ed.). *The Portable Jung.* New York: Viking Press, 1971.

de Casitllejo, Irene Claremont, *Knowing Woman.* New York: Harper & Row, 1975.

Grant, W. Harold, Thompson, Magdala, and Clarke, Thomas E., *From Image to Likeness: A Jungian Path in the Gospel Journey.* Ramsey, N.J., Paulist Press, 1983.

Johnson, Robert A., *He: Understanding Masculine Psychology.* New York: Harper & Row, 1977.

Johnson, Robert A., *She: Understanding Feminine Psychology.* New York: Harper & Row, 1977.

Johnson, Robert A., *We: Understanding the Psychology of Romantic Love.* New York: Harper & Row, 1983.

Jung, C. G., *Memories, Dreams and Reflections* (A. Jaffe, ed.) New York: Vintage Books, 1961.

Jung, C. G., *Psychological Types.* New York: Harcourt & Brace, 1923.

Jung, Emma, *Animus and Anima.* Irving, Tex.: Spring Publications, 1969.

Kelsey, Morton T., *Caring: How Can We Love One Another?* Ramsey, N.J.: Paulist Press, 1981.

Lawrence, Gordon, *People Types and Tiger Stripes.* Gainesville, Fla.: Center for Application of Psychological Type, Inc., 1982.

Marshall, Jeanie, and Hillers, Ellie (eds.), *Journal of Religion and the Applied Behavioral Sciences.* Frederick, Md.: Association for Creative Change, 1986.

McCaulley, Mary H., *Jung's Theory of Psychological Types and the Myers-Briggs Type Indicator.* Gainesville, Fla.: Center for Application of Psychological Type, 1981.

Myers, Isabel Briggs, *Gifts Differing.* Palo Alto, Calif.: Consulting Psychologists Press, Inc., 1980.

Myers, Isabel Briggs, and McCaulley, Mary H., *Manual: A Guide to the Development and the Use of the Myers-Briggs Type Indicator.* Palo Alto, Calif.: Consulting Psychologists Press, 1985.

Sanford, John A., *The Invisible Partners.* Ramsey, N.J.: Paulist Press, 1980.

Sanford, John A., *The Man Who Lost His Shadow.* Ramsey, N.J.: Paulist Press, 1983.

Sanford, John A., *The Man Who Wrestled with God.* Ramsey, N.J.: Paulist Press, 1974, 1981.

Sanford, John A., *Between People: Communicating One to One.* Ramsey, N.J.: Paulist Press, 1982.

Schemel, George J., and Borbely, James A., *Facing Your Type.* Wernersville, Pa.: Typrofile Press, 1982.

Stevens, Dr. Anthony, *Archetypes: A Natural History of the Self.* New York: Quill, 1982.

Thompson, Helen B.V.M., *Journey Toward Wholeness: A Jungian Model of Adult Spiritual Growth.* Ramsey, N.J.: Paulist Press, 1982.

von Franz, Marie-Louise, and Hillman, James, *Lectures on Jung's Typology*. Irving, Tex.: Spring Publications, 1971.

Welch, John O. Carm, *Spiritual Pilgrims*. Ramsey, N.J.: Paulist Press, 1982.

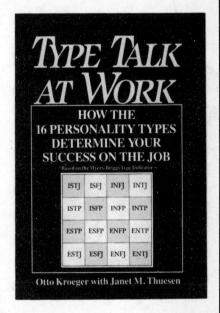